DIANA SHAW

ALMOST VEGETARIAN

A Primer for Cooks
Who Are Eating
Vegetarian
Most of the Time,
Chicken & Fish
Some of the Time
& *Altogether Well*
All of the Time

Illustrations by Kathy Warinner

Clarkson Potter/Publishers
New York

Published by Clarkson N. Potter, Inc., 201 East 50th Street New York, New York 10022. Member of the Crown Publishing Group.

Random House, Inc. New York, Toronto, London, Sydney, Auckland

http://www.randomhouse.com/

CLARKSON N. POTTER, POTTER, and colophon are registered trademarks of Clarkson N. Potter, Inc.

Manufactured in the United States of America

Design and illustration by Kathy Warinner, Aufuldish & Warinner, San Anselmo, Calif.

Library of Congress Cataloging-in-Publication Data
Shaw, Diana
    Almost vegetarian: a primer for cooks who are eating vegetarian most of the time, chicken and fish some of the time, and altogether well all of the time / Diana Shaw. — 1st ed.
        p.   cm.
    Includes index.
    1. Vegetarian cookery.   I. Title.
TX837.S4627   1994   93-41748
641.5'636—dc20   CIP

ISBN 0-517-88206-X

10   9

To the Memory of My Grandfather
ERAM J. AZIAN
For whom food was love
And in whose care we never went hungry

CONTENTS

ix Acknowledgments

2 Introduction

14 *Fresh Vegetable Directory*

31 *Selected Seasonings Directory*

42 Soups

62 Salads

78 Starters & Side Dishes
(That Can Make a Meal, Too)

108 Pasta, Risotto & *Focacce*

140 Vegetable Main Dishes

166 Poultry

188 Fish & Seafood

208 Desserts

210 *Fresh Fruit Directory*

231 Cookware and Utensils

235 Mail-Order Sources for Food

237 Bibliography

239 Index

Acknowledgments

Eating is one of the more personal pleasures in life, so perhaps it's no wonder that the people who like my recipes enough to edit, publish, and promote them are people with whom I share a good deal more than a taste for certain foods. Still, I feel lucky to be able to call my colleagues friends. In particular I'm thinking of Shaye Areheart and Kelly Hammond at Harmony Books, Kim Hertlein and Hilary Bass at Crown Publishers, my agents, Gail Hochman and Marianne Merola, and my favorite retailer, Ellen Rose of the Cooks Library in Los Angeles. I am also grateful to Kathy Warinner, Jane Treuhaft, and Susan DeStaebler for making this book look good.

I'm lucky above all to have Katie Workman as an editor. *Almost Vegetarian* was Katie's idea, and she put as much time, effort, and thought into it as I did, making sure I had the books and ingredients I needed (some trick, given that I was in Italy, and the postal service there is Europe's Bermuda Triangle), in addition to devoting precious weekends and after-hours to the manuscript.

I did most of the writing and recipe testing while living in Milan, where it's necessary to shop every day, and to stop at four or five different merchants to make a well-balanced meal. This seems quaint if you don't live in Italy, but it's enough to drive you crazy when you do. If I'm sane, it's because my husband, Simon, always *always* let me know that he appreciated my work. Simon tasted, listened, read, and gave his opinion with enough candor to help me correct my mistakes, and enough consideration to make me grateful for his criticism.

Finally, my parents' ongoing, unconditional generosity is a wonder to me, as well as the principal reason I've been free to pursue my heart's desire.

Almost Vegetarian

introduction

· · ● ○ ● · ·

Some Historical Background   What's Happened to Our Appetite?
Almost Vegetarians   On Cooking Well   General Cooking Tips   When
the Recipe Says   Notes on Nutrition for Almost Vegetarians   More Can
Be Less   Meatless Diets, While Often Healthy, Aren't Risk Free   You
Need Lots of Calcium, but You Don't Have to Drink Milk to Get It   Fat:
The Calories That Count   Low-Fat Menus   The Better Multivitamins
   High-Fiber Menus   We're Not Talking Miracles, but . . .   A Pinch
of Sugar   High-Carbohydrates Menus   About the Nutrition Information
   Nutritional Content per Serving   Some Additional Menus

Some Historical Background

In the late sixteenth century, the guests who attended a banquet in Rome put away a feast that today would send most of us screaming from the table. The four-course meal began with twelve "appetizers," including salted pork tongues, spit-roasted songbirds, spice cakes, biscuits, and pastries. Next came a dozen more dishes: fried sweetbreads, roasted skylark, pigeon, goat, cream of almond soup, and meat in aspic, to name a few. The next course featured boiled calves' feet, goat breast with fried onions, cabbage soup with sausages, and fat geese stuffed with almonds, cheese, and cinnamon sugar. There were also twelve desserts.

We don't even have to look back that far to see that our tastes have changed. Some popular family suppers of two decades ago—tuna casserole, for instance, made with canned mushroom soup, or panfried pork chops with a crushed cornflake crust—are not as appealing today as they were in their time.

What's Happened to Our Appetite?

We have become too familiar with the link between eating well and overall well-being to enjoy a meal without considering what we're doing to ourselves in the process. Knowing the benefits of low-fat, high-fiber, vitamin-rich foods, we have become partial to whole grains and fresh fruit and vegetables, choosing to eat less meat or none at all.

We have become part-time vegetarians.

Almost Vegetarians

. . . care that food is good in all respects; that it's nourishing, exciting, *and* delicious. Although we're particularly discriminating when it comes to fats—preferring foods that are poached, steamed, or lightly sautéed to those that are deep-fried, and favoring modest portions of poultry and fish over large helpings of pork or beef—we will never say "never" to the pleasure of a fresh mayonnaise or a sauce made from cheddar cheese or imported Parmesan.

The recipes that follow have been created and compiled with part-time vegetarians in mind. Many of them are vegetarian, and most of those that call for fish or poultry can be made with legumes instead. Throughout, you'll learn how to adapt recipes for meatless meals that are *not* bland imitations of the dishes that inspired them, but excellent in their own right.

Whether you're almost vegetarian or just interested in mastering the basics of good, healthy cooking, you'll find here the kind of dishes, guidance, and information you need to prepare foods in ways you will enjoy. Maybe you've heard plenty about the benefits of a diet low in fat and high in complex carbohydrates and want an effective incentive to switch to one. I hope you'll get that incentive from these recipes, which are meant, above all, to help you discover the pleasures of eating altogether *well*.

On Cooking Well

Cooking well isn't complicated. It takes only three things: appetite, enthusiasm, and good ingredients.

Appetite is fundamental. You'll cook best when you're eager to eat what you're making. Cooking what you love is like singing from the heart; you may be able to do a good enough job with any old song, but you'll do much better when the lyrics mean something to you.

Enthusiasm comes easily when you consider what good cooking does for you. First, it gives you confidence. When my gnocchi turns out chewy and light, when my swordfish is tender, and my risotto's just right, I feel as if I can handle anything. And even if I could name the chemical processes responsible for each result, it would still seem like wizardry to me. It's inspiring to think you can work magic from time to time.

Second, it helps you appreciate what matters in life. Convenience foods simply cut to the chase—as if the only point in preparing a meal is having something to eat. But when you cook, you discover the rewards in slowing down and taking time to smell the onions. Cooking is a succession of simple pleasures. Moreover, they're pleasures that can be shared and that multiply in the sharing. To know this is to be that much closer to contentment.

Finally—and vitally—it makes you healthy. When you cook you determine how *well* you'll eat, first by deciding what to make, then by choosing good ingredients and cooking them with care.

So much for what inspires enthusiasm for cooking. Here's what can kill it.

First, pressure.

Don't cook if you don't have time or if you're just not in the mood. You'll add salt instead of sugar; you'll drop your favorite plate; and you'll be miserable when you're through. If you decide to go ahead and cook anyway, keep it simple. Make one easy entrée and supplement it with a side dish, salad, and/or dessert from a reliable deli, speciality shop, or bakery.

Second, clutter.

Clean as you go. Clutter makes you tense, and a sinkful of dirty mixing bowls makes a mighty unpleasant chore. It's nice to be able to sit down at dinner and enjoy what you've prepared without facing the penance of a pile of unwashed cookware.

Third, chaos.

Be organized. Before you start cooking:

1. Read the recipe straight through so you'll know what's involved. It may contain a little surprise, such as a line after the first two steps saying "Cover and refrigerate overnight."

2. Set out your ingredients. This way, you'll know that you have everything you need before you begin (rather than getting halfway into the recipe before finding you've run out of an essential seasoning), and you'll have all of it within reach.

3. Set out enough bowls or dishes for each of the ingredients before you prepare them, such as a bowl for the chopped onions, another for the sliced peppers, another for the grated cheese.

4. Do all of the prep work—chopping, peeling, grating, and so on. You'll be able to assemble the dish swiftly, and you won't find yourself dicing carrots, for example, while the rest of your stir-fry burns.

General Cooking Tips

Your guests won't enjoy themselves if they see you're not having fun. The best way to make it look easy is to make it easy. These tips should help:

- Don't worry whether a dish you've made tastes the way it's *supposed* to taste: if it tastes good, it *is* good.

- When you use less fat in cooking than is called for in a recipe, spend more time stirring, and check the food more often, to avoid burning. I don't recommend nonstick sprays because I've found they make foods taste funny. I prefer to sauté in a small amount of unsalted butter or oil, often using so little that the calories I'd save using cooking spray are insignificant.

- Always have a garbage bag beside you, even if it means having several at various spots around the kitchen. This way you can keep your work space tidy without having to walk over to the trash every few minutes.

- Grate by hand if you're grating small amounts of cheese, potatoes, and so on, using a food processor for larger portions. If you need a half cup or less, it may take longer to clean the food processor than to grate the ingredient by hand.

- Don't feel as if you have to make the whole meal. You can buy some of the dishes or a dessert.

- It's easy to become known as a good cook. Have one specialty—one *really* good dish you know by heart.

When the Recipe Says

BAKE ✎ Put a food or a batter in a pan and place it in a warm oven (covered or not, depending on the recipe). Some foods, such as fish fillets and chicken parts, can dry out when they're baked, but wrapping them in soft lettuce leaves (for example, Boston or butter lettuce) will keep them moist. Oven temperatures vary; get to know your oven's idiosyncrasies so you can compensate—allowing more or less time, or adjusting to a higher or lower setting—when you're following recipes. You can do this by preparing a number of baked dishes and observing how much the actual baking times deviate from the times given in the recipes.

BLANCH ✎ Plunge the food into boiling water to cook it briefly, reducing the final preparation time of the dish. More detailed instructions for blanching are on page 144. An example of a dish that includes blanched vegetables is Grilled Assorted Vegetables (see page 143).

BRAISE ✎ Cook the food in a little butter or oil, then add liquid—usually wine or broth—cover the pan, and let it cook slowly. An example of a recipe that calls for braising is Braised Fish with Winter Greens (see page 192).

BROIL ✎ Cook the dish under direct heat, either in the oven or in a toaster oven. Because grilling involves cooking over direct heat, anything that can be broiled can be cooked on a grill, and vice versa. Broiling and grilling add no fat to food and actually melt away some of the fats on meat and fish. Make sure to broil on a raised rack so that the fat can drip into a pan underneath. Some broiled dishes are Barbecued or Broiled Turkey Burgers with All the Fixin's (see page 184) and Chicken Breasts (or Pressed Tofu) with Sweet Mustard Glaze (see page 176).

CHOP 🌿 Cut foods into small pieces, without worrying about achieving a uniform size or shape.

DICE 🌿 Cut food into small cubes (roughly ¼ inch).

MINCE 🌿 Chop very finely.

POACH 🌿 Cook a food in gently simmering water, stock, or bouillon. Poaching adds no fat to food, while an aromatic poaching liquid will infuse it with flavor. Poached Fish (see page 190) and poultry (see page 166) are excellent in salads.

PUREE 🌿 Process a food in a blender or food processor until it's smooth and thick. Be careful to stop when it reaches this consistency, or it will liquefy, that is, turn runny.

ROAST 🌿 Cook in the oven at a moderately low temperature. Roasting, like broiling, adds no fat. And if you place the food—chicken, for instance—on a raised rack inside your roasting pan, some of its fat will drip away as it cooks. Try Chicken Roasted with Garlic (see page 181).

SAUTÉ 🌿 Cook food quickly in a little bit of butter, oil, or stock over direct heat, just until it's softened or lightly browned. You can minimize the amount of fat by using a heavy anodized nonstick sauté pan (see page 231).

STEAM 🌿 Cook the food over gently boiling water until it's just crisp-tender, or as desired. Steaming adds no fat to foods, and allows vegetables to retain most of their nutrients. See page 148 for more detailed steaming instructions.

STEEP 🌿 Let an aromatic ingredient, such as tea or herbs, sit in hot liquid until it flavors the liquid. To make Basic Vegetable Broth or *Very* Basic Chicken Broth (see page 44 or 46), you steep a bouquet garni (see page 44) in the cooking water.

STEW 🌿 Place food in a well-seasoned broth or marinade, and cook it slowly over low heat in a tightly covered pot. Serve stews with plenty of the stewing liquid, which will contain many of the nutrients. Try the Chicken Stewed with Fennel, Tomatoes, and Saffron (see page 178).

STIR-FRY 🌿 Cook over very high heat, briskly stirring the ingredients so they cook evenly. This method doesn't require the addition of much fat. And because they're cooked so quickly, the vegetables retain most of their nutrients. Try the Vegetable-Tofu Stir-Fry (with Chicken) (see page 147).

Notes on Nutrition for Almost Vegetarians

For ages, food lovers thought of nutrition—if they thought of it at all—as something of a killjoy. But now it's a welcome part of meal planning. Here are some facts and related suggestions to help you balance your menus and your diet overall.

More Can Be Less

If you eat more foods, you may eat less *food*; when you have a lot of variety, you may want less volume. Many people find they fill up much faster when they have small portions of a number of different foods, especially bulky foods such as vegetable soups and salads, than when they have a large serving of a single dish.

Meatless Diets, While Often Healthy, Aren't Risk Free

But usually not, as long thought, for lack of protein. Protein has been so oversold that most Americans eat more than they need. And contrary to myth, extra protein doesn't build muscle; it burns off as energy or piles up as fat. If you eat legumes and dairy products along with whole grains, you're set for protein.

Meatless diets are more likely to lack B vitamins and iron. Make sure you compensate for B vitamins by eating lots of legumes, whole grains, and dark leafy vegetables.

B VITAMIN–RICH DISHES

Chickpea Curry (see page 156) with brown basmati rice

Rice Salad with Mango and Chickpeas (with or without Chicken) (see page 77)

Couscous with Vegetables (and Fish) (see page 197)

Don't rely on spinach for iron. Your body can't absorb enough iron from spinach to justify its reputation as a major source of that mineral. The best way to get iron from vegetables is to make a meatless stew such as chili with beans. The vitamin C in the tomatoes and bell peppers helps release iron from the beans.

IRON-RICH DISHES

Chili with Seafood or Beans (see page 204)

Chickpea Curry (see page 156)

Vegetable Ragu (see page 153)

Another risk involves fat. In going vegetarian, some people end up replacing one fatty protein source (red meat) with others, such as cheese and soy products. Instead, plan meals around legumes and low-fat or fat-free dairy foods, adding just enough of the fattier cheeses to give them some body and flavor.

You Need Lots of Calcium, but You Don't Have to Drink Milk to Get It

You can *cook* with it. Or you can eat or cook with low-fat or nonfat yogurt. Some legumes and green vegetables—notably broccoli and artichokes—also contain calcium in varying amounts.

ENRICH-QUICK SCHEME
The next time you make hot cereal, substitute skim milk for the water. Cook it over low heat and stir it often to prevent burning. Serve it with additional hot skim milk on top.

Skim milk and nonfat yogurt have fewer calories and more calcium—and more protein—than whole milk and whole-milk yogurt. Tofu and soy milk contain calcium, but lots of fat, too (one 4-ounce serving of tofu has 7 grams of fat, versus a trace amount in an 8-ounce serving of skim milk or nonfat yogurt).

CALCIUM-RICH DISHES
Spinach Fettuccine with Tangy Tofu Sauce and
Mushrooms (see page 118)
Tangy Spinach-Yogurt Soup (see page 48)
Peerlees Pureed Cauliflower Soup (see page 57)
Gnocchi with Leeks and Ricotta (see page 127)

Fat: The Calories That Count

Despite all the research devoted to it, metabolism remains a mystery. But it seems that the calories from fatty foods turn to fat more easily than calories from sugars and starches. Weight control seems to be a matter of eating *less fat, not fewer calories.*

The implications are delicious: you can reduce the amount of fat in your meals and enhance the flavor at the same time.

While butter and oils can make foods taste better, they can also overwhelm them. When you use less oil for sautéing, when you spread butter sparingly and dress salads lightly, you're bound to discover fresh, subtle tastes that had been smothered before.

Similarly, you can better appreciate the taste of butter and oils when you use them in smaller amounts. Rich foods taste best when they're balanced by crisp vegetables and good, earthy grains.

Further, with fewer fats on our plates there's room for more—and more imaginatively prepared—vegetables, fruits, grains, lean meats, and seafood.

I've tested all of the recipes in this collection with the intention of keeping the fat content as low as possible. Consequently, each recipe calls for the *minimum* amount of added fat necessary for good results—in some cases, none at all. Most of these dishes contain so little fat per serving that you can stay well within (and often way below) the present nutritional guidelines regarding fat consumption.

Low-Fat Menus

. . . . . .

Cold Sweet Potato Soup (see page 61)
Asian Snow Pea and Mussel Salad (see page 75)
Seasonal Clafouti (see page 219)

Tangy Spinach-Yogurt Soup (see page 48)
Beet Risotto (see page 132)
Chocolate Pudding in Fresh Orange Shells
(The Emperor's New Dessert) (see page 222)

Chickpea Curry (see page 156)
or Spicy Black Beans with Fresh Plums (see page 157)
Fruit Yogurt Soufflés (see page 218)

High-Fiber Menus

. . . . . .

Rice Salad with Mango and Chickpeas
(with or without Chicken) (see page 77)
with whole-grain bread
Seasonal Clafouti
(see page 219) with prunes

Lentil Salad with Sun-Dried Tomatoes and
Feta Cheese (see page 74)

Tossed salad (see page 64)
Chickpea Curry (see page 156) with brown rice
Apple Crepes (see page 216)

The Better Multivitamins

It seems that broccoli, brussels sprouts, cauliflower, and cabbage (known as cruciferous vegetables for their cross-shaped flowers) contain vitamin compounds that stimulate a sort of search-and-destroy mission aimed at cancer-causing molecules. This has never been confirmed beyond doubt, but it may be that preventing cancer involves developing a taste for crucifers, and then indulging it several times a week. Other vegetables in this category include turnips, rutabagas, collard greens, and kale.

What's more, cruciferous vegetables contain lots of soluble fiber, great for weight control because soluble fiber swells and makes you feel full. Soluble fiber may also help cleanse the bloodstream, while insoluble fiber, found in abundance in whole grains, dried fruits, and legumes, has the same effect on the digestive tract.

We're Not Talking Miracles, but . . .

There are foods that provide vitamins, minerals, fiber, and long-lasting energy, assuring a steady supply over several hours. They're complex carbohydrates, and they're versatile, delicious, and very, very satisfying. Because they taste so good and can be prepared in so many ways, current nutritional advice on the subject is easy to swallow and as easy to implement: shift away from fat-laden entrées to meals made up largely of foods from this category, such as whole grains, potatoes, pasta, and corn.

Simple carbohydrates shoot sugar straight into your bloodstream for a spurt of energy. They include fruits, milk, honey, syrups, and sugars. A slump will shortly follow unless you supplement your simple carbohydrate with a food or dish that is complex, such as bread with a glass of milk or milk over cereal. You'll get a quick boost from the sugars in the milk and longer-lasting energy from the carbohydrates in the bread or cereal grain.

A Pinch of Sugar

You'll find, when you look over the recipes, I have nothing against sugars (raw sugar, maple syrup, honey, and so on), which, in small amounts, aren't harmful to anyone whose ability to digest them isn't impaired. Sugar in itself isn't fattening, but it's often combined with ingredients that are. For example, fudge gets relatively few of its calories from sugar. The main culprits are the butter and cream.

Eating sugar may cause you to crave more of it, so that you eat too much and gain weight in the end. You can avoid this effect by eating lots of complex carbohydrates, which curb cravings by keeping your system satisfied. Most of the recipes in this collection calling for simple sugars also call for complex carbohydrates (such as whole wheat flour, stone-ground cornmeal, and rice) so that the craving cycle will not be activated.

High-Carbohydrates Menus

* * * * * *

Baked Stuffed Turnips (see page 93)
Poached Fish (see page 190) with assorted condiments
Strawberry Risotto (see page 220)

Sweet Potato Pancakes (see page 102)
Tandoori Spice Marinade for Chicken
(or Pressed Tofu) (see page 177)
Fruit Cups (see page 228)

Chilled Corn Chowder (see page 59)
White Beans and Fresh Tuna (see page 201)
Apple Crepes (see page 216)

Tossed salad (see page 64) with Basic Low-Fat
Cream-Style Dressing (see page 66)
Spicy Black Beans with Fresh Plums (see page 157)
Fruit Yogurt Soufflés (see page 218)

About the Nutrition Information

The nutrition information that follows each recipe is as accurate as possible, but not precise. I've made the calculations based on the ingredients I use, including brand-name products that may differ in content from those you tend to choose. Items such as enriched flours and grains, salt-free canned goods, and skim dairy products contain varying amounts of nutrients that will affect the totals in some categories to an extent.

Nevertheless, you can use the information to:

1. Plan well-rounded, healthy meals
2. Compare the nutritional values of vegetarian dishes with those made with poultry or fish

3. Supplement the information you get from product labels, so you can keep track of what you're eating in a day, week, or month

Nutritional Content per Serving

YIELD: The number of portions this recipe makes. The list below tells you what each portion contains.

CALORIES: To figure out how many calories are in a larger or smaller serving than that specified, multiply the number of calories by the yield given. Then divide that number according to how much of the whole amount you'll be having. For example, if you're going to eat half of it, divide by 2. If you want a quarter of it, divide by 4, and so on.

FAT (G): When a recipe calls for whole milk or low-fat dairy products, eggs, meat, or butter, some of this fat will be saturated. Otherwise it is mono- or polyunsaturated fat. Saturated fat has been found to clog arteries, while some unsaturated fats may have the opposite effect.

PROTEIN (G): RDA = Women 50 g, men 63 g. These numbers are recommended for people between the ages of 25 and 50.

CARBOHYDRATES (G): For most recipes in this book, the value here represents complex carbohydrates. (The exception is desserts.) This is good news (see page 9).

CHOLESTEROL (MG): Your total intake of cholesterol should not exceed 300 mg each day.

SODIUM (MG): The maximum amount of sodium, or salt, you consume should not exceed 2,900 mg each day.

BEFORE SALTING: A note on how the dish was prepared. You'll find these notes wherever an optional ingredient affects the nutritional content significantly.

% RDA: When a portion contains 20 percent or more of the recommended daily allowance for certain vitamins or minerals, you will find it mentioned here.

Some Additional Menus

All Vegetarian Menus

Tangy Spinach-Yogurt Soup
(see page 48)
Mushrooms and Bean Curd in
Thai Peanut-Coconut Curry Sauce
(see page 162)
Fruit Cups
(see page 228)

Cold Sweet Potato Soup
(see page 61)
Spinach Fettuccine with Tangy
Tofu Sauce and Mushrooms
(see page 118)
Seasonal Clafouti
(see page 219)

Chilled Cucumber Soup
(see page 60)
Summer Garden Risotto
(see page 134)
Peach Scone Cakes
(see page 219)

Tossed Salad for All Seasons
(see page 64)
Individual Potato Tortas
(see page 151)
Cabbage with Apples and Cheese
(see page 84)

One-Dish Dinners

Vegetable Ragu
(see page 153)

Cabbage Filled with Spinach,
Basmati Rice, and Fresh Salmon or
Spicy Lentil Puree
(see page 199)

Chunky Lentil Soup with Parmesan
(see page 56)

Chili with Seafood or Beans
(see page 204)

Rice Salad with Mango and Chickpeas
(with or without Chicken)
(see page 77)

Chicken Stewed with Fennel,
Tomatoes, and Saffron
(see page 178)

Menus for Mixed Company
(Some Vegetarian, Some Almost Vegetarian)

Aromatic Leek and Potato Soup
(see page 50)
Chicken Roasted with Garlic
(see page 181)
Lemony Risotto
(see page 130)
or Carrot-Ginger Risotto
(see page 129)
Red Cabbage and Onion Relish
(see page 106)
Sweet Baked Ricotta with Lemon or Pumpkin
(see page 221)

Mediterranean Eggplant and Peppers
(see page 81)
Poached Fish
(see page 190)
Winter Squash Gratin
(see page 86)
Braised Onions with Sweet Rice Stuffing
(see page 94)
Banana Ricotta Cream
(see page 224)

Special Occasion Menus

See Almost Vegetarian Holiday Dinner
(see page 186)

Chilled Tomato Timbales in
Tender Spinach Casing
(see page 89)
Monkfish with Mushrooms and Lentils
(see page 194)
Braised Onions with Sweet Rice Stuffing
(see page 94)
Sweet Baked Ricotta with Lemon or Pumpkin
(see page 221)

Carrot and Apricot Terrine
(see page 87)
Chicken Roasted with Garlic
(see page 181)
Foccace
(see page 138)
Seasonal Clafouti
(see page 219)

Aromatic Leek and Potato Soup
(see page 50)
Cabbage Filled with Spinach, Basmati Rice,
Fresh Salmon or Spicy Lentil Puree
(see page 199)
Winter Vegetables in Mellow Lemon Marinade
(see page 85)
Chocolate Pudding in Orange Shells
(The Emperor's New Dessert)
(see page 222)

Fresh Vegetable Directory
with a Taster's Tour of Recipes That Call for Them

A Fresh Fruit Directory with a Taster's Tour of Recipes That Call for Them starts at the beginning of the Dessert chapter, on page 210.

HOW TO CHOOSE FRESH VEGETABLES

Shopping is as critical as anything you'll do in the kitchen; be flexible and get what's fresh rather than setting your heart on a particular dish and buying the ingredients you need for it regardless of whether they're any good.

1. Look for vibrant colors and smooth, unblemished surfaces. Check for signs of aging and decay, such as wilting (on salad greens), molding (on mushrooms), and sprouting (on onions and potatoes).

2. Smell for an inviting aroma that's *true to type*—sweet and delicate for salad greens, for instance, earthy for mushrooms.

3. Feel for firmness, checking also for slime on the surface.

ARTICHOKES

These globes, with their spiked, calloused leaves, look fierce. But they're only bluffing. They have a heart that's tender and sweet.

The best artichokes are firm, plump, bright green in spring, and olive colored in fall. Some are streaked with purple, which is fine, and some are blotched with black, which is not. Squeeze the heads; if they squeak, they're fresh; if they rustle, they're not.

Peak season for artichokes occurs twice a year: spring and fall.

To store uncooked artichokes, wrap them in plastic and keep them refrigerated for up to 1 week. Sprinkle cooked artichokes with lemon juice, then wrap them tightly in foil or plastic, and they'll keep, refrigerated, for up to 3 days.

Try them pureed in a full-bodied Artichoke Soup (see page 47) or sautéed with garlic and herbs to fill poached chicken breasts (see Poached Chicken Breasts or Artichokes with Artichoke Stuffing, page 172).

ASPARAGUS

It's delicious, but that's not why grown men and women lose their heads when it first appears for sale. Liked for how it tastes, it's *loved* for what it means: spring is here at last.

The best asparagus has firm, slender stalks and tight, compact tips.

Peak season for asparagus is early spring through early summer. It peaks at different times throughout the country, so your market may carry asparagus from somewhere else before local crops are ready. You may be happier if you wait, because the more time asparagus spends in transit, the less taste it delivers.

To store asparagus, first remember that no matter what you do, it will lose flavor by the day and become tougher, too. Wrapped in plastic it will keep for up to 4 days, at most.

Try it on pasta with scallions, leeks, and mild soft cheese (see Pasta with Asparagus and Leeks, page 116) or in a golden baked omelette (see Herbed Asparagus Torta, page 80).

AVOCADO

Exceptionally good in sandwiches, salads, and tacos, the avocado is also an exception in two other ways: first, to the rule that fruit is sweet, which is why it's commonly served as a vegetable; second, to the rule that fruit has little fat and few calories. Avocados (sigh) are full of both.

The best avocados have ripened just enough to give slightly when you press them. The most common are Hass, from California, which have dark, rough, pockmarked skin, and various strains from Florida, which have smooth skin of either emerald or forest green. The Florida fruits have fewer calories and half as much fat as a Hass.

Peak season for avocados of some kind continues throughout the year. Hass hit their peak in the spring and summer, while Florida's crops kick in in fall.

To store unripe avocados, leave them out in a cool, dry place until they give when touched. For rapid ripening, place them in a paper bag along with a ripe banana. Refrigerated, ripe avocados will keep for up to 2 days. To store a cut avocado, sprinkle the exposed fruit with fresh lemon juice and wrap it tightly in plastic. Although it won't look very pretty, it will taste good for up to a week.

Try them sparingly—in small cubes to garnish Chili with Seafood or Beans (see page 204) or as a creamy and colorful component of Grilled Fajita Salad (with Turkey) (see page 182).

BEETS

They can be tangy and refreshing, or they can be cloying. The trick is to balance the sweetness of beets with something sharp and acidic, such as citrus juice, horseradish, plain yogurt, or low-fat sour cream. Or you can balance it with something mild, like potatoes.

The best beets are small (no larger than 2 inches in diameter), smooth, and round, with the leafy greens still attached. Check the tap root—the "tail" that extends from the bottom of each beet. It should be thin and firm, not stubby and tough.

Peak season is June through October.

To store uncooked beets, cut off the greens, leaving about 2 inches of stem. Put them in a plastic bag and refrigerate, in the crisper section, if possible. Cooked beets, wrapped in plastic or foil, will keep in the refrigerator for up to a week.

Try them in a sensational sweet Beet Risotto (see page 132), or with tender-crisp cauliflower and cabbage tossed with a creamy béchamel (see Wonderful Warm Winter Slaw, page 154), or use them to add color and zing to Wholly Wholesome Mashed Potatoes (see page 99).

BROCCOLI

It isn't universally popular. People who like it, love it, but those who don't, don't even want to hear about it much less eat it. I've never known persuasion to work in favor of a vegetable, so pointing out that broccoli is uncommonly high in vitamin C and calcium is likely to be futile if you're serving it to someone who simply hates the taste of it. Instead, try slipping them a small portion incognito, such as pureed into a pesto and served with fresh corn pancakes (see Sweet Corncakes with Mixed Pestos or Crab Filling, page 158).

The best broccoli is deep green with firm, narrow stalks ending in florets that have an even, tightly knit surface. If it's flowering or tinged with yellow, it's no longer good.

Peak season for broccoli is from mid-autumn through midspring, although good fresh broccoli is available throughout the year in most places.

To store broccoli, keep it refrigerated, unwashed and wrapped in plastic, for up to 4 days.

Try it steamed and topped with a creamy ginger herb sauce (see Spinach Fettuccine with Tangy Tofu Sauce and Mushrooms, page 118).

BRUSSELS SPROUTS

They rarely appear on anyone's list of favorite vegetables, probably because they're just as infrequently properly cooked. Boiled even a minute too long, they're acrid and mushy. But steamed until they're just cooked through, they taste like a cross between broccoli and cabbage, milder than the first and slightly stronger than the second. They also provide a serious dose of fiber.

The best brussels sprouts are small, pea green, and firm, resembling perfect miniature cabbages. Try to find them still on the stalk.

Peak season for brussels sprouts is early spring, although you can get them throughout the year. I suggest waiting for spring, when they're at their sweetest and most tender.

To store brussels sprouts, keep them refrigerated, unwashed, either in their tubs and covered in cellophane or in a plastic bag for up to 4 days.

Try them tossed with sharp cheddar cheese and sweet dried apples (see Wonderful Warm Winter Slaw, page 154), or spiked with nutmeg and pureed for Silken Vegetable Soup (see page 52).

CABBAGE

It's become so renowned as a food of last resort—a critical source of nourishment during wartime and famine—that many people don't think of cabbage as long as something else (*anything* else) is available. And, like many maligned vegetables, its reputation has suffered from being overcooked. I would urge skeptics to think again, because cabbage is crunchy, sweet, and very, very good for you.

The best green cabbage is pale in color, with tender, but not spongy, leaves packed into a firm head. Red cabbage should be deep purple and lustrous, and Savoy cabbage should have springy leaves and a head like a bud about to burst into bloom.

Peak season for cabbage is virtually year-round, with supplies slightly higher in winter.

To store cabbage, keep it in the crisper section of the refrigerator, unwashed and wrapped in plastic, for up to 10 days.

Try it as a tender casing for spinach, rice, and salmon or pureed lentils (see Cabbage Filled with Spinach, Basmati Rice, and Fresh Salmon or Spicy Lentil Puree, page 199), or sautéed with onions and dried cherries as a stuffing for chicken or a topping for grilled fish or vegetables (see Chicken Legs Filled with Sweet Shredded Cabbage, page 180).

CARROTS

The vitamin A in carrots, while linked to good vision, can't take the place of corrective lenses. But carrots may have critical benefits unrelated to eyesight. They may control blood cholesterol levels and help to confound cancer-causing enzymes. And although their effect on the eyes has been overstated, it would be hard to exaggerate their impact on soups, salads, entrées, side dishes, and desserts.

The best carrots are deep orange, small, firm, and well formed, without gnarls, knobs, or gashes. The kind kept chilled in plastic may be fresher than carrots sold in bunches with the greens attached.

Peak season for carrots is summer and fall.

To store carrots, keep them unwashed and unpeeled, in the crisper section of the refrigerator. Keep them away from apples, which let off a gas that causes carrots to rot.

Try them sweetened with apricot puree and baked with ricotta cheese (see Carrot and Apricot Terrine, page 87) and layered with spinach and smooth lemon sauce in a novel lasagna (see Carrot and Spinach Lasagna with Lemon Sauce, page 123).

CAULIFLOWER

Its principal shortcoming is also the cauliflower's greatest asset. It's bland, so while it doesn't add much flavor to anything, it is much affected by whatever's added to it.

The best cauliflower is densely packed, firm, and pearl white, and the surface of the florets has an even texture.

Peak season for cauliflower is autumn, although like many sturdy vegetables, it's available throughout the year.

To store cauliflower, keep it unwashed and wrapped in plastic, in the crisper section of the refrigerator. Handle it gently, or it may bruise.

Try it pureed and layered with spinach and golden squash in a cheese-dusted cold-weather dish (see Winter Squash Gratin, page 86).

CELERY

At its best, celery is crunchy and slightly sweet, adding texture to salads and flavor to broths. It's largely water, which accounts for the appealing idea that when you eat it, you burn more calories chewing it than you consume in the process. It's not quite true. Still, celery contains very few calories, so while it won't whittle away at the weight you have, you won't gain anything if you eat it *instead* of fattening foods.

The best celery is ice green, firm, and crisp.

Peak season is ongoing.

To store celery, keep it, unwashed and wrapped in plastic, in the crisper section of the refrigerator for up to 1 week.

Try it as an aromatic seasoning for Basic Vegetable Broth (see page 44) and *Very* Basic Chicken Broth (see page 46), as a stuffing for chicken in crunchy Chicken Legs Filled with Sweet Shredded Cabbage (see page 180), or as a topping for Sweet Potato Pancakes (see page 102).

CORN

This vegetable stirs more regional chauvinism than any other grocery item. Every state that has a crop claims its corn is the best. There can't be any argument because they're all correct. Here's why: The best corn is the freshest corn, so homegrown will *always* taste better than imported. Iowa corn will taste better in Iowa than in Michigan. And vice versa.

The best corn comes in snug, moist, bright green husks, with a tassel of soft white or golden silk on top. The kernels at the tip should be small, and all should be firm and arranged in uniform rows. White corn should have kernels like small pearls. Yellow corn kernels should be wider, plumper, and have a deep sunny shade.

Peak season for corn is late summer and early fall. You may be able to find fresh corn from Florida during the winter, but unless you live in that state, it will probably be tasteless and tough. So think regional and eat seasonal.

To store corn, first remember that it won't keep its pure sweet flavor for any length of time no matter what you do. After a few days, the sugars turn to starch, and the corn becomes tough, flat, and, eventually, sour. But kept in its husk, refrigerated, corn will be good for cooking for up to 4 days.

Try it in light savory pancakes (see Sweet Corncakes with Mixed Pestos or Crab Filling, page 158), in a summer soup seasoned with ginger and basil (see Chilled Corn Chowder, page 59), and in a very simple lunch salad (see Potato, Corn, and Egg Salad with Chives, page 69).

CUCUMBER

Otherwise unremarkable, cucumber has a dubious distinction. It is the subject of an infamous slur, a facetious recipe, attributed to Dr. Johnson, that goes like this: "A cucumber should be well sliced, and dressed with pepper and vinegar, and thrown out as good for nothing." Nevertheless, cucumbers still flourish in cuisines as diverse as Chinese, Persian, and Thai, prized for their refreshing contribution to salads, sandwiches, and cold summer soups.

Some people like them seeded but not peeled, while others peel them, and don't bother about the seeds. If the cucumber is small and unwaxed, just slice it and serve.

The best cucumbers are firm, with dark green skin of an even tone. European cucumbers are longer, thinner, and crispier with fewer seeds than American cukes.

Peak season for cucumbers is from May through July, although you can get them throughout the year.

To store cucumbers, keep them refrigerated in the crisper section for up to 5 days.

Try them in a creamy cold soup (see Chilled Cucumber Soup, page 60).

EGGPLANT

A pulpy texture and neutral flavor make eggplant a popular stand-in for meat in cuisines of all kinds. Many conventional recipes involving eggplant call for frying or sautéing it before adding it to the dish. I prefer to bake this high-fiber vegetable for two reasons. First, you can taste the eggplant itself, rather than the oil used to prepare it. And second, eggplant absorbs more fat during cooking than any other vegetable, going from next to no fat calories to as many as 700 in 1 minute.

The best eggplants are slender, firm, and shiny rather than squat, soft, and dull. I prefer the small, narrow Japanese eggplant (about 5 inches long and 1½ inches in diameter) because it's not bitter and doesn't need salting.

Peak season for eggplant is July through October, although you can get it throughout the year in many places.

To store eggplant, keep it refrigerated, wrapped in plastic, for up to 5 days.

Try it in a habit-forming side dish with red peppers and onion (see Mediterranean Eggplant and Peppers, page 81) and as a mild foil for sharp sautéed radicchio in the simple Baked Eggplant and Radicchio Sandwich (see page 147).

FENNEL

Also sold as anise, fennel is what celery would be if celery could fulfill its potential. Anything celery can do, fennel does better. It's crispier when raw, sweeter and more tender when cooked. Use it wherever you'd ordinarily use celery: in broths, salads, soups, poaching liquid, and sautéed dishes of all kinds.

The best fennel has firm, unblemished bulbs and feathery stalks, all of which can be used.

celery contains very few calories, so while it won't whittle away at the weight you have, you won't gain anything if you eat it *instead* of fattening foods.

The best celery is ice green, firm, and crisp.

Peak season is ongoing.

To store celery, keep it, unwashed and wrapped in plastic, in the crisper section of the refrigerator for up to 1 week.

Try it as an aromatic seasoning for Basic Vegetable Broth (see page 44) and *Very* Basic Chicken Broth (see page 46), as a stuffing for chicken in crunchy Chicken Legs Filled with Sweet Shredded Cabbage (see page 180), or as a topping for Sweet Potato Pancakes (see page 102).

CORN

This vegetable stirs more regional chauvinism than any other grocery item. Every state that has a crop claims its corn is the best. There can't be any argument because they're all correct. Here's why: The best corn is the freshest corn, so homegrown will *always* taste better than imported. Iowa corn will taste better in Iowa than in Michigan. And vice versa.

The best corn comes in snug, moist, bright green husks, with a tassel of soft white or golden silk on top. The kernels at the tip should be small, and all should be firm and arranged in uniform rows. White corn should have kernels like small pearls. Yellow corn kernels should be wider, plumper, and have a deep sunny shade.

Peak season for corn is late summer and early fall. You may be able to find fresh corn from Florida during the winter, but unless you live in that state, it will probably be tasteless and tough. So think regional and eat seasonal.

To store corn, first remember that it won't keep its pure sweet flavor for any length of time no matter what you do. After a few days, the sugars turn to starch, and the corn becomes tough, flat, and, eventually, sour. But kept in its husk, refrigerated, corn will be good for cooking for up to 4 days.

Try it in light savory pancakes (see Sweet Corncakes with Mixed Pestos or Crab Filling, page 158), in a summer soup seasoned with ginger and basil (see Chilled Corn Chowder, page 59), and in a very simple lunch salad (see Potato, Corn, and Egg Salad with Chives, page 69).

CUCUMBER

Otherwise unremarkable, cucumber has a dubious distinction. It is the subject of an infamous slur, a facetious recipe, attributed to Dr. Johnson, that goes like this: "A cucumber should be well sliced, and dressed with pepper and vinegar, and thrown out as good for nothing." Nevertheless, cucumbers still flourish in cuisines as diverse as Chinese, Persian, and Thai, prized for their refreshing contribution to salads, sandwiches, and cold summer soups.

Some people like them seeded but not peeled, while others peel them, and don't bother about the seeds. If the cucumber is small and unwaxed, just slice it and serve.

The best cucumbers are firm, with dark green skin of an even tone. European cucumbers are longer, thinner, and crispier with fewer seeds than American cukes.

Peak season for cucumbers is from May through July, although you can get them throughout the year.

To store cucumbers, keep them refrigerated in the crisper section for up to 5 days.

Try them in a creamy cold soup (see Chilled Cucumber Soup, page 60).

EGGPLANT

A pulpy texture and neutral flavor make eggplant a popular stand-in for meat in cuisines of all kinds. Many conventional recipes involving eggplant call for frying or sautéing it before adding it to the dish. I prefer to bake this high-fiber vegetable for two reasons. First, you can taste the eggplant itself, rather than the oil used to prepare it. And second, eggplant absorbs more fat during cooking than any other vegetable, going from next to no fat calories to as many as 700 in 1 minute.

The best eggplants are slender, firm, and shiny rather than squat, soft, and dull. I prefer the small, narrow Japanese eggplant (about 5 inches long and 1½ inches in diameter) because it's not bitter and doesn't need salting.

Peak season for eggplant is July through October, although you can get it throughout the year in many places.

To store eggplant, keep it refrigerated, wrapped in plastic, for up to 5 days.

Try it in a habit-forming side dish with red peppers and onion (see Mediterranean Eggplant and Peppers, page 81) and as a mild foil for sharp sautéed radicchio in the simple Baked Eggplant and Radicchio Sandwich (see page 147).

FENNEL

Also sold as anise, fennel is what celery would be if celery could fulfill its potential. Anything celery can do, fennel does better. It's crispier when raw, sweeter and more tender when cooked. Use it wherever you'd ordinarily use celery: in broths, salads, soups, poaching liquid, and sautéed dishes of all kinds.

The best fennel has firm, unblemished bulbs and feathery stalks, all of which can be used.

Small bulbs (about 2 inches at the base) are sweetest.

Peak season for fennel is fall and winter.

To store fennel, keep it wrapped in plastic in the crisper section of the refrigerator for up to 4 days.

Try it chopped, leaves and all, to season Basic Vegetable Broth and *Very* Basic Chicken Broth (see page 44 and 46); as a principal flavoring in Chicken Stewed with Tomatoes, Fennel, and Saffron (see page 178); or to complement eggplant, tomatoes, and zucchini in Vegetable Ragu (see page 153).

GARLIC

Said to cure everything from colds and toothaches to cancer and heart disease, garlic has also been prescribed to remedy demonic possession. Whether it has these effects is not altogether clear, but there's no doubt that it works wonders on foods of all kinds. It's a principal seasoning in almost everything worth eating, this side of dessert. The deep, sweet, and pungent flavor is impossible to replace, which is why the motto of cooks the world over might be "No garlic, no dinner."

The best garlic comes in firm plump heads with large unblemished cloves, with a blush of purple. The head should have some weight. If it's light and flaky, it's probably dried out, and if it's sprouting it's too old. Don't buy prepared minced garlic, which tastes sour and tinny.

Peak season for garlic is ongoing. You can get good garlic throughout the year.

To store garlic, keep it in a cool, dry place for up to 3 weeks. It will keep best in the refrigerator, wrapped in plastic and placed in the crisper section.

Try it with lemon zest, parsley, and rosemary to season roast chicken (see Chicken Roasted with Garlic, page 181), ground with fresh herbs and cheeses for a creamy condiment for soups and pastas (see pestos, page 160 and 161), or roasted and pureed into Wholly Wholesome Mashed Potatoes (see page 99).

LEEKS

Related to onions, leeks are used in similar ways. They have a complicated flavor but a mellow disposition that readily yields to strong ingredients. So the less you mix in with them, the more you'll appreciate the way they taste.

The best leeks are thick (about 1½ inches in diameter) and firm and are stark white at the base, darkening gradually to deep green. Grit can lodge in the underlayers, so clean them well before you cook with them.

Peak season for leeks is winter, but you can get good leeks throughout the year.

To store leeks, refrigerate them, unwashed and wrapped in plastic, for up to 5 days.

Try them steamed as a delicate casing for a light, savory custard (see Gingered Leek and Fennel Flans, page 90), in a creamy topping for pasta (see Gnocchi with Leeks and Ricotta, page 127), or with herbs and potatoes in a classic soup (see Aromatic Leek and Potato Soup, page 50).

LETTUCES

Long before becoming mere props for salad dressings, lettuces were served cooked more often than raw. Why that's no longer true is baffling, since most taste terrific that way.

The best lettuces *look* the best. The leaves are fresh and uniformly bright, not wilted, slimy, or brown around the edges.

Peak season for most lettuces is ongoing. Radicchio and Belgian endive are best in the winter, while spring is prime time for more tender greens.

To store lettuces, place them in a perforated plastic bag in the crisper section of the refrigerator for up to 3 days.

Try them in cooking, to season fish and keep it moist (see Braised Fish with Winter Greens, page 192), in a simple, scrumptious Baked Eggplant and Radicchio Sandwich (see page 147), or in a creamy-crunchy topping for toast and poached fish (see Endive and Leek Fondue, page 105). Also see "Tossed Salads for all Seasons," page 64.

MUSHROOMS

When prepared in ways that play up their texture, mushrooms can pacify meat cravings safely (no fat! no cholesterol!) and at relatively low cost.

Some Mushroom Varieties

•Button mushrooms are the most widely cultivated kind of mushroom in the United States, and so the easiest to come by. They have a faint, sweet flavor when raw, and a strong earthy taste when cooked. Unfortunately, cooking also causes them to release a lot of liquid. So when sautéing button mushrooms, be sure to take them off the heat as soon as they've colored and cooked through. (You can test them with a paring knife; they should be easy to pierce and evenly colored throughout.) Whenever you're adding sautéed button mushrooms to a sauce, transfer them with a slotted spoon, so excess liquid will drain away and won't dilute the final dish. Alternatively, carefully tilt the sauté pan and drain off the liquid.

- Cremini, also known as Italian brown mushrooms, look like tawny button mushrooms and have a flavor that's similar, but sweeter. Cremini don't lose as much liquid as buttons during cooking, so you may try substituting them if your mushroom sauces tend to turn out runny. Now that they're cultivated in the United States, they're easier to find.
- Morels, spongy, dark brown, and shaped like little pinecones, have a deep, smoky taste. Now that they're being cultivated in this country, fresh morels are more widely available. But they're still expensive. Dried morels (which you can get by mail from American Spoon Foods—see page 236) add wonderful flavor to dishes but don't provide the chewy sensation you can enjoy with fresh. For the maximum morel experience, combine a handful of fresh ones with as many dried.
- Oyster mushroom cultivation has taken off in this country, so these white, rangy, clustered (that is, joined at the stem in a bouquet) mushrooms are almost as widely available as common button mushrooms. Chewy and very mild, they're best sautéed and served along with other vegetables in a highly seasoned sauce.
- Porcini are rarely sold fresh in this country. And even in Italy, where they're plentiful in late fall, they're expensive and served as something special. For instance, pasta with porcini hardly ever contains anything more than those two ingredients, plus some olive oil and garlic. Risotto with porcini is the same simple thing with rice instead of pasta. And at the height of the season, it's customary in some places to serve a big cap of a porcino sautéed with garlic and strewn with fresh herbs as a main course.

  Dried porcini aren't cheap, but unlike fresh porcini, they are available here (see page 236). What's more, they're tastier than fresh because drying concentrates and intensifies the flavor. Mix the dried mushrooms with fresh portobellos or cremini, and you can enjoy the good firm texture of fresh mushrooms and the incomparable flavor of porcini.
- Portobello is a flat-topped mushroom, with a cap that can be enormous (up to 6 inches in diameter). Large or small, the portobello is hearty, with an earthy flavor similar to that of button mushrooms, but much deeper. Of the two, I prefer portobello because it becomes chewy as it cooks and releases less liquid, so I can better control the consistency of the sauce. Try them on the grill.
- Shiitakes, which once grew only abroad, are now being cultivated widely in the United States. The happy consequence is that you can find these yeasty-tasting mushrooms at

ordinary supermarkets throughout most of the country. Unlike many other mushrooms, shiitakes absorb rather than release liquid when cooked, becoming plump and chewy as they're stir-fried or sautéed.

The best mushrooms are firm and dry, with no soft brown spots or slime on the surface. The head should sit firmly on the stem, not wobble. They should have an inviting earthy smell. Check the underside for fuzzy mold.

Peak season for mushrooms occurs in the late fall and early spring, but you can get many kinds of fresh mushrooms throughout the year.

To store loose mushrooms, wrap them in a damp paper towel, put them inside a paper bag, and keep them in the crisper section of the refrigerator for up to 3 days. Leave packaged mushrooms in their container. Refrigerated, they'll keep for up to 5 days.

Try them by the dozens in the sensational Monkfish with Mushrooms and Lentils (see page 194), sautéed with garlic and parsley in Mushroom Barley (see page 102), or with vegetables of all kinds in a spicy (yow!) curry sauce (see Mushrooms and Bean Curd (and Scallops) in Thai Peanut-Coconut Curry Sauce, page 162). You can get the most from mushrooms by combining fresh and dried in the same dish: dried for an intense flavor, and fresh for texture. (To sample how this works, try the Many Mushrooms Farfalle on page 114).

ONIONS

Fundamental and indispensable, onions are to cooks what mortar is to masons. The character of onions changes so drastically as they cook, they taste utterly different from one moment to the next.

The best onions are firm with close-fitting skin. Watch out for sprouting, soft spots, and graying under the skin.

Peak season for onions is ongoing. (The exceptions are the sweetest varieties, such as Vidalia and Maui Sweet, which are available only in the spring and summer.)

To store onions, keep them at a cool room temperature, away from direct sun. Or put them, wrapped in a paper bag, in the crisper section of the refrigerator on their own so their odor doesn't affect other foods. They'll keep for up to 3 weeks.

Try them filled with sweet and nutty rice stuffing (see Braised Onions with Sweet Rice Stuffing, page 94); sautéed until melting, then mixed with nectarines, pine nuts, and honey (see Nectarine Relish, page 107); or seasoned with parsley to flavor Braised Fish with Winter Greens (see page 192).

PEAS

There's more protein in peas than in any fresh vegetable other than lima beans. Peas of all kinds taste best when they are very, very fresh.

Some Pea Varieties
- Green shell peas are mushy, a texture that's hard to match with other foods. Consequently, they're best in casseroles and other catchall dishes such as Vegetable Ragu (see page 153). Look for fat, firm, unbroken pods.
- Sugar snap peas are aptly named. Crunchy and sweet, they're delicious in the Vegetable-Tofu Stir-Fry (with Chicken) (see page 147). Look for bright green pods with an even row of peas. Sugar snap peas are often mistaken for . . .
- Snow peas, which taste like sugar snap peas, have edible pods, but are smaller and more tender. Look for bright green pods that are pliant but not limp. Try them with mussels and a light, gingery dressing in Asian Snow Pea and Mussel Salad (see page 75).

Peak season for peas of all kinds is early spring through mid-summer, although you can get them year 'round.

To store peas, keep them refrigerated in the crisper section of the refrigerator, unwashed and, in the case of green shell peas, unshelled, for up to 4 days.

PEPPERS

Different colors denote different flavors, so across the color spectrum bell peppers have little in common with one another besides their shape. Yellow peppers are mild and sweet. Orange peppers are sweet with a pungent finish, and red are the reverse. Green bell peppers are so strong that you should use them only when you really want their distinctive flavor, because they will dominate the dish.

The best peppers of any color are firm, with a natural sheen (ask whether they've been waxed). Check for soft spots around the stem, where decay often begins.

Peak season for peppers is summer, although good peppers (mostly imported) are available throughout the year.

To store peppers, refrigerate them in a paper bag in the crisper section for up to 10 days.

Try them in an irresistible side dish with baked eggplant and onions (see Mediterranean Eggplant and Peppers, page 81); strewn over savory potato patties (see *Pissaladière*-Inspired Potato Tarts, page 97); pureed with feta cheese in an exquisite appetizer (see Roasted Red Pepper Terrine, page 88).

POTATOES

Spuds have been maligned for far too long, rumored to be fattening in what amounts to a case of misattribution: fried potatoes, for example, are fattening because they're *fried*, not because they're potatoes. And plain potatoes, mashed, are benign fast-burning carbohydrates and virtually fat free until you add butter and cream.

Most of the vitamins, minerals, and fiber are in the skin, so try to prepare potatoes in ways that involve leaving it on. For instance, don't peel potatoes before you add them to soups or stews.

Garden Variety Potatoes

- Russets are brown, oblong, and often called baking potatoes due to their most common use. Because they're dry and firm, russets make the best gnocchi (see page 124).
- Long white potatoes, which are shaped like russets but have a thin, glossy skin, are excellent mashed and in potato salad.
- Round white or round red potatoes are the ones to use in soups and stews.
- New potatoes are tiny and sweet, and best simply boiled or roasted until tender and eaten plain or sprinkled with fresh herbs.

Specialty Spuds

- All Blue or Blue Bliss potatoes are creamy and sweet. Boil them as you would round reds.
- Finnish Golden Wax and Yukon Gold have a rich and buttery flavor that make them worth seeking out, and also worth the extra you'll pay per pound when you find them. Boil them, mash them, or use them for salads.

The best potatoes of any kind are firm and well formed. Don't buy them if they're shooting sprouts (a sign of age) or if they're green in spots (a sign of toxin). I've found that organic potatoes are sweeter and creamier than conventionally grown spuds, which usually spend more time in storage.

Peak season for most potatoes is perpetual; you can get them throughout the year. New potatoes, however, are available only from February through October.

To store potatoes, keep them in a cool, dry place, preferably so that air can circulate around them. Here's where a hanging wire basket would come in handy. Or you can simply put them in your refrigerator, turning them over every few days. Most potatoes will keep for up to 3 weeks, but new potatoes become tough and flat tasting after 3 days.

Try them in onion-smothered patties baked to a golden brown (see *Pissaladière*-Inspired Potato Tarts, page 97); as chewy dumplings in a tangy, creamy Parmesan sauce (see Gnocchi with Sun-Dried Tomatoes (and Chicken), page 126); with cottage cheese and chives in Wholly Wholesome Mashed Potatoes (see page 99).

PUMPKIN

(see Winter Squash)

SCALLIONS

Sautéed in sesame or peanut oil with garlic and ginger, and seasoned with soy sauce, scallions give Far Eastern foods their characteristic flavor. Relatively mild, scallions can take the place of onions in cooking as well as in salads and sandwiches.

The best scallions have firm white bulbs at the root and deep green stems. They should be firm, not limp.

Peak season for scallions is ongoing.

To store scallions, keep them refrigerated in the crisper section of the refrigerator for up to 5 days.

Try them with bean curd in a peanut-coconut curry (see Mushrooms and Bean Curd (and Scallops) in Thai Peanut-Coconut Curry Sauce, page 162); with mild cheese, asparagus, and leeks (see Pasta with Asparagus and Leeks, page 116).

SHALLOTS

They resemble large cloves of garlic, but shallots taste more like piquant onions. For a new twist on an old dish, substitute shallots where you'd ordinarily use onions or scallions.

The best shallots look like large tawny garlic cloves. They should be firm and smooth, with close-fitting skin.

Peak season for shallots is ongoing.

To store shallots, keep them in a dry place at a cool room temperature, away from direct sun. Or put them in the crisper section of the refrigerator. Either way, they'll keep for up to 2 weeks.

Try them with ginger and garlic in Mushrooms and Bean Curd (and Scallops) in Thai Peanut-Coconut Curry Sauce (see page 162).

SPINACH

A good-natured green, spinach is an agreeable companion to eggs, cheeses, and vegetables of most kinds. Well known as a source of vitamins, it's less widely considered a source of pleasure. This may be because it's often served in a soggy heap, rather than lightly steamed and seasoned with care.

The best spinach is dark green, with firm, unblemished leaves. It's best bought loose, rather than cello-packed.

Peak season is ongoing.

To store spinach, put it, unwashed, in a perforated plastic bag, and place it in the crisper section of the refrigerator for up to 3 days.

Try it as a tender casing for fresh tomatoes in summery Chilled Tomato Timbales in Tender Spinach Casing (see page 89), sautéed with onions to season Braised Fish with Winter Greens (see page 192), or with lively herbs in fragrant Tangy Spinach-Yogurt Soup (see page 48).

SWEET POTATOES

Commonly known as yams, sweet potatoes are neither potatoes nor genuine yams. You can fix them as you would ordinary potatoes—mashed, baked, or boiled. But because their flavor is so much more distinct, they call for altogether different seasonings. While you might prepare regular potatoes with savory herbs such as rosemary and chives, or sharp cheeses such as cheddar or Parmesan, sweet potatoes benefit from flavors such as orange, maple, cinnamon, nutmeg, and ginger.

The best sweet potatoes are heavy, firm, and smooth. Sweet potatoes come in two varieties, the more common the moist-flesh potato, which has a dark skin and smooth pulp. This is the kind known as yams. The other sweet potato is pale, with a floury pulp similar to that of long white potatoes.

Peak season is fall and early winter.

To store sweet potatoes, first remember that, unlike ordinary potatoes, they don't keep well. Store them at a cool room temperature (no more than 55° F.), well away from direct light and heat, for up to 1 week. *Don't refrigerate them.*

Try them in the closest thing to creamy pumpkin pie (see Cold Sweet Potato Soup, page 61) or tempered with plain potato, flavored with spices, and baked on a griddle (see Sweet Potato Pancakes, page 102).

TOMATOES

There are two distinct types of tomatoes: The kind we get only in late summer and the kind we get the rest of the year. The first are so good, I think they should be called something else so we won't expect the second to taste anything like them.

The best tomatoes are firm enough to maintain their shape, but soft enough to give when you squeeze them. They should be a deep, rich orange-red, without black spots or white fuzz. And they should have an appetizing aroma.

Peak season for tomatoes is late summer and early fall. You can get imported fresh tomatoes throughout the year, but most will be bland by the time they reach the market. When tomatoes aren't in season locally, imported Italian tomatoes (especially Pomi brand, which is sold in boxes) are a good alternative for cooking.

To store unripened tomatoes, leave them at room temperature until they soften and turn deep red. Ripe, they'll keep at a cool room temperature (up to 65°F.) for up to 3 days. Don't refrigerate tomatoes. The cold turns them mealy and sour.

Try them on pasta or fish in the two versions of Perfect Tomato Sauce (see page 112); with sharp feta cheese and chickpeas or shrimp (see Fresh Tomatoes and Feta Cheese with Shrimp or Chickpeas, page 203); or with roasted garlic, basil, and cheese in Summer Garden Risotto (with Scallops) (see page 134).

TURNIPS

It's true that turnips are tossed dutifully into soups and stews usually because they're called for, not because they're loved. But a good turnip is supremely smooth, like a perfect boiled potato but lighter and sweeter.

The best turnips are firm and weighty, with cream-colored skin and a rose- or lavender-colored band on top.

Peak season for turnips is winter.

To store turnips, put them in a plastic bag and refrigerate them for up to 5 days.

Try them filled with potato and pumpkin puree (see Baked Stuffed Turnips, page 93) or combined with a dozen other garden delights in My Favorite Minestrone with Creamy Pesto (see page 54).

WINTER SQUASH

Many types look more like decorations than things you'd have for supper, and you may not want to deface the lovely shells even for the sake of a very good side dish. The solution is to buy some for the table and some to serve.

The best pumpkins are small, because they're sweeter and more manageable than the giants. They should be firm, with smooth skin of an even color.

Peak season for pumpkin is autumn and early winter.

Try it in creamy, sweet Pumpkin Risotto (see page 133) or in a cheesecake-style pudding (see Sweet Baked Ricotta with Lemon or Pumpkin, page 221).

To store pumpkins keep them at a cool room temperature for up to 8 days.

The best **other winter squash** (such as acorn, butternut, golden nugget) have a dull—not glossy—rind of deep color and a sturdy knob of stem attached.

Peak season for most winter squash (except pumpkin, see above) is late summer through late winter.

To store winter squash, keep it at a cool room temperature for up to 5 days, or refrigerated for up to 10.

Try them pureed with potato and cauliflower and baked until golden brown (see Winter Squash Gratin, page 86).

YELLOW SUMMER SQUASH

(see Zucchini)

ZUCCHINI

Grown in quantities far exceeding its usefulness or desirability, zucchini has little nutritional value or flavor, but it comes in handy for adding bulk and color to vegetable stews, soups, and sauces.

The best zucchini are deep green, firm, and no more than 6 inches long. Small zucchini are best because they contain relatively little water, which accumulates as they grow. (Some would argue that yellow summer squash are the best zucchini, since they are similar, but have more color, flavor, and bite.)

Peak season for zucchini is summer.

To store zucchini, keep them refrigerated for up to 5 days.

Try them with other seasonal vegetables and herbs in Vegetable Ragu (see page 153).

FRESH BASIL

Fresh basil tastes sweet at first bite and turns spicier as you chew. It's not to be used sparingly, but showered on salads, pastas, sandwiches, pizzas, and tomatoes.

Dried basil tastes only vaguely like fresh and isn't, strictly speaking, a substitute for it. Yet it's pleasant tasting in its own right, and a good seasoning for soups, sauces, and pastas, especially when combined with dried oregano.

Store basil wrapped in a damp paper towel then sealed in a plastic bag in the crisper section of the refrigerator for up to 5 days.

Try it in Creamy Pesto (see page 55), Perfect Tomato Sauce (see page 112), and Chilled Corn Chowder (see page 59).

FRESH CHIVES

Fresh chives taste like sprightly onions, without the complications (no tears, no bad breath). The best have a clean, savory aroma, something like the mingling of scallions and freshly mowed lawn. They should be firm, not droopy. Dried chives have no taste, but frozen minced chives are widely available and are a good substitute for fresh.

Store chives in the refrigerator for up to 3 days.

Try them in Wholly Wholesome Mashed Potatoes (see page 99) and Chilled Cucumber Soup (see page 60).

FRESH CORIANDER (CILANTRO)

Fresh coriander (cilantro) is also called Chinese parsley because it resembles flat-leaf parsley and is commonly used in Asian cooking. Although they look alike, the herbs are rarely interchangeable in recipes. Not everyone is mad about cilantro's distinct taste—sharp and citruslike—so use it sparingly, adding more or less as you or your guests prefer.

Dried cilantro has virtually no flavor.

Store cilantro, like parsley, with stems submerged in a tall glass of water in the refrigerator. Use only the leaves for cooking.

Try it in Cilantro Pesto (see page 161), Tandoori Spice Marinade for Chicken (or Pressed Tofu) (see page 177), and Chickpea Curry (see page 156).

DRIED, GROUND CUMIN

Ground cumin, deep and musky with a lemony finish, is a marvel of a kind. Most spices with such a strong, distinct flavor have limited popularity. But people cook with cumin all over the world. The Spanish put it in sausage, the French in cheese, the Germans in pickles, the Thais in curry, the Russians in bread, the Tunisians in couscous, the Mexicans in chili.

Try it in Chickpea Curry (see page 156), Hummus (see page 72), Baba Ganoush (see page 71), and in Sweet Potato Pancakes (see page 102).

FRESH AND DRIED DILL

Fresh or dried, dill is a high-spirited herb that adds kick to cold soups and salads. This is a good thing because fresh dill has a shorter shelf life than most other herbs.

Store dill in the refrigerator for 2 days.

Try it in Tangy Spinach-Yogurt Soup (see page 48) and in Fresh Tomatoes and Feta Cheese with Shrimp or Chickpeas (see page 203).

DRIED FENNEL SEED

Dried fennel seed adds a licorice nip to foods, often echoing the milder, sweet flavor of fresh fennel in the same dish. Use very little because fennel seed should rarely do more than suggest that it's present.

Try it in Chicken Stewed with Fennel, Tomatoes, and Saffron (see page 178).

FRESH GINGER

Fresh ginger is the zippy signature seasoning in curries, stir-fries, and North African stews. The best ginger is plump, juicy, and aromatic. Dried ginger can't substitute for fresh in cooking, but it's excellent for baking.

Store ginger for up to a month, wrapped tightly in plastic, and kept in the refrigerator.

Try it in Cold Sweet Potato Soup (see page 61), Chickpea Curry (see page 156), and Gingered Leek and Fennel Flans (see page 90).

FRESH AND DRIED OREGANO

Equally flavorful fresh or dried, oregano comes from two distinct plants found on two separate continents, Europe and North America. Yet the flavor is similar enough to justify calling the two herbs by the same name and using them interchangeably. Like dill, oregano is nearly as good dried as fresh, as long as the dried herb hasn't been sitting around for too long.

Store oregano wrapped in a damp paper towel and sealed in a plastic bag in the crisper section of the refrigerator for up to 5 days.

Try it in Tangy Spinach-Yogurt Soup (see page 48) and in Chili with Seafood or Beans (see page 204).

FRESH PARSLEY

Parsley is so often served as a garnish that to think of using it as a real seasoning takes either a leap of imagination or an inspirational experience. It hadn't occurred to me until I was served a piece of fish dressed with onions that were green from having been sautéed with parsley. This combination is now a mild addiction. I prefer the milder flat-leaf (Italian) parsley to the bitter curly kind. Dried parsley has a terrible tinny taste. Don't use it.

Store parsley in a tall glass of water in the refrigerator for no more than 3 days. Use only the leaves for cooking; put the stems into vegetable broth.

Try it on Braised Fish with Winter Greens (page 192), Chicken Roasted with Garlic (page 181), or Chilled Tomato Timbales in Tender Spinach Casing (page 89).

FRESH ROSEMARY

Fresh rosemary has a powerful piney taste and an incomparable appetizing fragrance. Don't use rosemary leaves whole unless you wrap them in a bouquet garni (see box, page 44). Instead, strip the leaves from the branch, crush them with the side of a knife blade, and mince them. Try to use only fresh rosemary. Dried, it doesn't quite do the trick.

Store rosemary in the refrigerator for up to 5 days.

Try it in My Favorite Minestrone with Creamy Pesto (page 54), in Chicken Roasted with Garlic (page 181), and on *Focacce* (page 138).

DRIED SAFFRON

Sold in threads or powder, saffron is so much more expensive than other spices that you may wonder why it costs as much as it does. The rust-colored powder or threads that turn foods deep yellow and utterly delicious come from the stigmas of the saffron crocus. This in itself doesn't affect the price. The fact that it takes seventy thousand stigmas to make a pound of the spice is what does it. And all of those stigmas must be harvested by hand.

Beware of cheap imitations, which add color to the dish, but no flavor. The taste of saffron is so powerful and specific, if a dish calls for it, you can assume it really needs it. So put off making any such dish if you don't have saffron on hand.

Try it in Chicken Stewed with Fennel, Tomatoes, and Saffron (see page 178) and Basic Risotto (see page 128).

FRESH AND DRIED SAGE

Whether fresh or dried, sage is strong and a little does a lot to deepen the flavor of foods such as vegetable broth, chicken breasts, or firm-fleshed fish. It's best used with restraint and in combination with complementary herbs such as thyme. Dried sage is milder than fresh, so for mild flavor, use just a pinch.

Store sage wrapped in a damp paper towel, sealed in a plastic bag in the crisper section of the refrigerator.

Try it in Herbed Asparagus Torta (see page 80) and Monkfish with Mushrooms and Lentils (page 194).

FRESH AND DRIED TARRAGON

Tarragon, either fresh or dried, has been flavoring food since the 1200s, but it is still subject to trends, going through cycles of neglect and rediscovery. Don't wait for the next round of tarragon mania to test its effect on salad dressings and marinades. More recipes call for dried tarragon than fresh.

Store tarragon wrapped in a damp paper towel sealed in a plastic bag in the crisper section in the refrigerator for 4 days.

Try it in Chicken Breasts (or Pressed Tofu) with Sweet Mustard Glaze (see page 176).

DRIED THYME

Dried thyme, along with parsley and bay leaf, is a definitive component of bouquet garni, the bundle of herbs used to flavor broths and sauces (see page 44). Like tarragon, it's more commonly used dry than fresh.

Store thyme in a plastic bag in the crisper section in the refrigerator wrapped in a damp paper towel, sealed in a plastic bag, for 4 days.

Try it in Basic Vegetable Broth (see page 44) and Very Basic Chicken Broth (see page 46) and in Chicken Breasts (or Pressed Tofu) with Sweet Mustard Glaze (see page 176).

Legumes

Health enthusiasts, eager to endorse a nourishing food, put their credibility on the line when they say that beans taste good. The problem is that beans, as many people know them, are mushy and bland. Of course beans *can* taste very, very good, but it takes some work to make that happen.

First, you must be able to tell them apart.

When they're raw, there's little color to distinguish any given dried bean from your average pebble, much less from a dried bean of another kind. Yet few beans are interchangeable in recipes. Pinto beans and kidney beans taste similar enough to swap, as do cannellini beans and Great Northerns. But the sweet black bean has little in common with the peanutty chickpea, which, in turn, tastes nothing like the earthy lentil. Although their nutritional composition is pretty much alike, for culinary purposes, a bean isn't a bean any more than a fruit is an apple.

To familiarize yourself with the characteristics of different legumes, try them in dishes such as:

- Spicy Black Beans with Fresh Plums (see page 157)
- Tangy Spinach-Yogurt Soup (see page 48)
- Chili with Seafood or Beans (see page 204)
- Chickpea Curry (see page 156)

Second, you need to choose and cook your legumes with care. As with many other vegetables, legumes that are organically grown taste much better—more true to type—than conventionally grown beans, perhaps because they spend less time in storage. You'll get a cleaner bean flavor if you cook legumes yourself rather than use canned beans. But when you're stuck for time, use canned beans with no added sugar and salt, and always drain the beans and rinse them well before adding them to your dish.

Third, it's worth taking extra steps to deal with discomfort. Soaking the beans in advance, then changing the water for cooking should alleviate the gastric and social distress associated with them. Also, it helps to add legumes to your diet gradually, so your system has time to adjust.

HOW TO SOAK BEANS
❶ ❷ ❸

❶ Rinse the beans in a sieve and pick through them, throwing out any pebbles or discolored beans you may find.

❷ Put them in a large pot and add enough water to cover them by at least an inch.

❸ Cover and refrigerate overnight. Drain any remaining water, and add fresh water for cooking.

QUICK-SOAK METHOD
❶ ❷ ❸

❶ Rinse the beans as above, put them in a large pot, and add water to cover by an inch.

❷ Bring the water to a boil over medium-high heat, cover, lower the heat, and simmer for 2 minutes.

❸ Turn off the heat and let the beans sit, covered, for 1 hour. Drain the soaking water, and add fresh water for cooking.

Soybeans, a Special Case

Beans on average have 120 calories per half-cup serving. However, soybeans have more, about 175 per half cup, because they contain 9 grams of fat, compared with 3 grams of fat in the same amount of chickpeas and less than 1 gram of fat in most other popular beans, including lentils, black beans, white beans, kidneys, and pintos.

Soybeans also contain twice as much protein per half-cup serving (17 grams), and double the calcium of other legumes.

Because they have little flavor and tend to

Once you've found how good legumes taste, you'll be glad to know how good for you they are. Legumes are high in complex carbohydrates, fiber, B vitamins, and iron. And except for soybeans (see below), they have little fat, if any.

Legumes also have about as much protein per ½-cup serving as a comparable amount of a skim dairy product such as milk, cottage cheese, or yogurt (9 grams). This is still a lot less protein than an equivalent portion of fish or poultry, which contains approximately 30 grams per 3½-ounce serving. And while fish and poultry are more expensive than beans, you don't have to choose between economizing and eating well. Luckily, beans go splendidly with poultry and fish, so you don't need as much of the more expensive chicken, salmon, or shrimp to make a meal that's nourishing and delicious. Try the Monkfish with Mushrooms and Lentils (see page 194), Grilled Fajita Salad (with Turkey) (see page 182), and White Beans and Fresh Tuna (see page 201).

HOW TO COOK BEANS
❶ ❷ ❸

For each ½ cup soaked beans, do the following:

❶ Put the beans in a large stockpot, and add 4 cups water (for cannellini beans add only 3 cups).

❷ Bring to a boil over medium-high heat, skimming off any foam that forms on the surface.

❸ Turn down the heat to medium-low, cover the pot, and simmer until you can pierce the beans with a knife. This will take anywhere from an hour (kidney beans, pinto beans, chickpeas) to an hour and 40 minutes (black beans, white beans).

Note: To cook lentils, refer to specific recipes.

be mushy, plain soybeans don't inspire the kind of dishes that can be made with better-tasting legumes, such as black beans, lentils, and chickpeas. They become more promising once they're ground with water into soy milk, which is then treated with coagulant and left to harden into tofu.

If You Think You Hate Tofu . . .

You're not alone. While it's meant to be bland, some people find that it's not bland enough, tasting either soapy or something like plastic. But I've found several brands of organic tofu that have a pleasant, clean taste that's very close to neutral. And while I can't claim to love it unconditionally, I *do* love it in dishes such as Mushrooms and Bean Curd (and Scallops) in Thai Peanut-Coconut Curry Sauce (see page 162) and Spinach Fettuccine with Tangy Tofu Sauce and Mushrooms (see page 118).

Buy the freshest tofu you can find, preferably with a "sell by" date at least 10 days ahead. Don't buy it if there are bubbles or bulges in the plastic wrapper.

To store a package of tofu once you've opened it, drain the water, replace it with fresh water, cover, and refrigerate. Change the water daily. Throw out the tofu if it changes color or starts to smell sour.

Soaking Beans . . .

This serves two functions. It cuts the cooking time by up to half and makes the beans easier to digest. When you throw out the soaking liquid, you're getting rid of much of the indigestible sugars that cause gas. It's been said that you're tossing out the flavor, too, but I've found this untrue. What's more, the beans retain their nutrients.

Rice

Rice can be brown or white, amber, mahogany, tan, or pearl; short grain, medium, or long; aromatic or converted; organic or not. Some taste rich, Wehani brand, for instance; some light and sweet, such as organically grown short-grain brown rice; and some are fragrant and smoky, like Texmati, basmati, and jasmine; some others, medium- and long-grain white, for example, just taste like rice.

Although most rices can be stored indefinitely, brown rices contain oils that can go ran-

THE MORE NOURISHING RICE

Brown rice has more zinc, niacin, folacin, and vitamin B$_6$ than white rice, even white rice that's been enriched. This is because it still has its bran layer, which, in white rice, has been removed.

Brown rice can take twice as long as white to cook. You can cut the cooking time in half by soaking the rice in water to cover for 6 hours or overnight.

cid, and all rice is subject to insect infestation. I keep some of my rices in airtight canisters away from direct heat and sunlight. I have more varieties of rice than canisters, though, so I keep the rest in the refrigerator, where it's safe from bugs and heat triggered spoilage.

When choosing a rice, here are some things to consider:

- The shorter the grain, the plumper the rice will be. If you want fluffy rice, choose long grain. If you want chewy rice that's a little bit sticky, use short grain.
- Long-grain white rice has long been *the* rice to serve with Chinese food because it's too neutral to interfere with the flavors of other ingredients and because it soaks in the sauces so nothing goes to waste.
- Jasmine, basmati, and Texmati—known as aromatic rices—have a faint smoky aroma while they're cooking and a toasted flavor that complements curries of all kinds.
- Medium-grain white rice goes well with chili, since the grains are long enough to hold their own, yet soft enough to hold the sauce. It's also good for baked rice puddings.
- Arborio rice is the rice to use for risotto and paella because it absorbs more liquid than any other, swelling so it becomes plump and chewy.
- Ordinary brown rice has a mild, nut-like flavor and goes best with dishes that are slightly sweet. Brown basmati rice has a distinct smoky flavor, closer to white basmati than plain brown rice.

HOW TO STEAM PERFECT RICE
❶ ❷ ❸

Yields 1 to 1½ cups cooked rice

❶ In a heavy saucepan, combine ½ cup of rice with the appropriate amount of water (see below).

❷ Bring to a boil over medium-high heat.

❸ Cover, turn down the heat to low, and cook, without stirring, for the appropriate amount of time (see below).

Brown rice: 1 cup water / 40 minutes
Converted: ⅔ cup water / 30 minutes
Long or medium-grain white rice: ¾ cup water / 20 minutes
Short-grain white rice: ½ cup water / 15 minutes
White basmati rice: ½ cup water / 20 minutes
Brown basmati rice: ¾ cup water / 40 minutes
Texmati white rice: ¾ cup water / 20 minutes
Texmati brown rice: 1 cup water / 40 minutes
Wehani brand: 1 cup water / 45 minutes
Wild rice: 2 cups water / 55 minutes

- Converted rice has been steamed before milling, so vitamins that would otherwise go out with the bran are sealed in the grain yielding a more nourishing rice. The process also makes the rice slick, so the grains don't stick when they cook. It is not the same as instant rice, which has been fully cooked then dehydrated.
- Wehani brand rice cooks up plump and chewy. Because it tastes rich and sweet, it's a good side dish for light entrées, making the meal more substantial by adding flavor and bulk without fat.

- Wild rice has such a strong flavor that you can combine it with less expensive white or brown rice and enjoy the taste as much as you would if you were to eat it straight. Try preparing ⅓ cup wild rice with ⅔ cup white or brown rice (a smoky rice, such as Texmati, will boost the wild rice flavor).

Inquisitive Cooks Want to Know . . .

Q. *Why is wild rice more expensive than most other rices?*
A. Wild rice grows in shallow lakes and marshes in conditions that are more difficult to duplicate than the paddies where other rices are grown. Consequently, wild rice is not easily cultivated, which makes it relatively scarce and, so, expensive. It also requires extensive processing to bring out the nutty flavor and give it its deep brown color. While more expensive than most other rices, it is also more nourishing, richer in protein and B vitamins, than any common rice.

. . . gives flavors a lift, making sauces sparkle. Because much of the liquid burns off during simmering, people tend to assume that bad wine or vinegar works as well as the good stuff. In fact, quality counts, because it's the residue that flavors the food.

So-called "cooking wine," sold in supermarkets, is more of a marketing gimmick than an ingredient worth buying. A better approach to choosing a cooking wine is to select a wine to serve with supper, and use some of that in your dish. Most recipes call for so little wine that you might not miss it at the table.

If you're not planning to serve wine with dinner, and you don't want to buy a good bottle for the sake of one recipe, try using a wine vinegar in its place. Just use about ¼ as much vinegar as wine in the same color as the wine called for in the recipe. In other words, substitute a rich red wine vinegar (such as balsamic vinegar or red wine vinegar with tarragon) for red wine, and white wine vinegar, perhaps seasoned with lemon or mixed herbs, for white wine. As you begin to discover how vinegars affect foods, experiment with the various flavors that are now widely available. (See pages 235–36).

To sample what vinegars do to dishes, try Vegetable Ragu (see page 153), White Beans and Fresh Tuna (see page 201), Beet Risotto (see page 132).

About Balsamic Vinegar . . .

If you read food magazines regularly, you may have noticed that all of them run, from time to time, a piece about balsamic vinegar. Such an article is likely to deal with grapes, must (freshly pressed grape juice), and big wooden barrels (used to ferment the must), as well as the distinction between artisanal (premium grade, made from very good grapes in very fine barrels in very small quantities) and commercial (mass-produced) blends.

While interesting, this obsession with the process probably owes more to the fact that it's easier to describe how balsamic vinegar is made than how it tastes. You're left to infer that it's special enough to justify all the fuss about barrels and such, but with no firm idea of what you're in for when you splash it onto your salad or into your skillet.

This is necessarily so. In the case of a condiment so unique and complex, adjectives are bound to be inadequate and possibly misleading. The best I can do is to say that at its best, balsamic vinegar is so like a hearty, grapy red wine, it's nearly a toss-up between putting it into your salad, stew, or sauté and serving it in a goblet alongside. But when you cook with it, you'll find that its sharp finish (subtle compared with most wine vinegars) makes the rich, deep flavors of other ingredients resonate, sending them echoing down your throat.

To sample its flavor and its effect on foods, try balsamic vinegar in Lentil Salad with Sun-Dried Tomatoes and Feta Cheese (see page 74), Chicken Breasts (or Pressed Tofu) with Sweet Mustard Glaze (see page 176).

Cost-Conscious Cooks Want to Know . . .

Q. Should you pay a lot for a small bottle of artisinal balsamic vinegar when for far less you can get a larger quantity of a commercial brand?

A. Not necessarily. Just as wine is never just wine, all balsamic vinegar isn't alike. And as with wine, the quality of the grapes, as well as the nature of the processing method and environment, determine how good the vinegar will be and how much it will cost. Yet many modestly priced balsamic vinegars are as good as some of the more expensive "boutique" brands. If you can afford to taste around, try some from each category. Otherwise, do sample a number of the less expensive brands, ranging around four dollars per 12-ounce bottle, to find one you like.

Oils

Olive oil of the best quality makes you a better cook as soon as you start using it. Now that everyone's (rightly) wary of fats, some (wrongly) believe that oil is what you use *only* when you don't have a nonstick pan.

Olive oil is much more than that. It's an ingredient that also acts to bind other flavors, making the whole dish taste richer and far better than it would without it.

It's easy to remember what to look for when you're shopping for good olive oil: green, as in olives and dollar bills. Good oil, marked "extra virgin," is a pale sea green and often very expensive. But it actually works out to be economical, since the richer the oil the less of it you need to flavor your food. Much of the best olive oil comes from Tuscany and Umbria in Italy, although some high-quality oil is starting to trickle out of California's wine country. (For recommendations and sources, see pages 235–36.)

Cost-Conscious Cooks Want to Know . . .

Q. *Why does good olive oil cost so much?*
A. There are three reasons:
1. Olives are plentiful, but good olives are rare.
2. To preserve their flavor, they must be picked by hand.
3. To yield the best oil, extra virgin, the olives must be stone pressed in small batches, a process that produces less volume than steel pressing, used for lower grades of oil.

And Health-Concious Cooks Inquire . . .

Q. *Is olive oil good for you?*
A. In moderation. Olive oil is 100 percent fat, and while everyone needs some dietary fat, many people get as much as they need from foods without adding more in the form of cooking oils and condiments. However, the fats in olive oil are monounsaturated and polyunsaturated, which have been found to lower the amount of cholesterol in the blood. This is much better than saturated fats, such as butter or palm or coconut oils, which cause cholesterol levels to rise.

Other Oils

You'll need other types of oil as well. Olive oil isn't for every dish; its flavor doesn't complement curry spices, for instance, and it's not particularly pleasant in stir-fries.

Canola oil is perhaps the mildest-tasting oil around, and it's lower in unsaturated fat than any other. Because it's versatile and—in the small amounts needed for cooking—relatively healthy, I recommend it as an alternative to unsalted butter, in curries for instance.

Other mild-flavored, polyunsaturated oils are safflower oil, corn oil, and sunflower-seed oil.

At the other end of the spectrum, for a polyunsaturated oil that tastes like butter, try unrefined avocado oil (see pages 235–36). And walnut oil may be the richest-tasting oil going. Until recently, it was prohibitively expensive. But now that California producers have kicked in, it's widely available at a very good price. (See pages 235–36.) Combined with balsamic vinegar, it makes for one of the best dressings I've ever tasted. (See Lentil Salad with Sun-Dried Tomatoes and Feta Cheese, page 74).

Unrefined (also labled "cold-pressed") peanut oil is what I recommend for stir-fries and several other dishes. Unlike ordinary peanut oil, which is bland, it actually has a peanutty taste. For a superb stir-fry, cook with 2 parts unrefined peanut oil to 1 part unrefined sesame oil. (See pages 235–36.)

Soups

Basic Vegetable Broth ✣ Very Basic Chicken Broth ✣ Light Mushroom Broth for Risotto and Soups ✣ Artichoke Soup ✣ Tangy Spinach-Yogurt Soup ✣ Aromatic Leek and Potato Soup ✣ Panzanella Soup ✣ Tomato-Posole Soup ✣ Silken Vegetable Soup ✣ Wheat Berry Soup ✣ My Favorite Minestrone with Creamy Pesto ✣ Chunky Lentil Soup with Parmesan ✣ Peerless Pureed Cauliflower Soup ✣ Bell Pepper Soup ✣ Chilled Corn Chowder ✣ Chilled Cucumber Soup ✣ Cold Sweet Potato Soup

Many people don't expect much from soup, and I think cans are to blame. It's not just that canned soup is rarely very good; it's the cans themselves. We love convenience but have contempt for it at the same time, assuming that any food that can be obtained so easily is, by nature, second rate. I'm grateful for this bias, which I exploit often. Low expectations work in the favor of any competent cook, and if I manage to serve something even slightly better than the leading brand of chicken or tomato soup, I'm praised much more than I deserve.   Good soup hinges on two things: **Time.** Flavors need a chance to sink in, so often the best strategy is to serve the soup the day after you make it. (There are exceptions, such as Chilled Cucumber Soup, which calls for crushed ice. But many other cold soups taste better once they've chilled for twelve hours or so.) **Good ingredients.** Somehow, soup's become known as an appropriate place to put the scraps from the refrigerator. But ingredients matter as much here as in anything else you prepare. You can make good soup from leftovers, as long as you add some fresh vegetables, too, and choose flavorful legumes, potent herbs, and, when called for, a robust broth.

About Broth . . .

Broth adds a buffer layer of flavor when you use it instead of water as a base to make soup or to steam rice, vegetables, chicken, or fish. Homemade broth is what separates the more scrupulous cooks from . . . well, myself for one. I rarely make it now that I can choose among several good ready-made, all-natural, low-sodium broths at the market, including excellent fresh-frozen chicken and vegetable stock. Often I customize canned commercial broth in one of two ways: (1) pouring canned broth into a saucepan, adding a bouquet garni (see box, right), and simmering it gently, covered, for 30 minutes, or (2) pouring canned broth into a saucepan; adding some chopped aromatic vegetables such as leeks, carrots, celery leaves or fresh fennel, with the fronds attached, and coarsely chopped parsley with its stems; and simmering gently, covered, for 30 minutes.

Broth

Recipes that call for broth *or* water are misleading, suggesting that the result will be similar, when, in fact, made with broth, the

One incidental benefit of making your own broth is the aroma. It smells as if you're cooking something wonderful before you've really begun. This is heartening and highly motivating.

HOW TO MAKE A BOUQUET GARNI
❶ ❷ ❸

❶ Cut a 5-inch square from a piece of cheesecloth.
❷ Fill the center of the cloth with an assortment of dried herbs. The classic French bouquet garni contains parsley, bay leaf, and thyme. But you may want to add other herbs, such as sage, rosemary, basil, and oregano.
❸ Tie the bundle with string to hold it shut, and drop it into the broth to steep for 30 minutes.

dish will be better by far. It would also be misleading for me to suggest that you'll get the same results whether you cook with vegetable broth or chicken broth. Although you'll do very well with a very strong vegetable broth, you'll almost always get a deeper, richer flavor when the broth you use is made with chicken.

Basic Vegetable Broth

Makes 2 quarts

This is an all-purpose broth that can be a base for soups, risotto, and sauces. Consider this a rough suggestion rather than a strict recipe. You can sweeten it up by adding cabbage or fennel, deepen the flavor with the addition of fresh or dried mushrooms, or sharpen the taste with a battery of herbs. Whenever you improvise, just make sure you have plenty of aromatics, the strong-flavored vegetables that carry the broth: onions, leeks, scallions, carrots, and celery with its leaves, as indicated here.

20 minutes to prepare the vegetables
1 hour to simmer the broth

 Refrigerated in a covered container, this broth will keep for up to 10 days. You can keep it frozen indefinitely.

2 quarts water

1 large white or yellow onion, peeled and quartered

2 leeks, white part only, washed and sliced into rounds

6 scallions, white part only, chopped

4 celery stalks, including leaves, chopped

1 large turnip, peeled and chopped

1 head lettuce, such as butter lettuce or radicchio, torn into shreds

2 large carrots, peeled and chopped

1 large red or white potato, scrubbed and chopped

2 bay leaves

1 cup coarsely chopped fresh parsley, with stems

1 bouquet garni containing several sprigs fresh rosemary (see box, page 44), plus 2 teaspoons each dried thyme, oregano, and sage

Up to ½ cup minced fresh herbs (optional)

Handful dried morels or porcini mushrooms (optional; careful, this will make the broth very strong)

Salt and freshly ground pepper to taste

Combine all of the ingredients in a large pot. Cover, bring to a boil over medium-high heat, then reduce the heat and simmer, covered, over medium-low heat for an hour. If you need it right away, strain and use at once. If it's for later, let it sit, covered, in the refrigerator overnight before straining.

❧ Pour the strained broth into containers with tight-fitting covers and refrigerate or freeze.

Very Basic Chicken Broth

Makes about 4 quarts

Although I cook with chicken broth all the time, I admit I've never made a "proper" one, the kind that involves a cauldron of necks and gizzards and hours of boiling, skimming, and straining. Good ready-made chicken broth is easy to come by, and the fresh-frozen kind is nearly as good as homemade. Try different brands to find which you like best. Some brands contain herbs and spices, which will affect the taste of whatever you're making, maybe for better, and maybe not.

On the rare occasions when I make chicken broth I keep it this simple. You can substitute leeks, shallots, or scallions for some of the onions, playing around with the proportions as much as you'd like.

20 minutes to prepare the ingredients

1 hour to simmer the broth

 Refrigerated in a covered container, this broth will keep for up to 4 days. You can keep it frozen for several months.

4 quarts water

4 chicken wings (see Note)

2 chicken thighs (see Note)

1 cup giblets

6 onions, peeled and quartered

8 carrots, scrubbed and chopped

1 bunch celery, with leaves attached, chopped

8 garlic cloves, peeled and crushed

4 large red or white potatoes, scrubbed and quartered

2 bay leaves

1 cup coarsely chopped fresh parsley, with stems

1 bouquet garni, containing 2 sprigs fresh rosemary, 1 tablespoon dried thyme, and 6 fresh sage leaves, or 1 tablespoon dried sage (see box, page 44)

6 whole black peppercorns

2 teaspoons salt

HOW TO DEFAT CHICKEN BROTH
❶ ❷ ❸

The overnight method for defatting broth is as follows:

❶ Make and strain the broth as directed in the recipe.

❷ Cover it and refrigerate overnight.

❸ Remove the solid layer of fat that forms over the top.

Or if you need to defat broth for immediate use, follow these steps:

❶ Make and strain the broth as directed in the recipe.

❷ Using a large shallow spoon, skim off the pools of fat that rise to the top.

❸ Wait a couple minutes, place a piece of absorbent paper towel on the surface, then peel it off after about 3 seconds. The fat will adhere to the paper towel and come right off.

ombine everything except the salt in a large pot. Cover and bring to a boil over medium-high heat.

🍃 Add the salt, lower the heat, and simmer gently, covered, over medium-low heat, for 2 to 3 hours.

🌿 Turn off the heat, refrigerate the broth, covered, for 1 hour to let everything steep.

🍃 Skim off the fat, if you'd like (see box, page 46). Then strain the broth through a fine sieve and use it right away, or refrigerate, tightly covered, for up to 3 days, or freeze.

Note: If you're able to shop at a store where there's a butcher counter rather than just a refrigerator case, ask for "odd parts for broth," and you'll be given what you need.

Light Mushroom Broth for Risotto and Soups

Makes 1 quart

1 hour 10 minutes from start to finish

 Stored in a tightly covered container, this broth will keep for up to a week in the refrigerator, indefinitely in the freezer. For convenience, freeze in ice cube trays, then transfer the cubes to a tightly sealed plastic bag, so you won't have to defrost the whole batch when you need a smaller portion.

6 scallions, white part plus 1 inch of the green, sliced
One 1-inch piece of ginger, sliced
2 garlic cloves, sliced

1 medium onion, sliced
1 leek, white part plus 1 inch of the green, cleaned and sliced
4 dried porcini mushrooms
4 cups (1 quart) water

ombine all of the ingredients in a medium saucepan, cover and bring to a boil over medium-high heat. Turn down the heat to medium-low and simmer for an hour. Strain through a fine sieve.

🍃 Reserve the porcini for another use.

Artichoke Soup

Serves 6

If you like the idea of serving artichokes, but not the effort it takes to eat them, here's a dish that gives all the pleasure with none of the bother.

50 minutes from start to finish

 You can make this soup up to 2 days in advance, keeping it refrigerated in a tightly covered container. To reheat, transfer it to a heavy saucepan and set, uncovered, over medium-low heat, stirring often until warmed through, about 15 minutes.

1 red potato, peeled
6 baby artichokes, with at least 4 inches of stem attached
4 cups (1 quart) chicken or vegetable broth, homemade (see page 46 or 44) or canned
2 teaspoons fresh lemon juice
Salt and freshly ground pepper to taste

*b*oil the potato in water to cover over medium-high heat until it's cooked through, about 20 minutes.

🍃 Meanwhile, trim the bottom inch off the artichoke stems, and discard the sharp, tough outer leaves. Peel the stems with a paring knife or potato peeler. With kitchen shears, cut the points off the remaining leaves.

🍃 Cut off what remains of the stems and chop them. Place the artichokes and stems in a saucepan and add water to cover.

🍃 Boil gently over medium-high heat until the artichokes are very soft, about 20 minutes, adding more water as it boils away. (Or you can place the artichokes in a large glass bowl, add water to cover, and microwave at the highest setting until they're very soft, about 6 minutes.) Reserve the remaining cooking water, about ⅓ cup. Lift the artichokes out of the water with a slotted spoon and set them aside to cool. Save the stems and the cooking water, and set aside.

🍃 Slice the artichokes in half lengthwise, and using a paring knife, carefully scrape away the fuzzy choke.

🍃 In a food processor or blender, puree the artichokes with the stems and the reserved cooking water. Add the chicken broth and the potato and puree again.

🍃 Transfer the mixture to a large saucepan and cook over low heat, uncovered, stirring often, until warmed through, about 15 minutes. Just before serving, stir in the lemon juice and season with salt and pepper to taste.

[PER SERVING: CAL. 135 / FAT 0.1 G / PROTEIN 8.6 G / CARB. 23.8 G / CHOL. 0 / SODIUM 433 MG*] *VALUE GIVEN IS BEFORE SALTING. % RDA: 34.2 VIT. C.

SERVING SUGGESTIONS

Serve Artichoke Soup with Savory French Toast Sandwich (page 146), Baked Eggplant and Radicchio Sandwich (page 147), Chicken Roasted with Garlic (page 181), or Braised Fish with Winter Greens (page 192).

WINE LOVERS BEWARE . . .

Artichokes distort the flavor of other foods, making everything taste sweeter. So if you're planning a dinner to showcase a favorite wine, don't serve artichokes.

Tangy Spinach-Yogurt Soup

Serves 4 to 6

This nourishing yogurt-based soup is one of my house specials. While you have to watch over it just before serving, there's nothing to it up to that point, and it's well worth the attention it takes toward the end. It's good hot or cold.

1 hour from start to finish

This soup tastes better after a day or two. If you'll be serving it cold, you can make it up to 3 days in advance. If you're serving it hot, don't add the spinach until 30 minutes before serving. At that point, reheat the soup very slowly, preferably in a double boiler, so it won't separate. Once it's heated through, stir in the spinach, and serve the soup the moment the spinach turns bright green, after about 3 minutes.

1 tablespoon unsalted butter or canola oil

2 large white onions, thinly sliced

1 teaspoon coarse salt

½ cup minced fresh parsley

¼ cup minced fresh chives

¼ cup minced fresh dill, or 1½ tablespoons crumbled dried dill

1½ tablespoons crumbled dried oregano

½ cup uncooked green lentils, rinsed

1½ cups water

4 cups plain low-fat or nonfat yogurt

4 cups torn washed spinach leaves

Dash paprika

*i*n a large, deep saucepan, melt the butter or heat the oil. Add the onions, salt, parsley, chives, dill, and oregano, and sauté over low heat until the onion is limp, about 20 minutes. Add the lentils and stir well to blend.

🍃 Stir in the water. Bring to a boil over medium-high heat, cover, and simmer over low heat until the lentils are cooked, about 20 minutes. The lentils are done when they're tender all the way through, yet retain their shape. Turn off the heat.

🍃 In a large mixing bowl, whisk the yogurt until it's smooth and creamy. Whisk in about a tablespoon of the hot broth. Gradually add more broth, whisking after each addition, until half the broth is in the yogurt.

🍃 Whisk the yogurt mixture back into the saucepan. Add the spinach, and stir constantly over low heat until the spinach has turned bright green and the soup has warmed through, 8 to 12 minutes. Be careful not to bring the soup to the boiling point or the yogurt will separate.

🍃 Ladle the soup into serving bowls, and sprinkle each serving with a dash of paprika. Or chill right away, covered, and serve cold.

[PER SERVING: CAL.159.8 / FAT 2.1 G* / PROTEIN 11.1 G / CARB. 23.3 G / CHOL. 9.1 MG / SODIUM 604.8 MG**] *MADE WITH NONFAT YOGURT. **VALUE GIVEN IS BEFORE SALTING. % RDA: 48 VIT. A; 50 VIT. C; 40 CALCIUM.

Aromatic Leek and Potato Soup

Serves 4

I remember a music critic who'd automatically pan any concert where something familiar was played. He'd write off those performances as pandering to the audience, as if there were something wrong with giving people pleasure (or there were something wrong with music that had that effect). His reasoning, applied to drama, would mean that Shakespeare is no longer worth seeing. And applied to food, well, to serve this old chestnut would be beneath contempt.

While I like to be innovative, I'm also eager to please. So I serve it with pride every now and then.

50 minutes from start to finish

 You can make this soup up to 3 days in advance. If you'll be serving this soup hot, transfer it to a heavy saucepan or double boiler and reheat it, covered, slowly over medium-low heat.

4 large boiling potatoes, peeled and quartered

2 large leeks, cut in half, cleaned, and sliced into long thin strips

4 cups (1 quart) water

1 cup buttermilk, or 1 cup low-fat or nonfat plain yogurt, whisked until light and thin

Garnish

Salt and freshly ground pepper to taste

1 cup minced fresh herbs, such as chervil, parsley, chives, cilantro, dill, or a mixture

*i*n a large saucepan, combine the potatoes, leeks, and water. Bring to a boil over medium-high heat, cover, and turn the heat down to medium low.

🍃 Simmer until the potatoes are tender enough to cut with a spoon, and the leeks are equally soft. This should take about 40 minutes.

🥟 In a blender or food processor, puree the vegetables in the cooking water, doing this in batches if necessary, then return to the saucepan. Add the buttermilk or yogurt, and heat the soup slowly over low heat, uncovered, until just warmed through. Season with salt and pepper, and serve warm, sprinkled with the fresh herbs. Or, chill the soup, covered, and serve it cold.

[PER SERVING: CAL. 260 / FAT 0.7 G* / PROTEIN 6.2 G / CARB. 56.8 G / CHOL. 2.2 MG / SODIUM 59.2 MG**] *MADE WITH NONFAT BUTTERMILK. **VALUE GIVEN IS BEFORE SALTING. % RDA: 79.2 VIT. C; 23.2 IRON.

Panzanella Soup

Serves 4

This soup is more properly known as *Papas e Pomodoro*, a summertime staple in Tuscany. Because it's so hearty I prefer to eat it in winter, even though that means making it with tomatoes that come out of a can or a box rather than straight off the vine, as customary. My favorite tomatoes for this purpose are Pomi, imported Italian tomatoes that come in boxes, or Red Pack crushed whole tomatoes, which are sold by the can.

25 minutes from start to finish

 This soup must be served right away. (In any event, you won't want to wait to eat it!)

1 tablespoon extra virgin olive oil, plus more for serving

2 cloves garlic, thinly sliced

1 large onion, coarsely chopped

⅓ cup minced fresh basil or 2 tablespoons crumbled dried

2 tablespoons minced fresh oregano or 2 teaspoons crumbled dried

1 cup fresh tomatoes, peeled and chopped (see box, page 155) or 1 cup canned tomatoes, drained, peeled, and chopped

4 cups (1 quart) vegetable or chicken broth, homemade (see page 44 or 46) or canned

4 cups cubed bread, crust removed

½ cup freshly grated Parmesan cheese, or more, to taste

eat the olive oil in a wide saucepan over medium heat, and sauté the garlic, onion, basil, and oregano until the onions are soft and limp, about 8 minutes. Add the tomatoes, vegetable broth, and bread and stir, until the mixture is heated throughout and you have a coarse porridge.

🍃 Spoon into serving bowls and sprinkle grated Parmesan evenly over each. Serve while still steaming hot, with additional olive oil to be drizzled on at the table.

[PER SERVING (BEFORE ADDING ADDITIONAL OIL): CAL. 259 / FAT 8.4 G / PROTEIN 10.6 G / CARB. 35 G / CHOL. 8 MG / SODIUM 688 MG]

SERVING SUGGESTIONS
Serve Panzanella Soup with Potato Frittata (page 149) and Tossed Salad for All Seasons (page 64).

Tomato-Posole Soup

Serves 4

This soup contains corn in two forms: masa harina, a fine cornflour more commonly used for making tortillas, and hominy, dried corn minus the germ and bran. Straight from the can, hominy is a goopy mess. But in this southwest-style dish, it's something else.

45 minutes from start to finish

 You can make the pesto up to 5 days in advance, keeping it covered and refrigerated until ready to use. The soup is best hot off the stove.

2 cups vegetable or chicken broth, homemade (see page 44 or 46) or canned

½ cup masa harina, available at Latin and specialty markets, or by mail order (see pages 235–36)

1 tablespoon ground cumin

1 cup fresh or canned tomatoes, peeled and chopped

⅔ cup hominy (available at specialty markets and many supermarkets)

1 recipe Pesto for Posole Soup (recipe follows)

*i*n a saucepan combine the vegetable broth, masa harina, cumin, and tomatoes. Bring to a gentle simmer over medium heat and cook, stirring often, until thickened, about 25 minutes.

🍲 Add the hominy and cook until heated through, about 7 more minutes. Just before serving, swirl in the pesto. Ladle the soup into bowls and serve hot.

Pesto for Posole Soup
½ cup nonfat sour cream
¼ cup shredded sharp cheddar cheese
¼ cup minced fresh cilantro
½ garlic clove, grated

🍲 Combine all ingredients in a blender or food processor and blend until smooth.

[PER SERVING: CAL. 147 / FAT 2.7 G / PROTEIN 8.2 G / CARB. 23.5 G / CHOL. 7.5 MG / SODIUM 182 MG]

SERVING SUGGESTIONS
Serve Tomato-Posole Soup with Spicy Black Beans with Fresh Plums (page 157) or Grilled Fajita Salad (with Turkey) (page 182), and Apple Flan (page 217).

Serves 4 to 6

This adaptable recipe makes four soups that taste different, depending on the vegetable you use, each soothing and scrumptious and simple to prepare.

When a dish calls for only a handful of ingredients, each of them must be very good, in this case use the best cheddar and freshest vegetables you can find.

40 minutes from start to finish

You can make the vegetable puree up to 2 days in advance and refrigerate it, covered. While this may make the soup more convenient to prepare, it also makes it less nourishing. Cut or pureed vegetables lose nutrients more rapidly than those left whole until the last minute.

4 cups of one of the following: cauliflower florets, or small brussels sprouts or chopped spinach or broccoli florets
1 tablespoon unsalted butter
1 tablespoon all-purpose flour
3 cups warm low-fat or nonfat milk
⅔ cup shredded sharp cheddar cheese
Dash paprika if you're using cauliflower, or pinch ground nutmeg if you're using brussels sprouts, spinach, or broccoli
Salt and freshly ground pepper to taste

*S*team the vegetable of your choice until it's very soft. Cauliflower, brussels sprouts, and broccoli will take 7 to 10 minutes to steam. Spinach will take only 3 to 4 minutes.

Puree the vegetable in a food processor or blender, and set it aside.

 Melt the butter in a large saucepan. Stir in the flour and cook, stirring constantly, over medium-low heat, until it becomes a golden paste, around 2 minutes.

 Whisk in the warm milk, and stir over low heat until the milk thickens, about 10 minutes. Stir in the vegetable puree.

 Stir in the cheese and keep stirring until it melts and the mixture is smooth. Add the paprika or nutmeg, season with salt and pepper, and serve right away.

[PER SERVING (VALUES VARY ONLY SLIGHTLY WHEN MADE WITH ANY OF THE 4 VEGETABLES): CAL. 150 / FAT 6.4 G* / PROTEIN 9.3 G / CARB. 14.6 G / CHOL. 20.7 MG / SODIUM 378 MG**] *MADE WITH NONFAT MILK AND FULL-FAT CHEDDAR CHEESE. **VALUE GIVEN IS BEFORE SALTING. % RDA: 20 VIT. A; 108 VIT. C; 27.9 CALCIUM.

Wheat Berry Soup

Serves 4 to 6

Centuries after their glory days, wheat berries are making a comeback. In ancient times, wheat berries—unrefined kernels of wheat, containing the bran and germ that milling strips away— caught on in parts of the western world that had long depended on millet. No doubt fed up with the mealy paste they made from that grain, the Romans in particular welcomed this chewy, sweet, and nutty alternative. In fact, they liked it so much that long after other civilizations had worked out ways to refine and process wheat, the folks in Rome preferred it in its purest form. Even today you'll find *pane di farro* (wheat berry bread) in most bakeries in that region, and soups like this one on menus throughout the south of Italy.

2 hours to soak the wheat berries
20 minutes to prepare
2 hours to cook

 *You can soak the wheat berries overnight. You can refrigerate the soup in a covered container for up to 4 days, or freeze it for an indefinite period of time.*

1 cup navy beans
1 cup wheat berries
2 teaspoons extra virgin olive oil
1 medium onion, chopped
1 leek, white part and 1 inch of the green, cleaned and chopped
1 stalk celery, chopped (without leaves)
1 medium carrot, peeled and chopped
2 whole garlic cloves, peeled
4 cups (1 quart) vegetable or chicken broth, homemade (see page 44 or 46) or canned
1 bouquet garni, containing 6 celery leaves and 1 tablespoon crumbled dried thyme (see box, page 44)
1 bay leaf
2 teaspoons fresh lemon juice
Salt and freshly ground pepper to taste

Place the navy beans in a large bowl. Place the wheat berries in a separate bowl. Bring 6 cups of water to a boil in a large saucepan over high heat, and pour half of the water over the beans, and the rest over the wheat. Set both aside for two hours.

In a large deep saucepan, heat the olive oil over medium heat. Add the onion, leek, celery, carrot, and garlic. Stir until soft and fragrant, about 8 minutes. Drain the beans and add them to the vegetables. Stir to coat, about 1 minute. Add the vegetable broth, bouquet garni, and bay leaf. Cover the saucepan, turn up the heat to medium-high, and bring to a boil. Lower the heat to medium-low and simmer until the beans have cooked, about an hour.

Remove the bouquet garni and bay leaf, and transfer the soup to a food processor or blender. Blend in short pulses to make a chunky soup rather than a puree. Return the soup to the pan. Or, use an immersion blender to process the soup in the saucepan.

Drain the wheat berries and add them to the saucepan. Bring the soup to a boil again over medium-high heat, cover, lower the heat to medium-low, and simmer until the wheat berries are tender, about 50 minutes. Stir often to keep the wheat berries from sticking to the pot. Just before serving, stir in the lemon juice, and adjust the seasoning with salt and pepper to taste.

[PER SERVING: CAL. 341 / FAT 2.6 G / PROTEIN 11.7 G / CARB. 66.8 G / CHOL. 0 / SODIUM 22.2 MG] % RDA: 24.3 IRON.

SERVING SUGGESTIONS
Serve Wheat Berry Soup with Savory Mushroom Pie (page 164) or Savory Carrot Pie (page 163).

My Favorite Minestrone with Creamy Pesto

Serves 6

If I had to choose one dish to serve to everyone I love, I'd make this. If you've only had the thin, tinny-tasting commercial minestrone, you may wonder at my choice. But this robust stew is nothing like what commonly comes in cans or cafeterias. It takes time, but effort and results are in just proportion here.

This minestrone is so flavorful because it's two soups in one; it's built on a strong vegetable broth, which amplifies the flavors for a final dish that's rich and deep.

40 minutes to prepare, including the time it takes to make the vegetable broth
4 hours to simmer

 Make the vegetable broth and the beans up to 4 days in advance. Keep them refrigerated until ready to use. You can make the minestrone up to 3 days in advance, keeping it refrigerated in a tightly covered container. To reheat, transfer to a heavy saucepan, cover, and set over medium-low heat, stirring often until warmed through, about 20 minutes.

When I lived in Italy, basil ended up in my order each day, not because I asked for it but because my greengrocer just assumed that if I was going to be cooking at all, I'd be cooking with basil.

2 tablespoons extra virgin olive oil

1 large white or yellow onion, thinly
   sliced

1 red onion, thinly sliced

3 garlic cloves, peeled and crushed

1 leek, washed and chopped

4 celery stalks, including the leafy fronds,
   coarsely chopped, or 1 large fennel bulb,
   coarsely chopped

Two 3-inch sprigs fresh rosemary

½ cup chopped fresh Italian parsley

1 tablespoon crumbled dried oregano

2 teaspoons whole fennel seed

2 bay leaves

2 large red potatoes, peeled and chopped

2 turnips, peeled and chopped

4 carrots, peeled and chopped

½ pound winter squash, such as butternut,
   acorn, or pumpkin, rind removed and
   coarsely chopped

2 cups coarsely chopped peeled tomatoes,
   seeded and drained (about 5 fresh
   tomatoes), or one 16-ounce can, coarsely
   chopped

2 cups white beans, soaked overnight and
   cooked (see box, page 35 and 36), cooking
   liquid reserved, or 4 cups canned white
   beans, drained (rinsed if canned)

1 recipe Basic Vegetable Broth (see page 44)

Creamy Pesto

½ cup grated imported Parmesan cheese

1 small garlic clove, crushed

1 cup chopped fresh basil

½ cup Neufchâtel cheese (see Note) or yogurt
   cheese (see box, page 133)

1 cup uncooked short pasta, such as ditalini

Salt and freshly ground pepper to taste

*i*n a large pot, heat the olive oil. Add the onions, garlic, leek, and celery or fresh fennel. Sauté over medium heat until they soften, about 10 minutes. Add the rosemary, parsley, oregano, fennel seed, and bay leaves, and stir well to blend.

✎ Add the potatoes and turnips, along with the carrots and winter squash. Pour in the tomatoes, and stir again.

✐ Add the beans with their cooking liquid, or the drained canned beans. Then add the vegetable broth and stir well. Bring to a boil over medium-high heat, reduce the heat to low, cover, and simmer, stirring often, for 2 hours.

✎ Meanwhile, make the Creamy Pesto. In a small bowl, blend together the Parmesan, garlic, basil, and Neufchâtel cheese or yogurt cheese to make a thick paste. Refrigerate, covered, until you're ready for it.

✐ Near the end of the soup's cooking time, prepare the pasta according to package directions. When it's done, drain it well and stir it into the soup. Season with salt and pepper.

✎ Ladle the soup into bowls that are deep and wide. Stir a heaping spoonful of the

CHEAT THE CLOCK

Pestos are easy to make, and as easily compensate for weak broth or bland ingredients. Store-bought pestos make things easier still and work as well as homemade, provided you find a brand that you like.

topping into each serving and swirl it so that basil floats throughout.

Note: Neufchâtel cheese is a naturally low-fat cream-style cheese, which is usually sold in the same section of the dairy case as cream cheese. I recommend it because I've found that it has a cleaner, fuller taste than any of the "light" or nonfat cream cheeses I've tried. But if you've found a brand you like, you can substitute low-fat or nonfat cream cheese in this recipe and in others that call for Neufchâtel.

[PER SERVING: CAL. 574.4 / FAT 11.3 G / PROTEIN 22.5 G / CARB. 93.6 G / CHOL. 20 MG / SODIUM 628.1 MG*] *VALUE GIVEN IS BEFORE SALTING. % RDA: 146.7 VIT. A; 100 VIT. C; 44 IRON; 31 CALCIUM.

[PER SERVING FOR CREAMY PESTO: CAL. 80.7 / FAT 6.1 G / PROTEIN 5 G / CARB. 1 G / CHOL. 20 MG / SODIUM 199.5 MG]

Chunky Lentil Soup with Parmesan

Serves 4 to 6

Here's the dish to serve when the mercury's low and your mood's down with it. Rice, vegetables, and cheese make this lentil soup uncommonly hearty. Add bread, and you'll have dinner.

1 hour from start to finish

As many as 4 days in advance, you can make the soup up to the point where the rice is added, keeping it refrigerated in a tightly covered container. An hour before serving, transfer the soup to a saucepan, and proceed with the recipe. You can freeze it for up to 3 months.

1 tablespoon extra virgin olive oil
1 large white or yellow onion, sliced
4 garlic cloves, crushed and minced
4 carrots, peeled and chopped
3 large celery stalks, including leaves, coarsely chopped, or 1 small fennel bulb, including fronds, coarsely chopped
3 cups torn washed spinach leaves or Swiss chard
1½ quarts Basic Vegetable Broth (see page 44) or canned broth, with seasonings adjusted (see Note)
1 cup drained canned tomatoes, pureed in a blender or food processor, or 1 cup imported Italian tomato puree
1 cup uncooked green lentils, rinsed
¼ cup uncooked white rice, preferably medium grain
½ cup grated imported Parmesan cheese
½ cup minced fresh Italian parsley
Freshly ground pepper to taste

*h*eat the olive oil in a large pot. Add the onion, garlic, carrots, and celery or fennel, and sauté over medium heat until everything's very soft, about 20 minutes.

Stir in the spinach or chard, and cook, stirring, until it turns bright green, about 2 minutes more.

Add the vegetable broth, pureed tomatoes, and lentils. Stir well, cover, and simmer for 15 minutes over medium-low heat. (If you're making the soup a few days before you're going to serve it, transfer it to a covered container and refrigerate it at this point.)

Stir in the rice, cover again, and let the mixture simmer, stirring occasionally, for 20 minutes more, or until the rice is cooked through.

Meanwhile, combine the Parmesan cheese and parsley.

Stir the Parmesan-parsley mixture into the soup, making sure to blend it throughout. Season with pepper. Ladle the soup into serving bowls and serve right away.

Note: If you're using canned broth, steep fresh herbs in it first. Heat the broth with a bouquet garni containing 2 teaspoons each rosemary, tarragon, and thyme (see box, page 44). Simmer, covered, for 30 minutes, then discard the bouquet garni and proceed with the recipe.

[PER SERVING: CAL. 204.5 / FAT 4.4 G / PROTEIN 12.7 G / CARB. 27.3 G / CHOL. 5.3 MG / SODIUM 534.5 MG] % RDA: 174 VIT. A; 62 VIT. C; 23.2 IRON.

Peerless Pureed Cauliflower Soup

Serves 4

In a perfect world, all of the most nourishing foods would also be the best tasting. But this isn't a perfect world, and we have millet to remind us of that. Millet contains more B vitamins and iron than rice or wheat and a good amount of protein, too. But it's also mushy and bland, which explains why peoples in the ancient world who'd thrived on it for centuries switched to other grains as soon as they became available.

But the very qualities that make millet unappealing on its own, make it ideal for this dish. Its flavor doesn't interfere with the mild taste of cauliflower, and it purees easily into a soothing porridge-like soup.

45 minutes from start to finish

 This soup can be made up to 3 days in advance and kept refrigerated, tightly covered. Reheat gently over medium-low heat, taking care not to boil.

1 pound cauliflower, separated into florets
2 cups vegetable or chicken broth, homemade (see page 44 or 46) or canned
1 scallion, white part only, minced
½ cup millet (available at natural food stores and some supermarkets)
1 large egg yolk
1 cup evaporated skim milk
1 cup skim milk
2 tablespoons fresh lemon juice
¼ cup minced fresh chives

Steam the cauliflower until tender. (For steaming directions see box, page 144.) Whichever steaming method you choose, stovetop or microwave, use ½ cup water.

Meanwhile, in a large saucepan bring the vegetable broth to a boil over medium-high heat. Add the scallion and millet, turn the heat down to medium-low, cover and simmer until the millet has cooked, and most of the liquid has been absorbed, about 25 minutes. Turn off the heat.

In a mixing bowl whisk the egg yolk into the evaporated skim milk. Add two tablespoons of the hot millet to the milk mixture and whisk well. Add another two tablespoons, whisk, then stir in ¼ cup more. Whisking constantly, slowly pour the milk mixture back into the saucepan with the remainder of the millet mixture. Gradually stir in the skim milk.

Drain the cooking water from the cauliflower and add to the saucepan. Puree half the cauliflower with an immersion blender, a food processor, or blender, and add that as well. Stir in the remaining florets along with the lemon juice and chives. (If the florets are larger than bite size, first cut them in half).

 Gently heat over low heat, stirring often and taking care not to bring to a boil. Serve warm.

[PER SERVING: CAL. 216 / FAT 2.6 G / PROTEIN 10.7 G / CARB. 37 G / CHOL. 48 MG / SODIUM 88 MG]

SERVING SUGGESTIONS

Serve Peerless Pureed Cauliflower Soup with Winter Vegetables in Mellow Lemon Marinade (page 85) or Chickpea Curry (page 156).

Bell Pepper Soup

Serves 4

Bell peppers are so ornamental I used to leave them on my counter until they withered. But this soup challenged my aesthetic priorities. It's so good that no pepper, no matter how colorful or well-formed, is safe from my saucepan.

50 minutes from start to finish

 *You can make this soup up to 3 days in advance, storing it tightly covered in the refrigerator and reheating slowly over medium heat.*

1 tablespoon extra virgin olive oil
2 cups chopped yellow onion
1 cup carrots, peeled and chopped
1 cup chopped celery
1 large red pepper, roasted, peeled, seeded, and sliced (see box, page 88)
1 large yellow pepper, roasted, peeled, seeded, and sliced (see box, page 88)
1 small round red or white potato (¼ pound), peeled and sliced
3 cups vegetable broth, homemade (see page 44) or canned

*h*eat the olive oil in a medium saucepan over medium-high heat. Add the onions, carrot, and celery, turn the heat down to medium and sauté until softened, about 10 minutes.

 Add the bell peppers and potato, and stir to coat with the other vegetables. Add the vegetable broth, bring to a boil, cover, and lower heat to medium-low. Simmer until the potato falls apart when you pierce it with a knife, about 8 minutes.

✐ Transfer the soup to a food processor or blender, and process in pulses until pureed. Serve hot.

[PER SERVING: CAL. 116 / FAT 3.4 G / PROTEIN 1.7 G / CARB.18.6 G / CHOL. 0 / SODIUM 42.5 MG] % RDA: 120.5 VIT. A; 260 VIT. C.

SERVING SUGGESTIONS
Serve Bell Pepper Soup with Baked Eggplant and Radicchio Sandwich (page 147) or Poached Chicken Breasts or Artichokes with Artichoke Stuffing (page 172), and Peach Scone Cakes (page 219).

Chilled Corn Chowder

Serves 4

Most corn chowders I've come across are meant to be served hot, but the season for fresh corn is rarely the time for a steaming bowl of anything. I love this chilled version, flavored with a cooling blend of ginger and fresh basil.

25 minutes to prepare
2 to 3 hours to chill

 You can make this soup up to 3 days in advance, keeping it refrigerated in a tightly covered container.

2 ears fresh corn, or one 12-ounce can corn kernels (in water), drained
½ tablespoon unsalted butter or canola oil
1 large shallot, diced
1 tablespoon grated fresh ginger
2 tablespoons minced fresh basil
3 cups vegetable or chicken broth, homemade (see page 44 or 46) or canned
1 tablespoon arrowroot or cornstarch
1 cup evaporated skim milk
Pinch cayenne pepper
Salt to taste
Ice cubes

Garnish
Diced red pepper
Chopped fresh basil

*i*f you're using fresh corn, scrape the kernels off the cob.

🍃 Heat the butter or oil in a large heavy saucepan over medium-low heat. Add the shallot, ginger, and basil, and sauté, stirring often, until the shallot softens, about 6 minutes.

✐ Stir in the corn kernels, and continue sautéing and stirring until their color deepens, about 4 minutes.

🍃 Pour in the vegetable broth, turn the heat up to medium to bring it to a simmer, then cover, lower the heat to medium-low, and simmer until the corn kernels turn very soft, about 10 minutes.

✐ Transfer the mixture to a food processor or blender, and puree. Return the puree to the saucepan.

🍃 In a mixing bowl, combine the arrowroot or cornstarch and milk, whisking well to

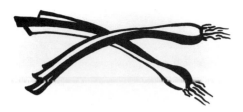

1 large cucumber, peeled, seeded, and chopped
1 scallion, white part only, minced
1 cup low-fat cottage cheese
½ cup plain nonfat yogurt
½ cup crushed ice
Minced fresh chives, dill, and/or mint to taste

blend. Stir it into the corn puree, and set it over medium-low heat, stirring often until it thickens, about 7 minutes. Stir in the cayenne pepper and salt.

🖎 Remove the soup from the heat, and pour it into a Pyrex or metal bowl. Fill another larger bowl with ice, and place the bowl with the soup inside it. Cover the soup with foil and place the whole thing in the refrigerator until thoroughly cool, 2 to 3 hours. (Stirring it occasionally will help cool it down.)

[PER SERVING: CAL. 118.3 / FAT 2.6 G* / PROTEIN 7.5 G / CARB. 15.3 G / CHOL. 6.8 MG / SODIUM 254.8 MG**] *MADE WITH NONFAT MILK. **VALUE GIVEN IS BEFORE SALTING.

*i*n a food processor or blender, blend together the cucumber, scallion, cottage cheese, and yogurt until smooth. Add the crushed ice and process again until the mixture thickens.

🖎 Distribute evenly between 2 serving bowls or mugs and top with the chives, dill, and/or mint. Serve at once.

[PER SERVING: CAL. 132.2 / FAT 1.2 G* / PROTEIN 18.5 G / CARB. 11.4 G / CHOL. 6.4 MG / SODIUM 505.2 MG**] *MADE WITH 1%-FAT COTTAGE CHEESE. **VALUE GIVEN IS BEFORE SALTING. % RDA: 21.1 CALCIUM.

Chilled Cucumber Soup

Serves 2

This refreshing summer soup is a cinch. A great dish for outdoor dining, it looks lovely in bright-colored bowls.

10 minutes from start to finish

 This soup can't be made ahead of time because it will become watery.

HOW TO SEED A CUCUMBER
❶ ❷ ❸

❶ Peel the cucumber with a potato peeler. If the peel is unwaxed, and you don't mind eating it, skip this step.
❷ Slice it in half lengthwise.
❸ Using a teaspoon, scoop out the seeds.

Cold Sweet Potato Soup

Serves 4

If you like pumpkin pie, here's a way to sneak a taste in the middle of summer. This cool, creamy soup has a startling similarity. It's also good served hot.

25 minutes to prepare
2 to 3 hours to chill

 You can make this soup up to 3 days in advance, keeping it refrigerated in a tightly covered container.

1½ cups vegetable or chicken broth, homemade (see page 44 or 46) or canned

1 yellow or white onion, minced

1 tablespoon grated fresh ginger

1 leek, white part only, cleaned and coarsely chopped

1 whole clove

1 generous pinch ground cinnamon

1 pinch mace or ground nutmeg

1 large sweet potato, peeled and finely diced

2 teaspoons maple syrup

2 cups evaporated skim milk

1 tablespoon arrowroot or cornstarch

Ice cubes

1 tablespoon fresh orange juice

our ¼ cup of the vegetable broth into a large heavy saucepan, and bring it to a simmer over medium-high heat. Turn the heat down to medium-low and add the onion, ginger, leek, clove, cinnamon, and mace or nutmeg. Cook, stirring often, until the vegetables turn very soft and the liquid is almost gone, about 8 minutes.

Add the sweet potato and the rest of the broth. Cover and simmer until the sweet potato is soft enough to puree, about 8 minutes. Transfer the mixture to a food processor or blender and puree.

Return it to the saucepan and stir in the maple syrup. In a mixing bowl, combine the milk and arrowroot or cornstarch, whisking well to blend. Stir the mixture into the puree and set over medium-low heat, stirring often, until thickened, about 7 minutes.

You can serve it hot off the stove or chill it by pouring it into a Pyrex or metal bowl, filling another, larger bowl with ice, and placing the bowl with the soup inside it. Cover the soup with foil and place the whole thing in the refrigerator until thoroughly cool, 2 to 3 hours. (Stirring it occasionally will help cool it down.) If hot or cold, stir in the orange juice just before serving.

[PER SERVING: CAL. 168.7 / FAT 0.1 G / PROTEIN 7.1 G / CARB. 33.9 G / CHOL. 1.8 MG / SODIUM 152.2 MG] % RDA: 42.1 CALCIUM; 26.8 VIT. C.

salads

· · · · · ·

Classic Reliable Oil and Vinegar   Walnut-Raspberry Vinaigrette   Sesame-Scallion Vinaigrette   Fat-Free Buttermilk Salad Dressing   Basic Low-Fat Cream-Style Dressing   Oil-Free Creamy Caesar-Style Salad   Warm Confetti Potato Salad   Potato, Corn, and Egg Salad with Chives   Basic Tahini Dressing   Baba Ganoush   Hummus   Beet Tabbouleh   Orange Tahini Dressing   Lentil Salad with Sun-Dried Tomatoes and Feta Cheese   Asian Snow Pea and Mussel Salad   Rice Salad with Mango and Chickpeas (with or without Chicken)

CHAPTER 2

I don't like to say I'm serving salad for supper because to some, the word "salad" suggests the meal will be meager. So I call it something else, preferably foreign, such as *mélange de poulet et avocat* instead of chicken salad, or *lenticchie con pomodori secchi e formaggio Greco*, aka salad with lentils, sun-dried tomatoes, and feta cheese. Despite the fact that conventional dressings jack up the calories by roughly 100 per tablespoon, salad has come to mean skimpy, and to say that you're going to serve it as a main course may be perceived as implying that your guests are too fat or that you couldn't be bothered with *real* food. But in many respects, a well-made salad would be hard to distinguish from a typical entrée, since it would contain a similar range of ingredients, flavors, textures, and nutrients. What I've chosen to call "salad" for the sake of this section are dishes that require several raw foods and are meant to be served chilled or at room temperature. Each, except the tossed salads, can be served as a main course on its own, or with soup before or after, with bread alongside.

Tossed Salads for All Seasons

Many things have been done in the name of salad that are, if not outright disgusting, then unpleasant enough. A number of them can be found on the shelf at most supermarkets, marked "dressing," and if you read the label, you'll know what I mean.

Not all bottled dressings are bad, and some—especially those sold in refrigerated sections—can be quite good. But it's really easy to make your own, and nice to claim credit when it turns out well.

Salad Tips

- To dress individual portions to taste, put the dressing in a spray pump or spritzer bottle and squirt the leaves. The spray gives a light, even coating.
- If you combine flavorful greens and fresh herbs, you'll need less dressing. Toss fresh herbs such as basil, parsley, chervil, and chives in with the lettuce, up to ¼ cup fresh herbs for each 1½ cups of salad greens.
- Smoother-tasting low-acid vinegars make it possible to use less oil in oil and vinegar dressings. When you use ordinary wine vinegar, you need about 3 measures of oil to each measure of vinegar to keep the dressing from tasting sour. But you can bring the ratio closer to 1-to-1 using balsamic vinegar, raspberry vinegar, or any flavored vinegar that has rice vinegar as a base. Using a rich oil, such as walnut, avocado, or a superpremium cold-pressed extra virgin olive oil, also makes it possible to lower the proportion of oil.

HOW TO DRESS A SALAD
❶ ❷ ❸

Folding the greens—gently turning the leaves to coat them—dresses a salad more evenly than tossing and with less damage to delicate ingredients.

❶ Make sure your greens are washed and dry (see box, page 66). Cut them into bite-sized pieces, and toss them well to combine.

❷ Have your dressing ready in a small pitcher or glass measuring cup. If it's an oil and vinegar dressing, give it a good stir.

❸ Fold the dressing into the salad by pouring slowly with one hand and gently but thoroughly turning the leaves with the other.

Dressings

Oil and Vinegar

Experiment with the ratio of oil to vinegar to find which you like most. The ideal proportion will vary, depending on the type of oil and vinegar you use, the manufacturer's and, of course, your preferences.

Here are several suggestions for dressings. Each of these dressings make enough for 3 cups of mixed greens. However, you can adjust to taste. These dressings can also be used to marinate vegetables for grilling. See page 143 for grilling instructions.

Classic Reliable Oil and Vinegar

Makes about ½ cup, enough for 4 servings

1 tablespoon extra virgin olive oil

2 teaspoons balsamic vinegar

Pinch crumbled dried oregano or tarragon

Salt and freshly ground pepper to taste

In a small mixing bowl or measuring cup, combine the ingredients and stir or whisk well right before serving

[PER SERVING: CAL. 30.1 / FAT 3.2 G / PROTEIN 0 / CARB. 0.1 G / CHOL. 0 / SODIUM 0 MG*] *VALUE GIVEN IS BEFORE SALTING.

Walnut-Raspberry Vinaigrette

Makes about ½ cup, enough for 4 servings

1 tablespoon walnut oil

1 tablespoon raspberry vinegar

Pinch finely grated orange zest

Salt and freshly ground pepper to taste

In a small mixing bowl or measuring cup, combine the ingredients and stir or whisk well right before serving.

[PER SERVING: CAL. 31 / FAT 3.2 G / PROTEIN 0 / CARB. 0.2 G / CHOL. 0 / SODIUM 0 MG*] *VALUE GIVEN IS BEFORE SALTING.

Sesame-Scallion Vinaigrette

Makes about ½ cup, enough for 4 servings

2 teaspoons dark sesame oil

1 tablespoon rice vinegar

½ garlic clove, grated

1 tablespoon minced scallions, white part only

Pinch fine-granulated sugar

In a small mixing bowl or measuring cup, combine the ingredients and stir or whisk well right before serving.

[PER SERVING: CAL. 31 / FAT 3.2 G / PROTEIN 0 / CARB. 0.2 G / CHOL. 0 / SODIUM 0]

Fat-Free Buttermilk Salad Dressing

Makes about ½ cup, enough for 4 servings

Go easy on the garlic, which could easily upset the flavors in this delicate dressing.

5 minutes from start to finish

 You can make this dressing up to 5 days in advance. Store tightly covered in a glass or heavy plastic container in the refrigerator.

⅓ cup part-skim ricotta cheese

3 tablespoons nonfat buttermilk

1 teaspoon grated fresh ginger

¼ teaspoon grated fresh garlic

1 teaspoon dijon mustard

2 tablespoons fresh orange juice

Combine all ingredients in a small bowl and whisk together by hand until smooth. Serve over mixed salad greens.

[PER SERVING: CAL. 27.5 / FAT 0 / PROTEIN 3.5 G / CARB. 3 G / CHOL. 0 / SODIUM 39 MG]

The phrase "nonfat buttermilk" may seem like a contradiction in terms. But originally buttermilk was the almost fat-free liquid left over from churning butter. Today it is not a by-product of buttermaking, but made intentionally from cultured skim milk.

Basic Low-Fat Cream-Style Dressing

Makes 1 cup

¼ cup part-skim ricotta cheese
¾ cup plain nonfat yogurt
2 teaspoons fresh lemon juice
½ garlic clove, grated
1 tablespoon minced fresh parsley
1 tablespoon minced fresh chives
Salt and freshly ground pepper to taste

*P*uree the ricotta cheese in a food processor or blender just until smooth. Add the yogurt, lemon juice, and garlic, and process again to blend.

Transfer to a mixing bowl or measuring cup and stir in the remainder of the ingredients.

Variations

Omit the chives and add 1 tablespoon minced fresh basil
   or
½ anchovy, rinsed, patted dry, and chopped, plus ½ teaspoon capers, rinsed and drained
   or
½ roasted, peeled, seeded, and chopped jalapeño and 1 tablespoon minced fresh cilantro

   Also, see Oil-Free Creamy Caesar-Style Salad, page 67.

[PER SERVING: CAL. 49.6 / FAT 1 G* / PROTEIN 4.5 G / CARB. 5.2 G / CHOL. 5.8 MG / SODIUM 57.3 MG**] *MADE WITH PART-SKIM RI-COTTA CHEESE. FOR LESS TOTAL FAT AND CHOLESTEROL, SWITCH TO NONFAT. **VALUE GIVEN IS BEFORE SALTING.

HOW TO CLEAN LETTUCE
❶ ❷ ❸

Washing the greens is as important as choosing a dressing, and many markets sell packaged greens that have been washed. When you buy a pack of greens, check the label to be sure they've been washed.

To clean leaf lettuces:

❶ Cut out the core and separate the leaves.
❷ Throw out the outer leaves, and dunk the rest in a large bowl of cool water. Swish them around with your hands, then lift them out one by one.
❸ Pat them dry with paper towels, or give them a good spin in a salad spinner.

Oil-Free Creamy Caesar-Style Salad

Serves 4 to 6

I rarely hear anyone order a Caesar salad without asking for a few alterations. Maybe it's the fish (*"no anchovies"*) or the croutons ("double, please") or the egg ("hold it") or the cheese ("do you have any cheddar?"). As long as everyone else feels so free to define Caesar salad, I'll go on and offer my own, which *does* call for anchovies, but does not call for oil. (Of course, you can omit the anchovies from this salad, too. This is an observation, not a recommendation.)

I also prefer fresh bread to the conventional fried croutons. Bread adds body, and it's more wholesome, too. Uncooked egg, an ingredient in the authentic recipe, would be too runny without oil, so I parboil it, also minimizing the risk of salmonella from raw eggs. Combined with yogurt, it makes a creamy dressing with enough body to cling to the lettuce leaves.

10 minutes from start to finish

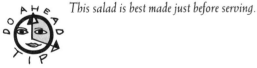

This salad is best made just before serving.

1 large egg in its shell
3 anchovy fillets, rinsed and patted dry (optional)
1 small garlic clove, peeled and crushed
2 tablespoons fresh lemon juice
¼ cup grated imported Parmesan cheese

⅔ cup nonfat ricotta cheese
2 tablespoons plain nonfat yogurt
Dash Tabasco sauce (optional)
2 heads romaine lettuce, washed and torn into bite-sized pieces
4 cups cubed fresh chewy French or Italian bread (see Note)
1 teaspoon grated lemon zest
Freshly ground pepper to taste

*f*ill a small saucepan with water, and bring it to a boil. Gently lower the egg into the water and boil for exactly 2 minutes. Lift the egg out with a slotted spoon and set it aside until cooled.

When the egg is cool enough to handle, peel it carefully and put it in the work bowl of a food processor or blender, along with the anchovies, if using, garlic, lemon juice, half the Parmesan cheese, the ricotta, yogurt, and Tabasco, if using. Process just until smooth.

Toss the lettuce and bread together in a large salad bowl. Sprinkle the lemon zest and remaining Parmesan on top, grind pepper over everything, and toss again. Pour on the dressing, toss thoroughly, and serve.

Note: If you can't get good fresh bread, cube the bread you have on hand, put it on a baking sheet, and bake it in the oven at 350° F. until it's toasted, about 7 minutes.

[PER SERVING: CAL. 213.5 / FAT 7.1 G* / PROTEIN 12.1 G / CARB. 21.4 G / CHOL. 86.9 MG / SODIUM 436.6 MG**] *MADE WITH NON-FAT YOGURT. **VALUE GIVEN IS BEFORE SALTING. % RDA: 35.4 VIT. A; 43.7 VIT. C; 321 CALCIUM.

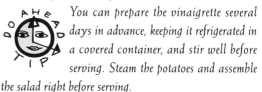

Warm Confetti Potato Salad

Serves 4

Use organically grown potatoes that haven't been sprayed with pesticides, and you won't have to peel the skins, which lend color and extra fiber to this dazzling side dish.

25 minutes from start to finish

You can prepare the vinaigrette several days in advance, keeping it refrigerated in a covered container, and stir well before serving. Steam the potatoes and assemble the salad right before serving.

1 pound small low starch potatoes (boiling potatoes of 2 inches in diameter maximum) with different color skins, if available
1 red pepper, roasted, peeled, seeded and sliced (see box, page 88)
1 yellow pepper, roasted, peeled, seeded and sliced (see box, page 88)
1 tablespoon extra virgin olive oil
2 teaspoons white wine vinegar
1 tablespoon minced fresh chives or scallion, white part only
4 cups mesclun (see box, left) or mixed lettuces such as radicchio, oak leaf, romaine, Boston

Place a steamer basket into a large saucepan and add water until it barely touches the bottom of the steamer. Put the potatoes into the steamer, arranging them evenly. Cover the pan and bring to a boil over medium-high heat. Lower the heat to medium and steam until the potatoes are tender enough to be pierced with a knife, about 15 minutes. Check often, adding more water as necessary.

🥔 Let the potatoes cool slightly, and roughly slice each into four pieces. Place the pieces in a large mixing bowl, and toss with the peppers, oil, vinegar, and chives. Arrange the lettuce evenly on four serving plates, and distribute the potato mixture equally among them. Serve warm or at room temperature.

[PER SERVING: CAL. 165 / FAT 3.3 G / PROTEIN 2.2 G / CARB. 30.2 G / CHOL. 0 / SODIUM 14 MG] % RDA: 26. VIT. A; 152 VIT. C.

SERVING SUGGESTIONS
Serve Warm Confetti Potato Salad with Barbecued or Broiled Turkey Burgers with All the Fixin's (page 184) or Baked Eggplant and Radicchio Sandwich (page 147).

Potato, Corn, and Egg Salad with Chives

Serves 4

This is the perfect potato salad: full of flavor, free of oil. Partial to starches, I love it for lunch; but it's a great side dish, too, with cold chicken or fish.

40 minutes to prepare

 3 hours to chill
You can make this salad up to 3 days in advance.

8 new potatoes (about 1 pound), scrubbed
6 ears frozen corn, shucked (if you're going to cook them in the microwave, leave them in the husk), or 2 cups frozen corn kernels, thawed
4 large eggs, in their shells
1 scallion, white part only, minced
1 celery stalk, diced
¼ cup minced fresh chives
2 tablespoons minced fresh dill, or 2 teaspoons crumbled dried dill
1 cup plain nonfat yogurt
1 tablespoon Dijon mustard
1 tablespoon fresh lemon juice
1 teaspoon grated lemon zest
1 teaspoon light honey
1 small garlic clove, grated
Pinch paprika
Salt and freshly ground pepper to taste

 ring a large pot of water to a boil and cook the potatoes over medium heat until they're cooked through, about 20 to 30 minutes depending on size. Drain them and set them aside

to cool while you prepare the rest of the salad.

🌿 If using ears of corn, bring another large pot of water to a boil. Drop in the corn and cover. When the water returns to a boil, turn off the heat. After 5 minutes, lift out the ears with tongs and put them in the refrigerator to cool. Or cook unshucked corn in the microwave, 2 ears at a time, at the highest setting. Cook each pair for 2 minutes, then turn the ears halfway, and cook for at least 2 minutes more. (How long it takes to cook depends on the strength of your oven. They're done when the kernels are glossy and bright yellow.) Set aside to cool before stripping off the husk, or prepare frozen corn according to package directions.

🍃 Bring saucepan of water to a boil and add the eggs, letting them simmer over medium-low heat for 5 minutes. Drain them and refrigerate to cool.

🌿 In a large mixing bowl combine the scallion, celery, chives, dill, yogurt, mustard, lemon juice, lemon zest, honey, garlic, and paprika. Stir well to blend.

🍃 Coarsely dice the potatoes and scrape the kernels off the corncobs. Add them to the mixing bowl. Peel and dice the boiled eggs and add them, too. Gently stir until well combined, and season with salt and pepper. Chill, covered, for at least 3 hours before serving.

[PER SERVING: CAL. 317 / FAT 1.2 G / PROTEIN 6 G / CARB. 69 G / CHOL. 46 MG / SODIUM 38 MG]

Two Tahini Salads

It is a good thing that tahini (the paste made from ground sesame seeds) tastes best when it's well diluted, because tahini is very rich, and if it had to be eaten at full strength I would either have to give it up or reconcile myself to weighing a good deal more than I should. But tahini is pretty pungent on its own, and it happens that the very ingredients that make it taste terrific also make it more wholesome. Lemon juice and nonfat yogurt lighten the flavor and spread the densely packed calories—120 per tablespoon—over a number of servings.

This tahini dressing is my favorite topping for Grilled Assorted Vegetables (see page 143). I love it on salad greens, too, and on chilled boiled new potatoes, as well as in the eggplant salad and chickpea dip below.

TO STORE FRESH HERBS

Don't wash them until you're about to use them.

For up to 3 days:

Wrap them in a damp paper towel and place them in a plastic bag.

Refrigerate in the crisper section.

For up to a week:

Place them in a jar or container with a tight-fitting lid, stems down.

Add about 2 inches of water.

Cover the container and refrigerate.

Basic Tahini Dressing

Makes about ¾ cup

1 tablespoon tahini (sesame paste; see pages 235–36)

2 tablespoons fresh lemon juice

⅔ cup plain nonfat yogurt

½ garlic clove, grated

2 teaspoons ground cumin

1 teaspoon paprika

2 tablespoons minced fresh cilantro

*i*n a small mixing bowl, combine the tahini and lemon juice to make a thin, smooth paste.

🍃 Add the yogurt and stir until smooth. Stir in all the remaining ingredients.

[PER SERVING: CAL. 48.3 / FAT 1.8 G* / PROTEIN 2.9 G / CARB. 4.8 G / CHOL. 1 MG / SODIUM 33.2 MG**] *MADE WITH NONFAT YOGURT. **VALUE GIVEN IS BEFORE SALTING.

Baba Ganoush

Makes 1½ to 2 cups

This simple, refreshing eggplant salad goes well with grilled foods.

4 Japanese eggplants, washed and tops trimmed

1 recipe Basic Tahini Dressing (see left)

*h*eat the broiler.

🍃 Pierce the eggplants in several places with the tines of a fork and place them on a tray. Put them underneath the broiler and broil until the skin buckles, 4 to 6 minutes. Carefully turn them over and broil until the skin on the other side buckles, about 3 to 5 minutes.

🍃 Remove them from the oven and let them cool completely. (You can put them in a paper bag and refrigerate them to speed this along.)

🍃 Strip off the skin, and scoop out as many seeds as possible. Chop the pulp and transfer it to a mixing bowl.

🍃 Add the tahini dressing and stir until well combined. Serve at room temperature, or chill for several hours and serve cold.

[PER SERVING: CAL. 156.5 / FAT 0.5 G* / PROTEIN 3.5 G / CARB. 34.5 G / CHOL. 0.3 MG / SODIUM 30.5 MG**] *WHEN THE TAHINI DRESSING IS MADE WITH NONFAT YOGURT. **VALUE GIVEN IS BEFORE SALTING. % RDA: 20 VIT. C.

Hummus

Makes 2 cups

I serve this as a dip with pita bread and crisp raw vegetables; a sandwich filling with sprouts, roasted peppers, and cherry tomatoes; and a side dish with grilled poultry, fish, or vegetables and with steamed potatoes.

2 cups cooked chickpeas, drained (rinsed if canned)

1 recipe Basic Tahini Dressing (see page 71)

 n a mixing bowl, mash the chickpeas with a potato masher or the back of a wooden spoon.

Add the tahini dressing, and stir well to blend thoroughly.

[PER SERVING: CAL. 122 / FAT 2.2 G / PROTEIN 6.1 G / CARB. 19 G / CHOL. 0 / SODIUM 26 MG]

Beet Tabbouleh

Serves 4

Not that I'd *ever* extend an insincere invitation, but if I had to offer to host people out of sheer obligation, the surest way to receive their regrets would be to mention that beets will be on the menu. My informal popularity poll indicates that beets are total losers, ranking even below brussels sprouts, which is about as low as it goes. Small wonder. Commonly pickled in acid, served in tepid cinnamon syrup, or shredded over iceberg lettuce in a cynical attempt at salad, they haven't had a chance. Beets, which can be delicious, are so often made to taste so terrible, I suspect a conspiracy among beet-lovers to corner the crop for themselves.

If you've never liked beets, this recipe may work the miracle of making you crave them. And if you enjoy them already, prepare for a treat.

15 minutes to prepare

1 hour to soak the grains

 Both the dressing and the dressed tabbouleh will keep well covered and refrigerated for up to 4 days.

⅓ cup water

1 cup bulghur wheat

1 recipe Orange Tahini Dressing (see page 73)

2 cups shredded cooked beets (about 2 small beets; see box, page 154)

1 cup cooked chickpeas, rinsed and drained if canned

¼ cup minced scallions, white part only

2 tablespoons currants

2 tablespoons minced fresh cilantro

2 tablespoons minced fresh dill

2 tablespoons minced fresh chives

1 tablespoon toasted sesame seeds (see page 77)

3 tablespoons sour cream, low-fat or nonfat if desired

*b*ring the water to a boil in a covered saucepan over high heat. Stir in the bulghur, bring to a boil again, cover, and turn off the heat. Let it sit, without lifting the cover, for an hour.
❧ Meanwhile make the dressing. Pour the bulghur into a fine sieve, and press out the excess moisture. Allow the bulghur to cool completely. Put it in a large mixing bowl, along with the Orange Tahini Dressing, beets, chickpeas, scallions, currants, cilantro, dill, chives, sesame seeds, and sour cream. Stir well and serve right away at room temperature, or chill and serve cold.

[PER SERVING (USING NONFAT SOUR CREAM): CAL. 276 / FAT 1.2 G / PROTEIN 10.1 G / CARB. 55.8 G / CHOL. .2 MG / SODIUM 63.1 MG]

SERVING SUGGESTIONS
Serve Beet Tabbouleh with Peerlees Pureed Cauliflower Soup (page 57) or Chicken Roasted with Garlic (page 181).

HOW TO WASH FRESH HERBS
❶ ❷ ❸

❶ Wait until you're just about to use them.

❷ Fill a small bowl with water and swish the herbs well.

❸ Blot them dry with absorbent paper towel.

Orange Tahini Dressing

Makes 1¼ cups

¼ teaspoon grated fresh garlic

1 tablespoon tahini

1 cup nonfat buttermilk

2 tablespoons fresh orange juice

2 teaspoons fresh lemon juice

1 tablespoon ground cumin

1 teaspoon paprika

2 tablespoons minced fresh cilantro

❧ Combine all of the ingredients in a mixing bowl and whisk until smooth.

Lentil Salad with Sun-Dried Tomatoes and Feta Cheese

Serves 4

Balsamic vinegar gets the earthy legumes up on their feet, and pungent sun-dried tomatoes and feta cheese keep them hopping.

10 minutes to prepare

30 minutes to cook

You can make this salad, leaving out the feta cheese, up to 3 days in advance. Keep it refrigerated in a covered container, then add the feta cheese, and toss well before serving. The flavors will become more pronounced over time.

Sun-dried tomatoes are more commonly dried in a factory, but whatever the method, the process concentrates the flavor so that each piece is a jolt of sheer tomato taste.

You can buy them packed in oil or dry packed. I prefer dry packed because without the rich flavor of the oil they're more versatile. You can reconstitute them in hot water, soften them with extra virgin olive oil for use in salads and pastas, or use them as they are in dishes such as Lentil Salad with Sun-Dried Tomatoes and Feta Cheese and the wonderful Gnocchi with Sun-Dried Tomatoes (and Chicken) on page 126.

2 whole cloves

1 white or yellow onion, peeled and halved

2 cups uncooked lentils, picked over and well rinsed

1 garlic clove, thinly sliced

1 bay leaf

1 large Belgian endive, cored and leaves separated

1 tablespoon balsamic vinegar

1 tablespoon walnut oil

6 large sun-dried tomatoes (dry packed), minced

1 cup crumbled feta cheese

¼ cup minced red onion

¼ cup minced celery or fennel

Freshly ground pepper to taste

Stick a clove into each half of the onion. Put them in a saucepan with the lentils, sliced garlic, and bay leaf. Add water to cover by 2 inches.

Cover and bring to a boil over medium-high heat. Turn the heat down to low and let the mixture simmer, covered, until the lentils are tender but not mushy, about 20 minutes. Check occasionally, adding water a little at a time if it's being absorbed too quickly.

When the lentils are cooked and the liquid has been absorbed, take the pan off the heat, remove the onion, cloves, and bay leaf, then transfer the lentils to a large glass or ceramic bowl and leave them to cool slightly. Meanwhile, set out 4 serving plates and arrange endive leaves in a star pattern around each one.

In a small bowl, whisk together the balsamic vinegar and walnut oil, and stir it into the lentils.

🦐 Toss in the tomatoes, feta cheese, red onion, and celery or fennel. Season with freshly ground pepper, and distribute the salad evenly, spooning it into the center of each of the 4 serving dishes. Serve warm or at room temperature.

[PER SERVING: CAL. 341.5 / FAT 14.9 G / PROTEIN 17.3 G / CARB. 32.9 G / CHOL. 50 MG / SODIUM 642.2 MG]   % RDA: 20.4 VIT. C; 26 IRON; 33.7 CALCIUM.

SERVING SUGGESTIONS
Serve Lentil Salad with Sun-Dried Tomatoes and Feta Cheese with fresh bread and Aromatic Leek and Potato Soup (page 50) or Silken Vegetable Soup (page 52).

Asian Snow Pea and Mussel Salad

Serves 4

A dish that's delicious *and* efficient. A dazzling broth does double duty here, steaming the mussels then dressing the salad.

40 minutes to prepare
3 hours to chill

You can prepare the mussels and the dressing 2 days ahead, provided you keep both covered and refrigerated. Blanch the snow peas about an hour before serving, so they'll have enough time to chill but not to turn rubbery.

1 cup Mirin (sweet rice wine for cooking, available at Asian specialty shops)
12 large garlic cloves, crushed
One 2-inch piece fresh ginger, peeled and thinly slivered
2 tablespoons fresh or dried chopped lemon grass (available at Asian markets)
½ cup minced fresh cilantro
6 scallions, including greens, chopped
3 pounds mussels in their shells, scrubbed and debearded (see box, page 122)
½ pound snow peas, trimmed

Garnish
Minced water chestnuts
Chopped toasted cashews or toasted almonds (see page 77)
Diced red bell pepper
¼ cup minced fresh cilantro

*I*n a large saucepan, combine the Mirin, garlic, ginger, lemon grass, cilantro, and scallions. Bring to a boil over medium-high heat.

🍃 Add the mussels, cover, turn the heat to low, and let them steam for 7 minutes, or until opened. Turn off the heat.

🍃 Using a slotted spoon, transfer the mussels to a large bowl. Discard any that haven't opened. Let the mussels cool slightly, then put them in the refrigerator, covered, until they're chilled through, about 3 hours.

🍃 Meanwhile, simmer the cooking liquid over low heat until it reduces by about ¼, about 6 minutes, then pour it through a sieve. Reserve the liquid and throw away the seasonings. Pour ¼ cup of the liquid into a medium skillet, and refrigerate the remainder, covered.

🍃 Heat the liquid in the skillet over medium heat, add the snow peas, cover and steam until they're just cooked, about 1 minute.

Using a slotted spoon, transfer them to a bowl, cover, and chill, at least 1 hour.

🍃 When the mussels are thoroughly chilled, remove all but 8 of them from their shells, and throw the rest of the shells away.

🍃 Distribute the snow peas evenly on 4 plates, and place equal amounts of shelled mussels on each. Garnish with the mussels in their shells, 2 per plate, the water chestnuts, cashews or almonds, red pepper, and additional cilantro. Drizzle with the reserved chilled Mirin mixture. Serve cold.

[PER SERVING: CAL. 226.7 / FAT 2.4 G / PROTEIN 16.0 G / CARB. 18.8 G / CHOL. 31.8 MG / SODIUM 334.7 MG] % RDA: 23.6 VIT. A; 67.4 VIT. C; 35.4 IRON.

Rice Salad with Mango and Chickpeas (with or without Chicken)

Serves 4

We had a young houseguest one summer who came into the kitchen while I was making this salad. She did a double take when I tossed the diced mango into the bowl. "I didn't know you could do that!" she said, awed. Chicken salad as she knew it was about celery and mayonnaise. It was a pivotal moment for her. Realizing there were no rules about chicken salad, she started to wonder what else was possible, taking notice of food with avid interest and pleasure.

50 minutes from start to finish

 You can poach the chicken up to 3 days in advance, provided you wrap it tightly and keep it refrigerated until ready for use. You can also make the salad and the dressing up to 2 days in advance, combining them up to 3 hours before serving. (Sooner, it may turn runny.)

1 boneless whole chicken breast, weighing about 1 pound (optional)

¼ cup slivered almonds (optional)

1 tablespoon tahini (sesame paste; see pages 235–36)

1 cup plain nonfat yogurt

¼ cup fresh orange juice

2 teaspoons grated lemon zest

2 teaspoons grated fresh ginger

1 small garlic clove, grated

1 teaspoon ground cumin

1 teaspoon paprika

1 ripe mango, peeled, pitted, and cubed

2 cups cooked chickpeas (if canned, rinse them thoroughly in cold water)

¼ cup sun-dried tomatoes (dry packed), minced

2 fresh tomatoes, diced

2 tablespoons minced fresh chives

2 cups cooked short-grain brown rice, cooled

*i*f you're including chicken, bring about 4 inches of water to a boil in a large saucepan. Add the chicken breast, cover, lower the heat, and simmer until it's cooked through, about 10 minutes. Transfer the breast to a plate and let it cool.

🍃 Meanwhile, heat the oven or a toaster oven to 350°F. Put the almonds on a piece of foil or a baking sheet and bake them until they're lightly toasted, about 5 minutes, shaking them occasionally to keep them from burning.

🍃 Put the tahini, yogurt, and orange juice into the work bowl of a food processor or blender, and process just until smooth. Add the lemon zest, ginger, garlic, cumin, and paprika, and process again to blend.

🍃 Cut the chicken, if using, into bite-sized strips and put it in a large mixing bowl, along with the mango, chickpeas, almonds, sun-dried tomatoes, fresh tomatoes, chives, and rice. Toss well.

🍃 Add the tahini dressing and mix thoroughly. Serve right away, or refrigerate for 3 hours to chill and serve cold.

[PER SERVING: CAL. 337.2 / FAT 6.5 G* / PROTEIN 21.9 G / CARB. 46.2 G / CHOL. 31.4 G / SODIUM 67.5 MG**] *MADE WITH NONFAT YOGURT. **VALUE GIVEN IS BEFORE SALTING. % RDA: 23.3 VIT. A; 50.1 VIT. C.

Starters & Side dishes

(That Can Make a Meal, Too)

· · · · · ·

Herbed Asparagus Torta ◊ Mediterranean Eggplant and Peppers ◊
Eggplant Pancakes ◊ Cabbage Cakes ◊ Cabbage with Apples and Cheese
◊ Winter Vegetables in Mellow Lemon Marinade ◊ Winter Squash Gratin
◊ Carrot and Apricot Terrine ◊ Roasted Red Pepper Terrine ◊ Chilled
Tomato Timbales in Tender Spinach Casing ◊ Gingered Leek and Fennel
Flans ◊ Pepper Filled Peppers ◊ Simple Baked Rutabagas ◊ Baked
Stuffed Turnips ◊ Braised Onions with Sweet Rice Stuffing ◊ Stuffed Grape
Leaves ◊ Pissaladière-Inspired Potato Tarts ◊ Potato Gratin ◊ Wholly
Wholesome Mashed Potatoes ◊ Red Potatoes in Saffron Marinade ◊ Sweet
Potato Pancakes ◊ Mushroom Barley ◊ Cheddar Buttermilk Spoon
Bread ◊ Endive and Leek Fondue ◊ Red Cabbage and Onion Relish ◊
Nectarine Relish

Side dishes are no longer the glorified garnishes they were when dinner, properly understood, meant meat. Now they can be the better part of a meal, or they can be the meal itself. There are several advantages to being able to cook a number of good side dishes. First, you can invite vegetarian friends to dinner where meat of some kind will be served. They can make a substantial meal of dishes that the others will have, in smaller portions, on the side. Also, you can give yourself time to prepare a generous dinner by starting a few days in advance, making a side dish or two each day. Many of these dishes taste better a day or so after they're made, since the seasonings will have had a chance to mingle and deepen.

With the side dishes out of the way, you'll be free to concentrate on the entrée, which can be a simple dish such as roast chicken or poached fish. The meal will be splendid, and you won't be too pooped to appreciate what you've done.

If You're Making a Meal of Side Dishes

- Balance for nourishment. Have at least one grain dish such as Mushroom Barley (see page 102), and one that includes beans or dairy products, such as Gingered Leek and Fennel Flans (see page 90). Check the ingredients to make sure you're not serving several dishes containing eggs or cheese, or that you're not offering more than three kinds of grain.
- Balance for texture, so you have one creamy dish, such as a terrine, one grainy, such as Braised Onions with Sweet Rice Stuffing (see page 94), and one crunchy, such as Winter Vegetables in Mellow Lemon Marinade (see page 85).
- Balance for color, so once filled, each plate looks appetizing.
- For optimum flexibility in meal planning, all of the dishes in this section are meatless. You can serve them to supplement a meal of chicken or fish, so that your vegetarian guests eat as well as everyone else. Or you can serve several together, perhaps with a salad, for an altogether meatless meal.

Herbed Asparagus Torta

Serves 3 or 4

This first course or light lunch dish is for real fans of asparagus, those devotees who take the "less is more" view of their favorite vegetable. What they mean is not less asparagus, of course, but that the less done to it, the more taste can come from it, *and* the less fuss to fix it, the more time there'll be to enjoy it.

15 minutes to prepare
35 minutes to bake

 You can make this dish up to 2 days in advance, keeping it refrigerated, tightly wrapped. If you make it in advance, serve it cold or at room temperature.

½ tablespoon unsalted butter or canola oil
1 red onion, minced
2 scallions, white part only, minced
1 tablespoon minced fresh sage leaves
1 tablespoon minced fresh chives
4 large eggs, lightly beaten
½ cup grated imported Parmesan cheese
1 cup part-skim ricotta cheese (see Note)
1½ cups asparagus tips, steamed (see box, page 148)

*h*eat the oven to 450° F.
  🌿 In a 6-inch ovenproof skillet, melt the butter or heat the oil, and sauté the onion, scallions, sage, and chives over medium-low heat until the onion is soft and translucent, about 7 minutes.
  🌿 Meanwhile, in a mixing bowl, combine

the eggs, Parmesan, and ricotta and beat with an electric mixer or wooden spoon until smooth.

🍃 Add the asparagus to the skillet and stir well to blend with the onion mixture. Pour the egg mixture on top.

🍃 Put the skillet in the oven and bake until a knife inserted in the center comes out clean and it is light brown on the bottom and firm all the way through, about 35 minutes.

Note: If the ricotta cheese is runny, let it drain for an hour; pour it into a strainer lined with a piece of cheesecloth or a paper coffee filter, set the strainer over a wide-mouthed jar or glass, and put it in the refrigerator.

[PER SERVING: CAL. 161.5 / FAT 9.4 G* / PROTEIN 12.9 G / CARB. 5.5 G / CHOL. 202.8 MG / SODIUM 215.9 MG**] *MADE WITH PART-SKIM RICOTTA. FOR LESS TOTAL FAT AND CHOLESTEROL, SWITCH TO NONFAT. **VALUE GIVEN IS BEFORE SALTING. % RDA: 26 CALCIUM.

SERVING SUGGESTIONS
Serve Herbed Asparagus Torta sliced in wedges as a first course, or for lunch with fresh bread and Aromatic Leek and Potato Soup (page 50) or Chilled Corn Chowder (page 59).

Mediterranean Eggplant and Peppers

Serves 6

I've never known anyone to stop at a single serving of this dish, so prepare plenty of it.

1 hour from start to finish

 You can make this dish up to 3 days in advance, keeping it refrigerated in a tightly covered container. To reheat, transfer it to a covered baking dish, and warm at 300° F. for about 20 minutes. (You don't have to reheat it, though, because it's also delicious cold or at room temperature.)

¼ cup extra virgin olive oil
2 large white or yellow onions, thinly sliced
2 fennel bulbs, stalks and fronds trimmed, thinly sliced
2 large yellow peppers, cored, seeded, and thinly sliced
2 large red peppers, cored, seeded, and thinly sliced
1 tablespoon crumbled dried oregano
1 tablespoon crumbled dried basil
2 teaspoons whole fennel seed
6 Japanese eggplants, cut into bite-sized cubes
2 tablespoons balsamic vinegar
Salt and freshly ground pepper to taste

*h*eat the oven to 425° F. In a large casserole or large heavy saucepan, heat the olive oil. Sauté the onions, fennel, yellow and red peppers, oregano, basil, and fennel seed over medium-low heat until the vegetables are soft and limp, about 40 minutes.

🍃 Meanwhile, spread the eggplant in a single layer on a nonstick or lightly oiled baking sheet and bake until tender, about 20 minutes.

🍃 Add the vinegar to the vegetables in the casserole, and stir over medium-low heat until most of it evaporates, about 2 minutes.

🍃 Stir in the eggplant, coating it well with the other vegetables. Stir until heated through, and season with salt and pepper before serving.

[PER SERVING: CAL. 161.3 / FAT 8.7 G / PROTEIN 2.2 G / CARB. 17.3 G / CHOL. 0 MG / SODIUM 78 MG*] *VALUE GIVEN IS BEFORE SALTING. % RDA: 22.1 VIT. A; 204.4 VIT. C.

SERVING SUGGESTIONS
Serve Mediterranean Eggplant and Peppers with Winter Squash Gratin (page 86), Roast Turkey (page 187), or Braised Fish with Winter Greens (page 192).

Eggplant Pancakes

Serves 4

This simple recipe calls for small Japanese eggplant because ordinary eggplant tend to be too bitter for seasonings as subtle as those used here. Serve this light, luscious side dish with poached fish, roast chicken, or any hearty soup.

40 minutes from start to finish

You can keep these pancakes for up to 3 days, wrapped tightly in plastic and refrigerated. To reheat, wrap in foil and heat in a 325°F. oven for 10 minutes.

1 large egg, lightly beaten
2 tablespoons all-purpose flour
2 tablespoons sour cream, low-fat or nonfat, if you'd like
½ pound Japanese eggplant, roasted, peeled, seeded and chopped (see page 71)
2 scallions, white part only, sliced
1 tablespoon toasted sesame seeds

*i*n a large mixing bowl, whisk together the egg, flour, and sour cream until smooth. Stir in the eggplant, scallions, and sesame seeds until well blended.

🍃 Heat a nonstick griddle over medium heat. When hot, add the eggplant batter ¼ cup at a time. Cook until bubbles form on the surface and the bottom has browned, about 7 minutes. Turn over and cook to brown the other side, about 4 to 5 minutes longer. Serve warm.

[PER SERVING (USING LOW-FAT SOUR CREAM): CAL. 55 / FAT 1 G / PROTEIN 3 G / CARB. 8.7 G / CHOL. 0 / SODIUM 25.2 MG]

SERVING SUGGESTIONS
Serve Eggplant Pancakes with Poached Fish (page 190) or Leek and Endive Fondue (page 105).

Cabbage Cakes

Makes 6 to 8 pancakes

A novel use for the common cabbage, this simple stovetop dish is astonishingly good. Serve with a salad for lunch or as a supper side dish with chicken or fish.

40 minutes from start to finish

These pancakes keep well for up to 3 days wrapped tightly in plastic and refrigerated. To reheat, wrap them in foil and without stacking them too thickly and warm them in a 325°F. oven until heated through, about 15 minutes.

3 cups losely packed thinly shredded green or red cabbage

1 large egg, lightly beaten

1 tablespoon milk, low-fat or nonfat if desired

2 tablespoons sour cream, low-fat or nonfat if you'd like

2 tablespoons all-purpose or whole wheat flour

¼ cup minced chives

team the cabbage on the stove top or in a microwave. (See steaming directions on page 148 or 144). Drain well in a colander.

In a mixing bowl, beat together the egg, milk, sour cream, and flour. Stir in the cabbage and chives.

Heat a nonstick griddle (lightly greased if foods tend to stick to yours anyway) over medium heat. When hot, give the batter a stir and drop 3 tablespoons for each cake onto the griddle, cooking up to 4 at a time. Cook until bubbles form on the surface, and the cake has browned underneath, about 5 minutes. Using a plastic spatula, turn to brown the other side, 3 to 4 minutes more. Repeat, stirring the batter before dropping it onto the griddle, until you've used up all of the batter. Transfer to a warm plate and serve right away.

[PER SERVING (USING NONFAT MILK AND LOW-FAT SOUR CREAM): CAL. 59 / FAT 1.6 G / PROTEIN 3.6 G / CARB. 7.9 G / CHOL. 68 MG / SODIUM 35 MG] % RDA: 51 VIT. C.

SERVING SUGGESTIONS
Serve Cabbage Cakes with Poached Chicken Breasts or Artichokes with Artichoke Stuffing (page 172), Chicken Breasts (or Pressed Tofu) with Sweet Mustard Glaze (page 176), or Monkfish with Mushrooms and Lentils (page 194).

Cabbage with Apples and Cheese

Serves 4 to 6

Imagination, a sense of humor, and sheer force of will can help you get through a dull winter day. But promising yourself something *this* good for dinner can be more effective.

30 minutes from start to finish

This dish is best made just before serving.

3 cups shredded green cabbage

1 tablespoon unsalted butter

1 tablespoon all-purpose flour

2 cups warm nonfat or low-fat milk

1 cup shredded sharp cheddar cheese

1 teaspoon caraway seeds

½ teaspoon dry mustard

1 cup diced dried apples, preferably organic
   unsulfured (see pages 235–36)

ring 2 inches of water to a boil in a saucepan. Add the cabbage, turn down the heat to medium-low, cover, and steam until tender but not mushy, about 12 minutes. Add water if necessary, a tablespoon at a time. Using a slotted spoon, lift the cabbage from the water, set it into a large sieve, and let it drain.

🍃 Meanwhile, melt the butter in a separate saucepan. Stir in the flour and cook over low heat, whisking constantly, until it's bubbly and golden, about 3 minutes. Whisk in the warm milk, raise the heat to medium, and

SERVING SUGGESTIONS
Serve Cabbage with Apples and Cheese with Poached Chicken Breasts or Artichokes with Artichoke Stuffing (page 172) or Mushroom Barley (page 102).

cook, whisking constantly, until the mixture thickens, about 10 minutes.

🍃 Stir in the cheddar cheese, and keep stirring until it melts to make a smooth sauce. Add the caraway seeds and dry mustard, and stir to blend.

🍃 Place the cabbage in a large mixing bowl with the dried apples. Pour the cheese sauce on top and toss well. Serve at once.

[PER SERVING: CAL. 177.9 / FAT 7.9 G* / PROTEIN 8.7 G / CARB. 16.5 G / CHOL. 26.8 MG / SODIUM 185.6 MG**] *MADE WITH NONFAT MILK AND WHOLE MILK CHEDDAR CHEESE. **VALUE GIVEN IS BEFORE SALTING. % RDA: 32.2 VIT. C; 26.4 CALCIUM.

Winter Vegetables in Mellow Lemon Marinade

Serves 4

The essential ingredient here is time, which allows the flavors to deepen and change in marvelous ways.

40 minutes to prepare
6 hours to chill

 You can make this dish up to 3 days in advance, keeping it refrigerated in a tightly covered container.

2 large russet potatoes, peeled

2 tablespoons extra virgin olive oil

2 teaspoons ground cumin

1 teaspoon salt

2 fennel bulbs, fronds attached, coarsely chopped

4 small white onions (the size of golf balls), peeled and quartered

2 garlic cloves, minced

1 carrot, peeled and coarsely chopped

1 lemon

2 whole cloves

ring enough water to cover the potatoes to a boil in a medium saucepan over high heat. Add the potatoes and boil over medium heat until just cooked through, about 20 minutes. Drain them and chop coarsely when cool enough to handle.

Meanwhile, in a large skillet, heat the olive oil. Add the cumin and salt, and sauté the fennel, onions, garlic, and carrot over medium-low heat until soft, about 20 minutes.

Squeeze the juice from the lemon into a large glass or ceramic bowl. Grate the zest from half the lemon over it and discard the rest of the peel.

Toss the cloves into the bowl, along with the sautéed vegetables and the potatoes. Mix well to combine.

Cover and chill for at least 6 hours and serve cold or at room temperature. Make sure to discard the cloves before serving.

[PER SERVING: CAL. 185 / FAT 4 G / PROTEIN 2.8 G / CARB. 39 G / CHOL. 0 / SODIUM 439.2 MG] % RDA: 34 VIT. A; 53 VIT. C.

Clove is not one of your recreational spices. It's much too strong for casual use. As a homeopathic treatment for toothache, it works by numbing the gums, paralyzing the taste buds in the process so that they're helpless to detect other flavors. To avoid inadvertently incapacitating your guests or yourself in this way, use cloves sparingly, and be sure to pick all of them out before serving.

SERVING SUGGESTIONS
Serve Winter Vegetables in Mellow Lemon Marinade with Chicken Roasted with Garlic (page 181), Poached Fish (page 190), or Herbed Asparagus Torta (page 80).

Winter Squash Gratin

Serves 4 to 6

This dish is so pretty I would almost say that it could double as a center-piece for a holiday buffet. But it tastes so good, it would last there about as long as an ice sculpture at a picnic on the Fourth of July.

50 minutes to prepare
15 minutes to bake

 You can make this gratin up to 3 days in advance, keeping it refrigerated and tightly wrapped. Reheat it in its original baking pan, covered with foil, at 300° F. for 20 minutes. Or take it out of the refrigerator 2 hours before serving and serve it at room temperature.

1 pound winter squash, such as butternut, acorn, or pumpkin

1 pound cauliflower, trimmed and cut into florets

2 tablespoons unsalted butter

2 tablespoons all-purpose flour

2 cups warm low-fat or nonfat milk

½ cup grated imported Parmesan cheese

½ teaspoon ground nutmeg

Salt and freshly ground pepper to taste

*h*eat the oven to 450° F. Cut the squash into quarters, scoop out the seeds, and wrap each piece tightly in foil. Bake until tender, about 40 minutes. Let it cool, cut off the rind, and cut the squash into small cubes.

🍃 Meanwhile steam the cauliflower until just cooked through (see page 148).

HOW TO COOK A WHOLE PUMPKIN OR WINTER SQUASH
❶ ❷ ❸

❶ Heat the oven to 425° F. Place the pumpkin or winter squash in a large, deep, heavy baking dish.

❷ Add enough water to the pan to come a third of the way up the side of the pumpkin or winter squash.

❸ Cover the pan tightly with foil and bake until the pumpkin or winter squash softens, about 45 minutes. Let the pumpkin or winter squash cool before cutting it open, removing the stem, and separating the seeds from the pulp.

🍃 In a medium saucepan, melt the butter. When it starts to sizzle, stir in the flour, and cook over low heat, whisking constantly, until the mixture is bubbling and golden.

🍃 Stir in the milk, turn the heat up to medium, and keep whisking until the mixture is smooth and thick, about 10 minutes. Take

SERVING SUGGESTIONS
Serve Winter Squash Gratin as a first course before Roast Turkey (page 187), or with Braised Fish with Winter Greens (page 192), or a tossed salad (page 64) for a light lunch.

it off the heat. Whisk in half of the cheese, and all of the nutmeg, salt, and pepper.

🍃 Place the cubed squash and the cauliflower in an 8-inch square baking pan, and pour the sauce on top.

🐚 Sprinkle the remaining cheese on top and bake for 15 minutes. Serve right away.

[PER SERVING: CAL. 146 / FAT 6 G / PROTEIN 7.4 G / CARB. 15 G / CHOL. 818 MG / SODIUM 180 MG]

Carrot and Apricot Terrine

Serves 6 to 8

This exquisite terrine is so sweet I suggest you serve it at brunch rather than dinner. It's as close to cheesecake as you can come and still call it a first course.

50 minutes to prepare
1 hour 30 minutes to bake
Chill 6 hours or overnight

This is a do-ahead dish because it must be chilled 6 hours or overnight. You can make it up to 3 days ahead, keeping it refrigerated, well wrapped.

8 carrots, peeled and sliced into rounds ⅓ inch thick
8 dried apricots, preferably organic
2 bay leaves
½ cup fresh orange juice, plus extra if necessary
3 large eggs, lightly beaten
1 cup grated imported Parmesan cheese
1 cup part-skim ricotta cheese
1 cup fine dried breadcrumbs
Pinch powdered ginger
Pinch ground nutmeg

*P*lace the carrots in a medium saucepan and add water to cover. Bring to a boil and let simmer, covered, until the carrots are very soft, about 40 minutes. Drain thoroughly and let them cool at room temperature.

🐚 Meanwhile, place the apricots and bay leaves in a separate saucepan and add ½ cup orange juice. Bring to a gentle simmer, cover, and cook on low heat until the apricots are mushy, about 30 minutes. Check often, adding more orange juice if necessary. Let cool at room temperature, and discard the bay leaves.

🍃 Heat the oven to 425° F. In a food processor or blender, combine the eggs, Parmesan cheese, ricotta cheese, and breadcrumbs. Transfer to a large mixing bowl.

🐚 Process the carrots and apricots together until smooth. Stir into the cheese mixture until well combined. Add the ginger and nutmeg and mix well.

Making a terrine is a way of combining your favorite ingredients and serving them in the most compact manner possible. Terrines look spectacular, a neat trick for pureed vegetables bound together with eggs and cheese. You can tinker with the type of cheese to modify the flavor and fat content, and alter the ratio of one vegetable to another to favor those you prefer.

✍ Lightly butter a loaf pan or terrine measuring 6 × 4 inches. Pour the carrot mixture inside and cover with aluminum foil. Place the terrine inside a larger, deeper baking dish and pour water into the larger dish so it comes halfway up the side of the terrine.

🌸 Bake for 1½ hours, checking often and adding more water as it evaporates. The terrine is done when a knife inserted into the center comes out clean. Let it cool completely at room temperature before refrigerating for 6 hours or overnight.

HOW TO ROAST A BELL PEPPER
❶ ❷ ❸

❶ Heat the broiler to its highest setting. Slice the pepper in half and take out the core and seeds.

❷ Place the halves skin side up on an oiled baking sheet, and put them under the broiler until the skin buckles and chars, 3 to 4 minutes.

❸ Using a fork, transfer the peppers from the baking sheet to a paper bag, and refrigerate for 15 minutes. The skin should peel off easily.

You can keep roasted peppers for up to 4 days, refrigerated and wrapped tightly in plastic. Or you can extend their refrigerator shelf life for up to a month by coating them lightly in extra virgin olive oil and refrigerating them in a sealed jar or tightly lidded plastic container.

SERVING SUGGESTINS
Serve Carrot and Apricot Terrine with Apple Crepes (page 216) for brunch, or with Chilled Corn Chowder (page 59) or Poached Chicken Breasts or Artichokes with Artichoke Stuffing (page 172).

✍ To serve, run a butter knife around the rim and gently turn it over onto a platter. French bread or toast can be served with it.

[PER SERVING: CAL. 204.7 / FAT 7.3 G* / PROTEIN 12.4 G / CARB. 21.2 G / CHOL. 120.2 MG / SODIUM 325.3 MG] *MADE WITH PART-SKIM RICOTTA. FOR FEWER CALORIES, LESS TOTAL FAT AND CHOLESTEROL, SWITCH TO NONFAT. % RDA: 274.7 VIT. A; 27.5 VIT. C; 26.7 CALCIUM.

Roasted Red Pepper Terrine

Serves 4 to 6

This terrine is delicious, dazzling, and incredibly easy. Serve it as an appetizer or a first course with bread or toast. Or have it for lunch, with salad or soup.

30 minutes to prepare
40 to bake

 You can make this terrine up to 2 days in advance, keeping it refrigerated, tightly wrapped. Remove it from the refrigerator 2 hours before serving, and let it come to room temperature before serving.

4 large red bell peppers, roasted, peeled, seeded, and sliced (see box, left)
2 large eggs, lightly beaten

½ cup crumbled Feta cheese

1 cup part-skim ricotta cheese or dry-curd
  cottage cheese

Pinch dried oregano, crumbled

Pinch dried basil, crumbled

*h*eat the oven to 450°F.

🖎 Put the roasted peppers into a food processor and process in short spurts to make a thick paste. Add the eggs, Feta cheese, ricotta or cottage cheese, oregano, and basil, and process in short pulses until smooth and well blended. Be careful not to run the processor at full power, or the mixture will become too thin.

🖉 Pour the mixture into an 8-inch round cake pan. Place this pan into a larger and deeper pan. Pour water into the outer pan so that it comes halfway up the inside pan.

🖎 Bake, uncovered, for 40 minutes, checking often and adding more water as it evaporates. If the top starts to brown, cover it loosely with foil.

🖉 The terrine is done when a knife inserted into the middle comes out clean. Remove the terrine from the outer pan, and let it cool to room temperature on a wire rack. To serve, run a butter knife around the rim and gently turn it over onto a platter.

[PER SERVING: CAL. 169.5 / FAT 8.9 G / PROTEIN 14.8 G / CARB. 6.5 G / CHOL. 164.5 MG / SODIUM 359 MG] % RDA: 70.1 VIT. A; 316.7 VIT. C.

The most flavorful dried herbs and spices are organic. Their shelf life is short, so buy them in small batches, or split the cost and the contents of a larger container with a friend.

Chilled Tomato Timbales in Tender Spinach Casing

Serves 4

Chilled steamed spinach filled with herbs and tomatoes is a refreshing alternative to salad, especially in late summer when the tomatoes are so good. The olive oil makes all the difference here, so use the best you can afford. If you have to cut back on fats, don't add the drizzle of oil at the end. Otherwise, consider this a course in how a very good olive oil can enhance the flavor of simple foods.

40 minutes to prepare
3 hours to chill

You can make the tomato filling up to 4 days in advance, keeping it refrigerated in a tightly sealed container. You can make the assembled timbales up to 1 day in advance, adding the olive oil just before serving.

4 large tomatoes, ripe but firm

5 tablespoons extra virgin olive oil (1
  tablespoon if you must cut back on fats)

2 shallots, minced

¾ cup minced fresh chives, plus additional for
  garnish

¾ cup minced fresh parsley

16 large spinach leaves, washed but not dried

Salt and freshly ground pepper to taste

*c*hop the tomatoes, discarding the stems and seeds.

🖎 Heat 1 tablespoon of the olive oil in a small skillet, and sauté the shallots over medium-low heat until soft, about 6 minutes. Add the ¾ cup of chives and the parsley and sauté for 5 minutes more. Add the tomatoes and continue to cook, over low heat, until they soften and start to break down into a sauce, about 7 minutes. Meanwhile bring a cup of water to a brisk boil in a small saucepan or the microwave.

🌿 Place the spinach leaves in a shallow pan and add boiling water to cover. Taking care not to tear them, lift the leaves out of the water when they've turned bright green, about 4 minutes. Transfer the leaves to a plate, being careful not to tear them, and let them rest until they're cool enough to handle.

🌿 Lightly oil the bottom and sides of four 4-inch tart pans or shallow porcelain ramekins. Lay 4 spinach leaves in each pan so they line the bottom and sides and hang over by several inches.

🍃 Fill each spinach-lined tart pan with an even amount of the tomato mixture. Fold the overhanging leaves over the top, sealing the tomatoes inside. Cover loosely with foil or plastic wrap and chill for at least 3 hours.

🌿 Pour an even amount of the remaining extra virgin olive oil onto each of 4 serving plates. Invert 1 spinach "packet" on top of each. Season with additional pepper, if you'd like, or sprinkle with more chives. Serve chilled.

[PER SERVING: CAL. 186.7 / FAT 12.8 G* / PROTEIN 2.8 G / CARB. 12.8 G / CHOL. 0 MG / SODIUM 64.6 MG**] *WHEN MADE WITH THE FULL AMOUNT OF OLIVE OIL CALLED FOR IN THE RECIPE. **VALUE GIVEN BEFORE SALTING. % RDA: 67.1 VIT. A; 101.6 VIT. C.

Gingered Leek and Fennel Flans

Serves 4

The ingredients hardly hint at how this dish tastes. The elusive flavor compels me to eat it with great concentration, ever intent on figuring out how these few, simple foods can be so dazzling in combination.

1 hour to prepare
50 minutes to bake and cool

 You can make these flans up to 2 days in advance. Keep them tightly wrapped and refrigerated, removing them from the refrigerator 2 hours before serving to let them come to room temperature. They don't reheat well.

1 large leek, cut in half lengthwise and washed
1 tablespoon unsalted butter
1 large fennel bulb, without fronds, trimmed and diced
1 teaspoon grated fresh ginger
Pinch salt
Juice of 1 lemon
2 large egg yolks
1 large egg white

ring about 2 inches of water to a boil in a large saucepan. Cut the leek in half crosswise, cover, and steam until it's tender all the way through, about 10 minutes. Lift the leek out of the water and set it aside on paper towels to drain and cool. Reserve the cooking water.

🍃 Meanwhile melt the butter in a skillet and add the fennel, ginger, and salt. Sauté over low heat until the fennel begins to soften, about 7

minutes. Add the lemon juice, cover, and continue to cook gently, stirring often, until the fennel is cooked through and very tender, about 40 minutes altogether. Add the reserved cooking water 1 tablespoon at a time to prevent sticking, if necessary.

Puree the fennel mixture in a blender or food processor. Transfer the mixture to a large mixing bowl and stir in the 2 egg yolks.

In a small bowl, beat the egg white until stiff. Fold it into the fennel mixture.

Heat the oven to 450°F., and lightly butter 4 shallow 3-inch ramekins. Carefully unroll and separate the leek layers. Line each ramekin with leek leaves, overlapping them slightly and making sure the leaves hang over the sides by at least ½ inch. Gently spoon the fennel mixture into the lined ramekins, distributing it evenly. Fold the leek leaves over to enclose the filling.

Place the ramekins in a deep baking dish and add enough water to come halfway up

SERVING SUGGESTIONS
Serve Gingered Leek and Fennel Flans with Poached Chicken Breasts or Artichokes with Artichoke Stuffing (page 172) or Poached Fish (page 190).

the sides. Put them in the oven and bake until a knife tests clean when inserted in the center, about 35 minutes.

Let the flans cool for 15 minutes. To serve, invert each on a plate. If they stick to the ramekins, wet a butter knife and run it gently around the flans to pry them loose.

[PER SERVING: CAL. 94.5 / FAT 5.8 G / PROTEIN 3.1 G / CARB. 7.2 G / CHOL. 144.8 MG / SODIUM 345.2 MG*] *VALUE GIVEN IS BEFORE SALTING. % RDA: 25.4 VIT. C.

HOW TO CLEAN A LEEK
❶ ❷ ❸

❶ Fill a long deep pan with water and add a few drops of lemon juice or wine vinegar.

❷ Cut off the root end and the top few inches of greens. (Most recipes call for the white part only, so save the green for broth, if you like.) Slit it lengthwise so it unscrolls.

❸ Loosen the layers, and soak the leek for about 10 minutes. Rinse it well with fresh water and pat it dry with paper towels.

Pepper Filled Peppers

Serves 4

It's only fair to warn you that if you serve this as a starter, you'd better have something good to follow. It's an appetizer in the truest sense, so tantalizing your guests will be primed for more and more and more. You'll get best results if you use firm, deeply colored bell peppers for this dish, which depends on them for flavor.

20 minutes to prepare

20 minutes to cook

 These peppers keep refrigerated, tightly wrapped, for up to 4 days.

4 large red peppers, halved, seeded, roasted, and peeled (see box, page 88)

4 large yellow peppers, halved, seeded, roasted, and peeled (see box, page 88)

1 small eggplant (⅓ pound), roasted, peeled, and seeded (see page 71)

2 cups part-skim ricotta cheese

⅔ cup grated imported Parmesan cheese

3 tablespoons minced fresh basil

1 teaspoon grated garlic

*h*eat the oven to 425°F. Place half of the red and half of the yellow peppers in the bowl of a food processor, along with the roasted eggplant, ricotta cheese, Parmesan, basil, and garlic. Process just until smooth.

🍃 Fill the remaining pepper halves with the cheese mixture and place upright in a shallow baking dish. Bake until lightly browned, about 20 minutes.

[PER SERVING: CAL. 135 / FAT 2.6 G / PROTEIN 15.4 G / CARB. 11.4 G / CHOL. 7 MG / SODIUM 260 MG]

Simple Baked Rutabagas

Serves 6

Rutabagas are doubly disadvantaged. First, the name. It sounds like a plumbing implement. Second, the size. They grow to obscene proportions. Add to that the unfortunate practice of coating them in wax, and you have one sorry vegetable. But what rutabagas lack in glamour, they have in beta carotene, Vitamin C, and flavor. They taste like concentrated turnips: firmer, sweeter, and richer. If you're still reluctant to try this vegetable, think of this as mashed baked potatoes only better.

25 minutes to prepare

45 minutes to bake

 You can make this dish up to 4 days in advance. Keep refrigerated, tightly covered, and reheat for 20 minutes, covered with foil, in a 325°F. oven before serving.

1 pound peeled rutabaga, diced

1 pound peeled medium-starch potatoes, such as Yukon Gold or Yellow Finn, diced

2 large eggs, lightly beaten

1½ cups low-fat cottage cheese

½ cup shredded cheddar cheese

2 tablespoons minced chives

SERVING SUGGESTIONS

Serve Simple Baked Rutabagas with Braised Fish with Winter Greens (page 192), Chicken Roasted with Garlic (page 181), or as part of the Almost Vegetarian Holiday Dinner (page 186).

*h*eat the oven to 375°F. Using the stovetop or microwave method (see page 148 or 144), steam the rutabagas and potatoes until soft enough to pierce easily with a knife. Transfer to a food processer and puree. Add the eggs, cottage cheese, and cheddar cheese, and process again until smooth. Blend in the chives.

🍃 Spread the mixture into an 8-inch square baking pan, and bake until firm, about 45 minutes. Let rest 15 minutes before cutting and serving.

[PER SERVING (USING LOW-FAT COTTAGE CHEESE): CAL. 196 / FAT 3.5 G / PROTEIN 13 G / CARB. 26 G / CHOL. 12.5 MG / SODIUM 323 MG]

Baked Stuffed Turnips

Serves 4

Until recently, turnips were one of several things I had never thought of cooking. There were 2 reasons for this: (1) They didn't look much like food to me, and (2) I wasn't aware of ever having eaten them before. Consequently, I wasn't hungry for them. And since I rely on appetite for inspiration, I was never inspired to cook with turnips.

But I get periodic bouts of self-improvement, when I tackle my mental blocks. In one such mood, I bought some turnips and filled them as follows, acquiring a taste for them in the bargain.

50 minutes to prepare
15 minutes to bake

 You can make the filling up to 4 days in advance, keeping it refrigerated, tightly wrapped. Complete the dish either just before serving or 1 day in advance (any more than that and the turnips will become soggy).

½ lemon

4 medium turnips, trimmed

½ pound firm winter squash, such as acorn, butternut, or pumpkin, cut into 2-inch slices

1 large white potato, peeled and quartered

1 tablespoon canola oil

½ cup minced fresh parsley

1 tablespoon white wine vinegar or vinegar with herbs

queeze the juice from the lemon into a large bowl. Peel the turnips and add them to the bowl, along with enough cold water to cover.

❧ Steam the squash (for steaming instructions, see page 144) until just cooked through, but not mushy, about 15 minutes. Peel away the rind and dice the rest of the squash.

✐ Over medium-high heat, bring water to a boil in a medium saucepan, and cook the potato until just cooked through, about 8 minutes. Drain, then finely dice.

❧ Heat the oil in a large skillet and sauté the squash, potato, and parsley over medium heat, stirring often, for 10 minutes. Splash the vegetables with the vinegar, stir well, and cook for 3 minutes more, until the vinegar evaporates. Turn off the heat.

✐ Meanwhile, in a large saucepan bring to a boil enough water to cover the turnips. Drain the turnips, put them in the saucepan and simmer until they're soft, about 15 minutes. Heat the oven to 425°F.

❧ Drain the turnips and hollow out the center of each to make a well. Fill them with the vegetables, pressing down to pack them in. The sides of the turnip will stretch, holding much more filling than you'd expect.

SERVING SUGGESTIONS
Serve Baked Stuffed Turnips with Chicken Roasted with Garlic (page 181) or Braised Fish with Winter Greens (page 192).

✐ Place the filled turnips upright in a baking pan and bake, uncovered, until the filling is firm and golden brown, about 15 minutes.

[PER SERVING: CAL. 133.3 / FAT 3.2 G / PROTEIN 1.7 G / CARB. 23.9 G / CHOL. 0 / SODIUM 86.4 MG*] *VALUE GIVEN IS BEFORE SALTING. % RDA: 60.4 VIT. C

Braised Onions with Sweet Rice Stuffing

Serves 4

The onion may be the most mutable vegetable. To say how it tastes depends first on whether it's white, yellow, or red. If white, whether small or large. If yellow, whether Vidalia or Spanish, fresh or "storage." Then it's a matter of whether the onion is raw or cooked; if cooked, then how and for how long. This dish features 2 distinct onion flavors: the faint celerylike taste when onions are boiled, and the improbable sweetness when they're sautéed gently for a long, long time.

40 minutes to prepare
45 minutes to steam and bake

 You can make the whole dish or just the filling up to 3 days in advance. To reheat, put the onions in a baking dish with ½ inch of water, cover with foil, and warm at 300°F. for 20 minutes.

8 white boiling onions (2 inches in diameter), peeled
1 whole clove
1 tablespoon extra virgin olive oil
1 large yellow onion, chopped

½ teaspoon salt

2 teaspoons ground cumin

½ teaspoon ground cinnamon

1 teaspoon crumbled dried oregano

½ cup uncooked medium- or long-grain white or brown rice

3 tablespoons currants

3 tablespoons pine nuts

1 tablespoon tomato paste

ring lightly salted water to a boil in a large saucepan. Add the boiling onions and the clove, and boil over medium-high heat until soft but not mushy, about 10 minutes. Lift the onions out with a slotted spoon, and set them aside on paper towels to drain and cool. Reserve 2 tablespoons of the cooking liquid.

🍂 Heat the olive oil in a large saucepan. Add the chopped onion and sauté over medium heat until soft and translucent, about 7 minutes. Halfway through the cooking time, add the salt, cumin, cinnamon, and oregano.

🍂 Add the rice, currants, and pine nuts and stir until thoroughly combined. Stir in the tomato paste.

🍂 Add ¾ cup of water. Raise the heat to medium-high, bring to a boil, cover, then turn the heat down to its lowest setting. Cook for 20 minutes without lifting the lid. Turn off the heat and let the rice sit, covered, for 10 minutes. Lift the lid and fluff the rice with a fork.

🍂 Heat the oven to 425°F. To stuff the onions, cut the tip off one end and gently squeeze the center out of each, leaving a sack about an inch wide at the opening. Using a

SERVING SUGGESTIONS
Serve Braised Onions with Sweet Rice Stuffing with Cold Sweet Potato Soup (page 61), Chicken Breasts (or Pressed Tofu) with Sweet Mustard Glaze (page 176), or Monkfish with Mushrooms and Lentils (page 194).

teaspoon or a butter knife, fill the middle of each onion with the rice mixture.

🍂 Pour the reserved cooking liquid into a baking dish and arrange the filled onions on top. Cover the baking dish with foil and bake for 15 minutes. To serve, carefully lift the onions out with a slotted spatula.

[PER SERVING: CAL. 266.3 / FAT 6.8 G / PROTEIN 5.2 G / CARB. 44.6 G / CHOL. 0 / SODIUM 318.3 MG*] *VALUE GIVEN IS BEFORE SALTING.

Stuffed Grape Leaves

Serves 6

Almost every family has heirloom recipes, and I'm particularly proud of mine. I learned how to make these grape leaves from my mother who learned from her great aunt who learned it from her aunt, and so on, back through the centuries in Armenia. Most Middle Eastern and some Mediterranean cultures have one or several versions of this dish, but none as good as these. If you think my preference has more to do with personal heritage than objective taste, try these and you may think differently in the end.

1 hour 30 minutes to prepare
1 hour 40 minutes to cook

 Always make these the day before you plan to serve them. Stuffed grape leaves improve with age, and will keep up to 4 days refrigerated wrapped in plastic. Wrap them in plastic then tin foil to freeze, and defrost at room temperature.

1 tablespoon extra virgin olive oil
3 cups chopped yellow onion (about 2 large onions)
1 tablespoon ground cumin
2 teaspoons ground cinnamon
1 teaspoon ground allspice
2 cups long grain brown or white rice
1 tablespoon tomato paste
¼ cup currants
1 cup cooked chickpeas, rinsed if canned
20 to 30 grape leaves, depending on size, well-rinsed

2 tablespoons fresh lemon juice
1½ cups vegetable or chicken broth, homemade (see page 44 or 46) or canned

*h*eat the olive oil in a deep saucepan over medium-high heat. Lower the heat to medium-low and sauté the onion, cumin, cinnamon, and allspice until the onion is very soft and fragrant, about 10 minutes.

Add the rice, tomato paste, and currants, and stir well to blend evenly. Add 3 cups of water if you're using white rice, and 4 cups if you're using brown rice. Raise the heat to medium-high, and bring the mixture to a boil. Cover, turn down the heat to medium-low and simmer until the rice is cooked, and all of the water has been absorbed, about 35 minutes for white rice and 50 minutes for brown. Let sit, covered, for 15 minutes, then stir in the chickpeas.

Place a grape leaf glossy side down, with the tip pointing up and the stem toward you. Place a heaping tablespoon of filling in the center of the leaf, then bring the lower portion up over it, then fold the sides over that. Roll it up toward the tip to make a little packet. Place it inside a lidded skillet, seam

> **SERVING SUGGESTIONS**
> Serve Stuffed Grape Leaves with Chicken and Lentil Stew (page 179) and Custard-Style Indian Pudding (page 227).

HOW TO BAKE POTATOES
❶ ❷ ❸

In a conventional oven:

❶ Heat the oven to 400°F. and scrub the russet potatoes to remove the surface dirt.

❷ Run a metal skewer lengthwise through the center of each potato (the metal conducts the heat so they'll bake faster).

❸ Bake, unwrapped, until they give when you squeeze or press them, about 50 to 60 minutes, depending on size.

In a microwave oven (for one 8-ounce russet potato):

❶ Scrub the potato to remove the surface dirt, prick it well with a sharp fork, and place it in the center of the microwave on a single layer of paper towel.

❷ Microwave the potato on high (100 percent) for 5 minutes, turn it halfway, then microwave for 5 minutes more.

❸ Remove it from the oven, wrap it in foil, and let it rest for 5 minutes.

Note: To microwave more than one potato, arrange the potatoes in a circle in the oven and increase the cooking time by 2 to 3 minutes per potato.

side down. Repeat until you've used up all the filling.

🍃 Sprinkle the lemon juice evenly over the grape leaves, and pour the broth over them. Place a heavy heatproof plate on top of the rolls and cover the pan with the lid. Bring to a boil over medium-high heat, then lower the heat and simmer until the grape leaves are tender, about an hour.

🍃 Let cool completely before serving at room temperature, or refrigerate and serve cold.

[PER SERVING: CAL. 295 / FAT 4 G / PROTEIN 8 G / CARB. 55 G / CHOL. 0 / SODIUM 27 MG] % RDA: 28 VIT. C; 15 IRON.

Pissaladière-Inspired Potato Tarts

Serves 4

I wish it were easier to pronounce. Otherwise I have no problems with Pissaladière, a paradise of onions sautéed until melted, baked on fluffy bread dough with a couple of anchovies, some olives, and maybe a roasted bell pepper or two. It's the kind of dish that makes it unnecessary for me to explain my enchantment with the south of France, where it's sold fresh for lunch everywhere every day. I decided to tinker with it, not to try to improve it, but to serve it as a side dish.

2 hours to prepare and bake

 You can make potato pissaladière up to 3 days in advance, keeping the tarts refrigerated, well wrapped in foil. If you make them ahead, serve cold, or at room temperature. (They don't reheat well.)

4 large russet potatoes, scrubbed

1 tablespoon extra virgin olive oil

1 onion, thinly sliced

2 large garlic cloves, crushed and minced

1 red pepper

1 yellow or green pepper

4 anchovy fillets, rinsed and patted dry (optional)

4 ripe unpeeled tomatoes, cored, seeded, and chopped

1 teaspoon capers, rinsed

2 large egg yolks

½ cup low-fat milk

½ cup semolina flour (see Note)

eat the oven to 425° F. Bake the potatoes in a conventional oven or the microwave (see page 97). Scoop out the insides, discard the skin, and mash the potatoes in a large mixing bowl. Leave the oven on.

❧ Meanwhile, heat the olive oil in a skillet. Sauté the onion, garlic, and peppers over low heat, stirring occasionally, until they're so soft they seem to be melting, about 40 minutes.

❧ Rinse the anchovies, if using, pat them dry, then mash them with a fork.

❧ Add the tomatoes, anchovies, and capers to the skillet. Cook until the juice from the tomatoes has evaporated, about 10 minutes. Turn off the heat and set aside.

❧ In a small bowl, beat together the egg yolks and the milk, and mash the mixture into the potatoes. Add the semolina, and continue mashing.

❧ Press ¼ of the potato mixture into the bottom of four 4-inch tart pans. Bake for 10 minutes, until the tops start to harden.

SERVING SUGGESTIONS
Serve Pissaladière-Inspired Potato Tarts with Tangy Spinach-Yogurt Soup (page 48) or Silken Vegetable Soup (page 52), or as a first course before Poached Fish (page 190).

❧ Spread the onion-tomato mixture evenly on top of each potato layer, and return the tart pans to the oven. Bake for 45 minutes more, until the potato crust has browned lightly. Remove from the oven and let cool on a wire rack for 15 minutes.

❧ To serve, run the blade of a blunt butter knife around the outer rim of each potato pissaladière, and carefully pry it out and onto a serving plate. Serve warm.

Note: Semolina, a hard grain flour, is the best flour for this job because the potatoes turn out firm. All-purpose flour would make them mealy.

[PER SERVING: CAL. 398 / FAT 6.9 G / PROTEIN 11.1 G / CARB. 71.2 G / CHOL. 139.2 MG / SODIUM 211.2 MG] % RDA: 38 VIT. A; 222.5 VIT. C; 28.7 IRON.

Potato Gratin

Serves 4

Made with skim milk, this is a lower-fat version of a dish that is typically quite rich. It tastes more of potatoes than others that include butter and cream. Save those for an occasional treat, and enjoy this one often.

20 minutes to prepare

30 minutes to bake and cool

This gratin tastes best hot from the oven.

2 cups plus 2 tablespoons skim milk

2 pounds very low starch potatoes (round red or round white potatoes), thinly sliced

1 clove garlic, crushed and minced

¼ teaspoon salt

1 tablespoon arrowroot powder or cornstarch

½ cup shredded cheddar cheese or Gruyère

¼ cup grated imported Parmesan cheese

*h*eat the oven to 375°F.

🍃 In a medium saucepan, combine 2 cups of the milk, potatoes, garlic, and salt. Bring to a simmer over medium-high heat, and cook until the potatoes are tender enough to pierce with a fork, about 10 minutes. Turn off the heat.

🌿 Using a slotted spoon, transfer the potatoes to a shallow baking dish (2 inches deep) or four individual ramekins 2 inches deep and 4 inches in diameter.

🍃 In a small bowl, stir together the arrowroot or cornstarch and the remaining 2 table-spoons milk to make a thick paste. Whisk the paste into the hot milk over medium heat until thickened, about 10 minutes. Stir in the cheddar cheese and pour over the potatoes. Sprinkle with the Parmesan and bake until browned and bubbly, about 15 minutes.

🌿 Let set for 10 minutes before serving.

[PER SERVING: CAL. 340 / FAT 3.5 G / PROTEIN 13 G / CARB. 63 G / CHOL. 12 MG / SODIUM 370 MG] % RDA: 60 VIT. C; 17 IRON; 32 CALCIUM.

Wholly Wholesome Mashed Potatoes

Serves 3 or 4

Mashed potatoes seem as if they mean well, but they actually involve some pretty bad faith. Typically, they call for masses of butter and cream, indicating a lamentable lack of confidence in potatoes themselves. I don't think fixing them in that way makes them taste any better, and I *know* it makes them no better for you.

These are really honest-to-goodness mashed potatoes. For best results, use organically grown russets, which tend to be creamier than conventional spuds.

30 minutes from start to finish if you bake the potatoes in a microwave

Up to 1 hour 10 minutes to prepare if you bake the potatoes in a conventional oven

These are best made just before serving, but you can make mashed potatoes up to 3 days in advance, keeping them refrigerated in a covered container. Reheat them by

placing them in a covered baking dish and warming in a 300°F. oven for 20 minutes. Just before serving, refresh them by mashing in an additional 1 tablespoon each skim milk and cottage cheese.

5 large russet potatoes, preferably organic
1 cup low-fat cottage cheese
½ cup nonfat or low-fat milk
Salt and freshly ground pepper to taste
Minced fresh chives (optional)

ake the potatoes either in a conventional oven or a microwave (see page 97; I usually do this in the microwave not only because it saves time, but because the skin peels away more easily).

🍃 Meanwhile, blend together the cottage cheese and milk in a small bowl until smooth.

🍃 Peel away the skin or scoop the potato out of the shells, whichever is easiest for you and yields the most potato. Throw away the skin and put the potato pulp in a large bowl.

🍃 While the potato is still hot, mash in the cottage cheese mixture until everything is well combined and there are no lumps left.

🍃 Season the potatoes with salt and pepper and the chives, if you'd like. Serve right away.

[PER SERVING: CAL. 289 / FAT 0.5 G* / PROTEIN 9.8 G / CARB. 59 G / CHOL. 2 MG / SODIUM 182.2 MG**] *MADE WITH NONFAT MILK AND LOW-FAT COTTAGE CHEESE. **VALUE GIVEN IS BEFORE SALTING. % RDA: 60 VIT. C.

Variations

Wholly Wholesome Mashed Potatoes with Beets

1 recipe Wholly Wholesome Mashed Potatoes
4 large beets, cooked and peeled
  (see box, page 154)

1 tablespoon minced fresh dill
2 teaspoons prepared horseradish (optional)
Minced fresh chives (optional)

🍃 Peel and dice the beets. In a large mixing bowl, stir them into the mashed potatoes, along with the dill and horseradish and chives, if using.

Wholly Wholesome Mashed Potatoes with Roasted Garlic

1 recipe Wholly Wholesome Mashed Potatoes
4 garlic cloves, unpeeled
2 tablespoons minced fresh parsley

🍃 Heat the oven to 425°F.

🍃 Wrap the garlic cloves, papery skin intact, in aluminum foil and place in a baking pan.

🍃 Roast until soft, about 20 to 25 minutes.

🍃 Let the garlic cool, then cut off the bottom of each clove and pinch with your fingers, squeezing out the pulp.

🍃 Mash the pulp into the potatoes, along with the parsley.

SERVING SUGGESTIONS
Serve Wholly Wholesome Mashed Potatoes with any chicken dish, especially Chicken Roasted with Garlic (page 181), Herbed Asparagus Torta (page 80), or Braised Fish with Winter Greens (page 192).

Red Potatoes in Saffron Marinade

Serves 4 to 6

Like most dishes made with saffron, these splendid potatoes are better after a day or two. This works out well if you're giving a dinner party during a busy week, because you can make this dish the day before, then serve it with an easy entrée.

40 minutes to prepare
6 hours to chill

 You can make this dish up to 3 days in advance, keeping it refrigerated in a tightly covered container.

2 tablespoons extra virgin olive oil
4 small white onions, sliced
2 garlic cloves, crushed and minced
1 large fennel bulb, including fronds, chopped, or 4 celery stalks, including leaves, chopped
2 teaspoons grated orange zest
1 bay leaf
1 tablespoon lemon vinegar (see pages 235–36) or 1 teaspoon fresh lemon juice

---

SERVING SUGGESTIONS
Serve Red Potatoes in Saffron Marinade with Chicken Roasted with Garlic (page 181) or Braised Fish with Winter Greens (page 192).

---

1 teaspoon powdered saffron, dissolved in 1 tablespoon hot water
4 large red potatoes, scrubbed and thinly sliced

Garnishes
Chopped fresh parsley (optional)
Diced tomatoes (optional)

*h*eat the olive oil in a large skillet. Add the onions, garlic, fennel or celery, orange zest, and bay leaf, and sauté over medium-low heat until the onion is limp and the fennel or celery is tender, about 20 minutes.

❧ Add the vinegar or lemon juice to the vegetables in the skillet, raise the heat to medium-high, and cook, stirring vigorously, until the liquid has evaporated, about 1 minute.

✐ Turn the heat down to medium-low, add the saffron in its soaking liquid and stir well to blend. Turn off the heat.

❧ Meanwhile, bring 1 cup of water to boil in a medium saucepan. Place the potatoes in a vegetable steamer, lower it into the saucepan, cover, and steam until just cooked through, about 15 minutes. Drain them and put them in a large glass bowl.

✐ Add the vegetable mixture to the potatoes and toss well. Cover the bowl and refrigerate for at least 6 hours, so the flavors have a chance to meld.

❧ Toss well before serving, either chilled or at room temperature, garnished with parsley and tomato, if you'd like.

[PER SERVING: CAL. 178 / FAT 4.3 G / PROTEIN 2.3 G / CARB. 32 G / CHOL. 0 / SODIUM 386 MG]

Sweet Potato Pancakes

Makes 6 pancakes

Sweet potatoes, straight up, are a little strong for my taste. But when they come cut with plain potatoes and seasoned with maple syrup and sweet spices, I could eat them every day.

25 minutes to prepare

 You can make this dish up to 3 days in advance, keeping it refrigerated in a tightly covered container.

1 large sweet potato, peeled and thinly sliced

2 medium red potatoes, peeled and sliced

½ cup soft breadcrumbs

2 tablespoons nonfat or part-skim ricotta cheese

2 teaspoons maple syrup

1 teaspoon ground cumin

Pinch ground cinnamon

Pinch ground nutmeg or mace

Place the sweet potato and red potatoes in separate heavy saucepans. Add water to cover, and bring each to a boil over medium-high heat. Cover each pan and turn the heat down to medium-low. Simmer until the potatoes are soft enough to pierce easily. Check often; the red potatoes will probably cook in about 5 minutes, the sweet potato in about 8 minutes.

Using a slotted spoon, transfer the sweet and red potatoes to a large mixing bowl. While they're still hot, mash them with a potato masher, or with the side of a large wooden spoon. Mash in the remaining ingredients, making sure everything is well combined.

Using your hands, pat the potato mixture into 6 cakes.

Heat a nonstick skillet or griddle over medium-high heat. Cook the pancakes until the bottoms have browned, about 5 minutes. Using a wooden or plastic spatula, turn them over and brown the other side, about 5 minutes more.

Serve hot, room temperature, or cold, with Red Cabbage and Onion Relish (see page 106), Nectarine Relish (see page 107), Chunky Maple Apple Sauce (see page 216), or with Cabbage with Apples and Cheese (see page 84).

[PER SERVING: CAL. 233 / FAT 2.2 G / PROTEIN 6.4 G / CARB. 46.4 G / CHOL. 9 MG / SODIUM 82.8 MG] % RDA: 35 VIT. C.

SERVING SUGGESTIONS
Serve Sweet Potato Pancakes with Tandoori Spice Marinade for Chicken (or Pressed Tofu) (page 177), Spicy Black Beans and Fresh Plums (page 157), or Mushrooms and Bean Curd (and Scallops) in Thai Peanut-Coconut Curry Sauce (page 162).

Mushroom Barley

Serves 6

Barley is a Big Grain with such a strong flavor you have to shower it with herbs, steam it in broth, and add to it other assertive ingredients (such as mushrooms) to season it.

10 minutes to prepare

50 minutes to cook

 You can make this barley up to 4 days in advance, keeping it refrigerated in a tightly covered container. To reheat it, transfer to a covered baking dish with 1 tablespoon of water, and place it in a 300° F. oven for 20 minutes.

1 tablespoon canola oil or unsalted butter

4 large garlic cloves, crushed and minced

1 cup minced fresh parsley

1 cup sliced, washed mushrooms, such as portobello, shiitake, or oyster

1 cup uncooked pearled barley

2 tablespoons dry white wine

2 cups vegetable or chicken broth, either homemade (see page 44 or 46) or canned

*i*n a medium saucepan, melt the butter or heat the oil. Sauté the garlic and parsley over medium-low heat long enough to flavor the butter or oil, about 3 minutes.

🍃 Add the mushrooms and cook, stirring constantly, until they darken and soften, about 3 minutes. Add the barley and the wine

and continue cooking and stirring for about 2 minutes more.

🍃 Add the broth, bring the mixture to a boil over medium-high heat, then lower the heat to medium-low, cover, and simmer for 40 minutes. Turn off the heat and let the barley rest, covered, for 10 minutes.

🍃 Fluff well with a fork before serving.

[PER SERVING: CAL. 124.5 / FAT 2.3 G / PROTEIN 4.3 G / CARB. 20.3 G / CHOL. 0* MG / SODIUM 110.1 MG**] *MADE WITH CANOLA OIL. **VALUE GIVEN IS BEFORE SALTING.

Cheddar Buttermilk Spoon Bread

Serves 6

I moved to the South in early adolescence, too late in life to develop a natural craving for the foods of that region and also too late to shake my appetite for things I couldn't get down there. I resented what foods there were simply because they weren't the foods I wanted. I didn't care if the corn bread was good. All that concerned me was that it wasn't bagels.

Eventually I assimilated to the extent that I came to love a few southern specialties, especially spoon bread, a creamy, sunny colored, side dish soufflé, made here with buttermilk and lemon zest for a lively kick.

5 minutes to prepare

45 minutes to bake

 This spoon bread must be served hot from the oven.

SERVING SUGGESTIONS

Serve Mushroom Barley with Chicken Legs Filled with Sweet Shredded Cabbage (page 180), White Beans and Fresh Tuna (page 201), or Cabbage with Apples and Cheese (page 84).

2 large eggs

½ cup yellow cornmeal, preferably stone
   ground

2 cups nonfat or low-fat buttermilk

2 tablespoons grated sharp cheddar cheese

½ teaspoon salt

1 tablespoon grated lemon zest

 eat the oven to 350°F.

❧ Put the eggs in a mixing bowl and whisk until well blended. Stir in the rest of the ingredients.

✑ Pour into a greased 1½ quart soufflé dish, and bake for about 45 minutes, until puffy and golden brown.

[PER SERVING (USING NONFAT BUTTERMILK): CAL. 167 / FAT 5.5 G / PROTEIN 11 G / CARB. 17.4 G / CHOL. 144.5 MG / SODIUM 410 MG] % RDA: 21.7 CALCIUM.

SERVING SUGGESTIONS
Serve Cheddar Buttermilk Spoon Bread with Wheat Berry Soup (page 53) or Chili with Seafood or Beans (page 204).

HOW I STOPPED WORRYING AND LEARNED TO LOVE SALT

As a birthday gift one year, a friend sent me a chef—a friend of hers who had turned a local dive into one of L.A.'s more acclaimed restaurants, and who was willing to give up his night off to make dinner in my apartment. I'd left the key so he could let himself in, and when I came home from work I found him turning my cabinets inside out. "I'm so glad you're home," he said. "Now you can tell me where you keep your salt." At the time I was sharing my place with someone who, citing recent research blaming sodium for everything from strokes to premenstrual syndrome, had persuaded me to get rid of it. I told the chef I had no salt, and he said that he wouldn't cook without it.

I went back out and bought some. We ate very well that night. For all the virtues of leaving it out, the fact remains that some salt makes some foods taste better. And unless your blood pressure is uncommonly sensitive to sodium, this is no bad thing. The trick is to learn to use salt in such a way that it makes other ingredients taste not salty, but more like themselves. This usually means adding very little during cooking, and none at all afterward. And if you're using ingredients such as anchovies, cheese, cured olives, commercial broth, canned tomatoes, or sun-dried tomatoes, they may be salty enough to season the dish.

Endive and Leek Fondue

Serves 4

Fondue refers to 2 very different dishes. One concerns sauce of some kind—cheese, stock, chocolate—cooked over a Sterno can. The other involves aromatic vegetables reduced slowly over low heat into a subtle dressing or side dish. This one is perfect for poached fish, and just as good as a topping for toasted bread or a condiment for grilled vegetables.

40 minutes from start to finish

 You can make the fondue up to 2 days in advance, keeping it refrigerated in a covered container until ready to use. Serve cold or at room temperature.

1 tablespoon unsalted butter

1 large leek, white part only, cleaned and thinly sliced

¼ cup minced fresh parsley or chervil

2 large Belgian endives, cored and chopped

2 tablespoons dry white wine, or 1 tablespoon lemon vinegar (see pages 235–36)

2 teaspoons Dijon mustard

1 tablespoon heavy cream or yogurt cheese (see box, page 133)

Salt to taste

*i*n a medium skillet, melt the butter and sauté the leek, parsley or chervil, and endives over low heat, stirring occasionally, until they seem to be melting, about 25 minutes.

Add the wine or vinegar, turn up the heat to medium high, and cook, stirring constantly, until most of the liquid evaporates, about 3 minutes.

Turn the heat down to medium-low, and stir in the mustard. Remove from the heat, and let it cool for about 5 minutes.

Stir in the cream or yogurt cheese and season with salt. Serve warm as a side dish or as a dressing for poached fish or spoon it over slices of toasted French bread for a lovely appetizer.

[PER SERVING: CAL. 60.8 / FAT 4.1 G* / PROTEIN 1 G / CARB. 3.6 G / CHOL. 12.8 MG / SODIUM 67 MG**] *MADE WITH BUTTER. FOR LESS CHOLESTEROL AND SATURATED FAT, USE OIL. TOTAL FAT WILL REMAIN THE SAME. **VALUE GIVEN IS BEFORE SALTING.

SERVING SUGGESTIONS

Serve Endive Leek Fondue with Chicken Breasts (or Pressed Tofu) with Sweet Mustard Glaze (page 176), Braised Chicken Breasts Tapenade (page 169), Poached Fish (page 190), or Milk Poached Fish with Chive Cream (page 193).

Red Cabbage and Onion Relish

Makes about 4 cups

When we were kids my brother and I were intent on finding the perfect condiment. What we sought was one food that would make anything else taste good (we had a special interest in its effect on green peas and mushrooms). We tested ketchup, mustard, mayonnaise, and even Blue Bonnet, a margarine whose ad jingle promised "Everything's better with Blue Bonnet on it." Nothing worked.

I don't know if this relish can make bad food taste good, but I'm certain it makes many things—even very good things—taste that much better.

30 minutes to prepare

30 minutes to steam and let cool

 You can make this relish up to 1 week in advance, keeping it refrigerated in a covered container.

1 small head red cabbage

1 tablespoon unsalted butter

2 red onions, thinly sliced

2 tablespoons minced fresh dill

1 tablespoon cider vinegar

¼ cup dried cherries

1 tablespoon light honey

 ear away and discard the tough outer leaves of the cabbage. Cut the core out of the head, and slice the rest. Bring a large pot of water with a steamer basket to a boil over medium heat and steam the cabbage until cooked through, about 15 minutes. Turn it into a colander to drain thoroughly.

🍃 In a large skillet, melt the butter. Sauté the onions and dill over medium heat, stirring often, until the onions are very soft, about 10 minutes. Add the drained cabbage and stir well to blend.

🍃 Stir in the cider vinegar, dried cherries, and honey. Cover and cook over medium-low heat, stirring occasionally, for 15 minutes.

🍃 Turn off the heat and let the relish rest for another 15 minutes so that the flavors can deepen. Serve at once or cover and serve well chilled.

[PER SERVING: CAL. 95.3 / FAT 2.2 G* / PROTEIN 1.1 G / CARB. 17.6 G / CHOL. 5.5 MG / SODIUM 10.8 MG**] *MADE WITH BUTTER. FOR LESS CHOLESTEROL AND SATURATED FAT, USE OIL. TOTAL FAT WILL REMAIN THE SAME. **VALUE GIVEN IS BEFORE SALTING. % RDA: 71.3 VIT. C.

SERVING SUGGESTIONS

Serve Red Cabbage and Onion Relish with Sweet Potato Pancakes (page 102), Barbecued or Broiled Turkey Burgers with All the Fixin's (page 184), Poached Fish (page 190), or Chicken Roasted with Garlic (page 181).

Nectarine Relish

Makes about 2 cups

Vegetables overcooked? Turkey burgers dry? Left the seasoning out of the Sweet Potato Pancakes? There's nothing wrong with anything that this relish can't remedy.

40 minutes from start to finish, most of it sautéing

 You can make this up to 5 days in advance. Keep it refrigerated in a covered container.

2 teaspoons canola oil or unsalted butter

1 large white onion, very thinly sliced

1 leek, white part only, cleaned and minced

4 ripe nectarines, peeled, pitted, and chopped

1 tablespoon fresh lemon juice

1 tablespoon cider vinegar

1 yellow or orange pepper, peeled, seeded, and cut into thin strips

1 whole clove

3 tablespoons dried cherries or raisins

3 tablespoons minced fresh chives

1 tablespoon minced fresh cilantro

1 tablespoon pine nuts

1 tablespoon honey

*i*n a large nonstick skillet, heat the oil or melt the butter over medium-high heat. Add the onion and leek and turn the heat down to medium-low. Sauté until very soft and limp, about 20 minutes.

❧ Stir in the remaining ingredients, cover, and simmer over medium-low heat, stirring often, until the nectarines cook down into soft pulp, about 25 minutes.

✒ Remove and discard the clove, then transfer the relish to a ceramic bowl and chill for several hours.

❧ Serve cold.

[PER SERVING: CAL. 104.4 / FAT 2.7 G / PROTEIN 1.7 G / CARB. 16.8 G / CHOL. 0* / SODIUM 5.6 MG] *MADE WITH CANOLA OIL. % RDA: 70 VIT. C.

SERVING SUGGESTIONS

Serve Nectarine Relish with Barbecued or Broiled Turkey Burgers with All the Fixin's (page 184), Grilled Assorted Vegetables (page 143), Chicken Roasted with Garlic (page 181), or Broiled Skate with Citrus Glaze (page 196).

Pasta, risotto & focacce

· · · · · · · ·

Perfect Tomato Sauce 🍃 Perfect Tomato Sauce, Too 🍃 Many Mushrooms Farfalle 🍃 Pasta with Asparagus and Leeks 🍃 Whole Wheat Penne with Cabbage and Cumin 🍃 Spinach Fettuccine with Tangy Tofu Sauce and Mushrooms 🍃 Mushroom Noodle Pudding 🍃 Quick Creamy Pasta 🍃 Linguine with Mussels and Shrimp 🍃 Carrot and Spinach Lasagna with Lemon Sauce 🍃 Gnocchi 🍃 Light(er) Béchamel Sauce with Parmesan 🍃 Gnocchi with and Sun-Dried Tomatoes (and Chicken) 🍃 Gnocchi with Leeks and Ricotta 🍃 Basic Risotto 🍃 Carrot-Ginger Risotto 🍃 Lemony Risotto 🍃 Beet Risotto 🍃 Pumpkin Risotto 🍃 Summer Garden Risotto (with Scallops) 🍃 Risotto with Mussels 🍃 Risotto with Shrimp 🍃 Focacce 🍃 Roast Garlic Pesto

In the store in Milan where I used to shop, pasta took up all of the shelf space on both sides of an aisle. There were fifteen brands, and each manufacturer made seventy to one hundred shapes. It looked to me like overkill. But to my neighbors, who ate pasta at least once a day, it was merely adequate. Every size, every shape has a particular purpose. And so I discovered that what goes *under* the sauce matters as much as what goes into it.   It's also important to have some basic utensils on hand. They include the following: a very large pot for boiling the pasta; a large colander for draining the pasta; a large earthenware or porcelain bowl for tossing the pasta with the sauce; wooden spatulas, spoons, or forks for tossing and serving the pasta; and an accurate kitchen timer.

On Cooking Well . . .

The difference between perfect pasta and disappointment can be a matter of:

1. Seconds

Pasta that's been cooked too long is mushy and bland. Ironically, if you follow the directions on the box given by most brands, you'll overcook it. So play it safe and when the pasta has cooked for four minutes fewer than the manufacturer suggests, fish out a strand and bite into it. If it's still hard in the center, cook it for a minute longer and test it again, repeating the process until it's done. It's done when it's pleasant to chew. (It's overdone if teeth aren't necessary at this point.)

2. Water

You need lots of water (roughly 5 to 6 quarts for every pound of pasta) so that the pasta will cook evenly without sticking to the pot (or itself), or becoming gummy.

3. Tailoring

Think of the relationship between pasta and sauce in terms of clothing: The pasta should wear the sauce. The sauce shouldn't be too bulky or too skimpy. For example, a clingy fresh tomato sauce is perfect on fine pasta such as angel hair, and a heavy ragu is best on thick pasta such as perciatelli and ziti.

4. A few dollars

Whether money can buy happiness is inconsequential; it *can* buy the ingredients for a perfect plate of pasta, which is close enough for me. Although some American brands are quite good, the best dry pastas, olive oils, and cheeses still come from abroad, which means they get slapped with an import tax and a higher price tag on arrival.

- **Extra virgin olive oil** (see page 40)
  Olive oil adds flavor that can't be imitated, omitted, or replaced, and in these recipes, relatively few fat calories. (Divide the amount of oil called for in a recipe by the number of servings it provides, and you'll find that each portion contains only a small amount of fat.) What's more, olive oil is unsaturated fat, which may lower cholesterol.

- **Fresh herbs,** or organically grown dried herbs (see "Selected Seasonings Directory," page 31).

- **Fresh tomatoes** or imported Italian tomatoes packed in boxes rather than cans. Use these whenever you can't find good fresh tomatoes. You should be able to find them at any store with a good supply of foods imported from Italy.

- **Imported Parmesan.** This isn't just a cheese. It's a safe, economical means to total contentment.

  Reggio Parmesan is the cheese I've used to test all of the recipes in this book calling for Parmesan. Its flavor is light but distinct, sweet and nutty. Don't bother with domestic Parmesan, which has no taste at all. Buy imported Parmesan in small blocks. The flavor starts to fade once it's been grated, so grate it yourself just before serving. You can preserve much of the flavor by wrapping chunks of Parmesan airtight in plastic wrap, and storing them in your freezer. For variety, try substituting imported asiago, which is milder than Parmesan, or provolone, which is a little bit stronger. Fat-free or low-fat ricotta is fine for cooking, but allow yourself, on occasion, to enjoy the fresh, sweet flavor of the real thing.

Inquisitive Cooks Want to Know . . .

Q. *Why does the serving size on pasta packages seem so small? Does this mean you're a glutton?*
A. No, it means the manufacturer is Italian. Americans tend to eat pasta for dinner, while Italians eat it as a first course. An Italian eating pasta as a starter would eat less than an American making an entrée of it.

Q. *But pasta is fattening, isn't it?*
A. Spaghetti with meatballs and sausage is fattening because of the meatballs and sausage, not the spaghetti. Most dried pastas contain flour and water, and no fat at all. The trick to less fattening pasta isn't to eat fewer noodles, but to modify the sauce.

Risotto

The problem with serving risotto as a first course—as in Italy—is that it raises expectations for what's to follow. And risotto is so delicious it can be hard to match. Consequently, you might prefer to make it the main course, following soup or salad.

PERFECT PASTA

1. Bring lots of water (5 to 6 quarts of water per pound of pasta) to a boil in a large pot with a lid. When the water is boiling, add 1½ tablespoons of coarse salt (see Note) and plunge the pasta into the water in one move. Cover the pot.

2. As soon as the water is boiling again set your timer for 4 minutes fewer than the time given on the package. Keep the water at a rolling boil, and stir the pasta occasionally with a wooden fork.

3. When the timer goes off, fish out a strand and bite into it. If it's pleasant to chew, it's done. If it's hard in the center, set the timer for another minute and test again.

4. Drain the pasta in a colander. Don't rinse it, and don't shake it completely dry.

5. Have the sauce ready in a large porcelain or ceramic bowl. Add the pasta and toss well, using a wooden fork and spoon. Serve right away.

Note: Salt brings out the flavor of the pasta, which would be bland without it. If you're worried about sodium, you'll be glad to know that very little salt clings to the pasta.

What makes risotto so special?

There are plenty of dishes that taste good, but here aroma, flavor, and texture come together in such a way they knock your socks off.

Moreover, risotto is good for you. It only seems rich, a deception pulled off by the type of rice involved and the way it responds to slow cooking, becoming beguilingly creamy without cream (or in those versions that call for cream, less than a teaspoonful per serving).

To tell if risotto is done, you need to look, feel, and taste.

LOOK ✎ The rice kernels should be clear, not chalk white at the core. They should seem to melt together into a thick, creamy porridge. If the kernels are still white, add more broth, stir until it's absorbed, check again, and repeat if necessary. Also, you shouldn't see any liquid on the surface. If you do, keep stirring over low heat until it's absorbed.

FEEL ✎ Bite into a kernel. It should be soft and chewy. Your teeth shouldn't grind up against anything. If it's not done, add more broth, stir until it's absorbed, check again, and repeat if necessary.

TASTE ✎ Adjust the seasoning, adding more cheese, lemon zest, or herbs, if you think the risotto needs it.

> **PLAYING FAVORITES**
> I prefer DeCecco pasta, not only because it tastes good, but because the suggested cooking times on the beautiful blue or orange packages are uncommonly accurate.

Perfect Tomato Sauce

Makes about 4 cups

There's only one trick to making fresh tomato sauce: getting good fresh tomatoes. If you can do that, you're all set.

You may be shocked to see that an anchovy is called for here. Please don't omit it unless you or guests of yours are strictly vegetarian. I promise you won't taste the anchovy, but you *will* appreciate its effect, which is to deepen the flavors as nothing else can.

30 minutes to prepare
30 minutes to simmer

 You can make this sauce up to 5 days in advance, keeping it refrigerated in a tightly covered container. You can freeze it indefinitely.

1 tablespoon extra virgin olive oil
2 large garlic cloves, crushed
1 white or yellow onion, thinly sliced
¼ cup minced fresh basil
¼ cup minced fresh parsley
1 bay leaf
1 anchovy fillet, rinsed and patted dry
10 fresh tomatoes (about 2 pounds), peeled, seeded, chopped, and drained

*i*n a large skillet heat the olive oil over low heat. Add the garlic and sauté, swishing it around until the oil starts to color, but without letting the garlic brown, about 3 minutes. Remove the garlic and throw it away.

☙ Raise the heat to medium and add the sliced onion, basil, parsley, and bay leaf. Sauté until the onion is soft and translucent, about 7 minutes.

✍ Mince the anchovy and stir it in to the onion mixture along with the tomatoes. Bring to a simmer, cover, and cook gently over medium-low heat, stirring occasionally, until the tomatoes break down into a sauce, about 30 minutes. The sauce will be pulpy.

☙ Remove the bay leaf and transfer the sauce to a food processor or blender (see Note). Process in 3 to 5 short pulses, until it's smooth. Be careful not to pulse it too many times or let the appliance run full speed, or the sauce will become too thin.

Note: For a thicker sauce pour the tomatoes into a fine-mesh sieve instead of a food processor. Hold the sieve over a large bowl and force the sauce through it using the back of a wooden spoon.

[PER SERVING: CAL. 80.4 / FAT 2.4 G / PROTEIN 2.0 G / CARB. 11.9 G / CHOL. 0.4 MG / SODIUM 46.5 MG*] *VALUE GIVEN IS BEFORE SALTING. % RDA: 29.1 VIT. A; 81.5 VIT. C.

Perfect Tomato Sauce, Too

Makes about 4 cups

This sauce tastes lighter than the other and is best on fine pasta such as angel hair and spaghettini. It also makes a nice condiment for Lemony Risotto (see page 130) and Poached Fish (see page 190). The delicate flavor is overwhelmed easily, so add little cheese or none at all.

30 minutes to prepare
30 minutes to simmer

You can make this sauce up to 5 days in advance, keeping it refrigerated in a tightly covered container. You can freeze it indefinitely.

1 tablespoon extra virgin olive oil
2 large garlic cloves, crushed
½ cup minced fresh basil
¼ cup minced fresh parsley
15 fresh tomatoes (about 3 pounds), peeled, seeded, chopped, and drained

*i*n a large skillet heat the olive oil over low heat. Add the garlic and sauté, swishing it around until the oil starts to color, but without letting the garlic brown, about 3 minutes. Remove the garlic and throw it away.

🍃 Raise the heat to medium and add the basil, parsley, and tomatoes. Bring to a simmer, cover, and cook gently over medium-low heat, until the tomatoes break down into sauce, about 30 minutes. The sauce will be pulpy, not smooth.

🍃 Transfer the sauce to a food processor or blender and process in 3 to 5 short pulses until it's smooth (see Note). Be careful not to pulse it too often or run the appliance at full speed, or the sauce will become too thin.

Note: For a thicker sauce pour the tomatoes into a fine-mesh sieve instead of a food processor or blender. Hold the sieve over a large bowl and force the sauce through it using the back of a wooden spoon.

[PER SERVING: CAL. 70 / FAT 2.3 G / PROTEIN 1.5 G / CARB. 10 G / CHOL. 0 / SODIUM 21.3 MG*] *VALUE GIVEN IS BEFORE SALTING. % RDA: 29.1 VIT. A; 77.6 VIT. C.

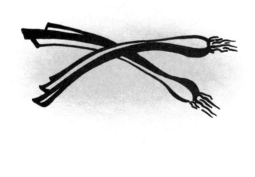

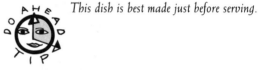

Many Mushrooms Farfalle

Serves 4

Dried mushrooms alone would be too flaccid; fresh button mushrooms alone would be too bland. Combined, they compensate for each other's shortcomings. Add some Parmesan and cream, and you'll forget some of life's shortcomings, too.

45 minutes from start to finish

This dish is best made just before serving.

5 ounces dried porcini mushrooms
1 tablespoon unsalted butter
1 garlic clove, minced
1 small white onion, thinly sliced
½ cup minced fresh parsley
½ pound fresh button mushrooms, washed and sliced
½ cup diced red pepper
2 tablespoons dry white wine
2 cups dried farfalle (bow-tie pasta)
1 tablespoon heavy cream
Grated imported Parmesan cheese to taste

*S*oak the dried porcini mushrooms in warm water just to cover for at least 20 minutes (or according to package directions), then drain them, reserving the soaking liquid and setting both aside.

🍃 In a large skillet, melt the butter. Sauté the garlic, onion, and parsley over medium heat until the onion is very soft, about 10 minutes.

Q. *Why are porcini so expensive?*
A. Porcini are relatively rare in the wild, and they're more difficult to cultivate than some other mushrooms, such as white and button.
Q. *Are they worth it?*
A. Since I once spent a full third of my weekly grocery budget on fresh porcini, without regret, I'm clearly impartial. Nothing tastes like them, so I can't describe their flavor, only their effect, which is to make your head spin.

🌿 Stir in the porcini, the button mushrooms, and the red pepper. Continue cooking until the button mushrooms have cooked through, about 6 minutes.

🌿 Add the wine and reserved mushroom liquid, turn up the heat to medium-high, and cook, stirring constantly, for 2 minutes more.

🌿 Meanwhile, cook the pasta according to package directions, and drain, leaving some water clinging to it. Transfer the pasta to a large serving bowl, and toss with the heavy cream. Pour the mushroom sauce on top and toss again. Add as much grated Parmesan as you'd like, and toss once more before serving.

[PER SERVING: CAL. 377.1 / FAT 5.1 G* / PROTEIN 12.2 G / CARB. 67.7 G / CHOL. 13.5 MG / SODIUM 580 MG**] *MADE WITH HEAVY CREAM. **VALUE GIVEN IS BEFORE SALTING. % RDA: 56.9 VIT. C; 25.4 IRON.

HOW TO CLEAN MUSHROOMS
❶ ❷ ❸

To keep mold from forming, don't wash mushrooms until you're ready to use them. And when you clean them, use as little water as possible, or it will seep into the mushrooms, affecting their flavor.

❶ Trim away the woody end of the stem, if there is one.

❷ Dampen a paper towel and squeeze it dry, or lightly wet a special mushroom-cleaning brush.

❸ Rub the mushroom well with the paper towel or the brush to remove all dirt from the surface.

Pasta with Asparagus and Leeks

Serves 3 to 4

"That tastes best that travels least."
—*Someone who knows her asparagus*

Asparagus is now cultivated all over the world and shipped from those places where it's in season to those where it's not, giving the cruel illusion that it's available year-round. Unfortunately, the stalks can be transported, but not the flavor. This, and all asparagus dishes, will taste best made with fresh asparagus grown close to home.

25 minutes from start to finish

This dish is best made just before serving.

½ tablespoon unsalted butter or canola oil

1 leek, white part only, washed and thinly sliced

4 scallions, white part only, minced

½ cup minced fresh parsley

2 tablespoons white wine, or 1 tablespoon lemon vinegar (see pages 235–36)

8 ounces dried short flat pasta, such as orcchiette

1½ cups steamed asparagus tips (see box, page 148)

1 tablespoon heavy cream or yogurt cheese (see box, page 133)

4 ounces taleggio or Muenster cheese, finely diced

*P*ut a large pot of water on to boil over medium-high heat for the pasta.

🍃 Meanwhile, melt the butter or heat the oil in a large skillet and sauté the leek, scallions, and parsley over low heat until the leek softens, about 10 minutes. Add the wine or vinegar and stir until most of the liquid has evaporated, about 2 minutes. Add salt to the pasta water and put the pasta in to boil.

🍃 While the pasta's cooking, add the asparagus to the leek mixture and toss swiftly to combine with the other ingredients. Turn off the heat.

🍃 Add the cream or yogurt cheese to the asparagus mixture and stir to blend.

🍃 Drain the pasta in a colander. Before it's thoroughly drained, set the colander back over the cooking pot, so that some of the pasta water drips into the pot. Toss the pasta back into the pot, adding the asparagus mixture and the taleggio or Muenster immediately. Stir vigorously with a wooden spoon until well combined, transfer to a serving bowl, and serve at once.

[PER SERVING: CAL. 461.2 / FAT 11.6 G* / PROTEIN 19.6 G / CARB. 67.1 G / CHOL. 30.1 MG / SODIUM 776.7 MG**] *MADE WITH WHOLE MILK CHEESE. **VALUE GIVEN IS BEFORE SALTING. % RDA: 26.6 VIT. A; 52.1 VIT. C; 27.8 IRON; 28.1 CALCIUM.

Whole Wheat Penne with Cabbage and Cumin

Serves 4

If you've tried only domestic brands, you might well assume that whole wheat pasta is, like soy dogs and carob chip cookies, a lamentable attempt by American health fanatics to offer a more virtuous version of a popular food. It's so coarse, pasty, and bland, calling it pasta is as audaciously inapt as referring to vinegar as fine wine.

But whole wheat pasta is neither new nor American. *Pasta integrale* (whole wheat pasta) has been eaten by Italians for centuries, not just because it's good for them, but because the kind they make tastes very, very good. The best imported whole wheat pastas have body and bite, and the faint nutty flavor of good hearty grain.

30 minutes from start to finish

This dish tastes best served right away.

2 teaspoons extra virgin olive oil

1 onion, thinly sliced

1 large carrot, peeled and thinly sliced

2 cups shredded red cabbage

1 medium red or white low-starch potato, peeled and sliced paper thin

1 teaspoon whole cumin seeds

4 ounces fontina or taleggio cheese, thinly sliced

3 cups imported dried whole wheat penne

*h*eat the olive oil in a large non-stick skillet over medium heat. When hot, add the onion, carrot, cabbage, potato, and cumin, and sauté until the onion is soft and limp, about 8 minutes. Cover and let steam until the cabbage is very tender and the potato has cooked through, about 12 minutes. Turn off the heat.

Meanwhile, cook the penne according to package directions. Drain, then quickly toss it into the skillet, along with the cabbage mixture and the cheese. Toss briskly with two wooden spoons and serve at once, in warmed bowls.

[PER SERVING: CAL. 520 / FAT 12.1 G / PROTEIN 20.1 G / CARB. 80 G / CHOL. 33 MG / SODIUM 255 MG]

SERVING SUGGESTIONS
Serve Whole Wheat Penne with Cabbage and Cumin with Bell Pepper Soup (page 58).

Spinach Fettuccine with Tangy Tofu Sauce and Mushrooms

Serves 4 to 6

. . . gets its tang from dill, cilantro, and ginger.

40 minutes from start to finish

You can make the tofu sauce up to 3 days in advance. To reheat it, transfer to a double boiler and warm it slowly over medium-low heat, stirring often. Make the vegetables and fettuccine just before serving.

½ tablespoon unsalted butter or canola oil

1 large white onion, thinly sliced

One 2-inch piece fresh ginger, peeled and grated

1 tablespoon minced fresh dill, or 2 teaspoons crumbled dried dill

2 tablespoons minced fresh cilantro

1 pound total mixed button and portobello mushrooms, cleaned and quartered

1 pound dried spinach fettuccine

1 cup soft tofu

2 cups plain low-fat or nonfat yogurt

2 teaspoons soy sauce

Dash paprika

Steamed vegetables of your choice in any combination: broccoli, carrots, cauliflower, cabbage, snap sugar peas (see box, page 148)

*h*eat the oil or melt the butter in a large skillet, and sauté the onion, ginger, dill, and cilantro over medium-low heat until the onion is soft and limp, about 20 minutes.

🖋 Meanwhile, bring a large pot of water to boil over medium-high heat for the pasta.

🖋 Add the mushrooms to the skillet and turn down the heat to low. Continue to cook, stirring constantly, until they soften and color and start to give up liquid, about 4 minutes. Remove from the heat and tilt the pan to drain away as much liquid as you can.

🖋 Meanwhile, add the fettucine to the boiling water and cook according to package directions.

🖋 While the pasta is cooking, blend together the tofu, yogurt, and soy sauce until smooth in a bowl. Stir into the onion and mushroom mixture. Heat very slowly over very low heat until just warmed through.

🖋 When the pasta is cooked, drain it well. Stir the paprika into the sauce and toss in a serving bowl the sauce with the fettuccine and the steamed vegetables. Serve at once.

[PER SERVING: CAL. 423.8 / FAT 5.2 G* / PROTEIN 22.3 G / CARB. 70.1 G / CHOL. 1.8 MG / SODIUM 0] *MADE WITH NONFAT YOGURT. % RDA: 80.7 VIT. C; 49.4 IRON; 33.1 CALCIUM.

COOKING WITH YOGURT

Like heavy cream, sour cream, and mayonnaise, yogurt can moisten, flavor, and bind other foods. But unlike the others, it adds few calories and little saturated fat while enriching the dishes with calcium and protein.

Choosing the Best Yogurt for the Job
The consistency and flavor of plain unsweetened yogurts vary from sour to sweet, runny to firm. Whole-milk yogurts have more true cream flavor than nonfat yogurts, and some nonfat yogurts seem much richer than they are thanks to pectin, a natural thickening agent. I've found that among national brands, Dannon nonfat is the mildest yogurt—in fact, it's perfectly mild—and, consequently, the best for general use.

Try several brands for yourself so you'll know which you like best for what purpose. You may find that you prefer a tart yogurt for some recipes, such as Tangy Spinach-Yogurt Soup (see page 48) and Chilled Cucumber Soup (see page 60), and a milder brand for others, such as the Chickpea Curry (see page 156) and the Rice Salad with Mango and Chickpeas (with or without Chicken) (see page 77).

Mushroom Noodle Pudding

Serves 4

If food is love, this dish is a big warm bear hug.

25 minutes to prepare
55 minutes to bake and cool

 You can make this noodle pudding up to 4 days in advance, keeping it refrigerated, tightly covered with plastic. To reheat, cover with foil and place in a 325°F. oven for 20 to 30 minutes.

2 teaspoons canola oil or unsalted butter
2 scallions, minced
1 small onion, minced
½ pound firm mushrooms, such as cremini, white button, or portobello, cleaned and sliced
¼ cup Light Mushroom Broth, vegetable broth, or chicken broth (see page 47, 44, or 46)
2 large eggs, lightly beaten
1 cup cottage low-fat cheese
½ cup sour cream, low fat or nonfat if desired
¼ cup shredded mild cheese such as mild cheddar, Monterey Jack, or muenster
Pinch paprika
Pinch crumbled dried dill
4 cups cooked pasta, such as penne or ziti, whole wheat if desired

*h*eat the oven to 425°F. In a skillet heat the oil over medium heat. When hot, add the scallions and onion. Turn down the heat to medium low, and sauté until the scallions and onion are soft and limp, about 8 minutes.

Add the mushrooms and sauté, stirring often, until they begin to give up liquid, about 6 minutes. Add the broth, turn up the heat to medium high, and let simmer for five minutes. Turn off the heat.

🐚 In a mixing bowl, beat together the eggs, cottage cheese, sour cream, and cheese. Using a slotted spoon, transfer the mushroom mixture from the skillet into the bowl and stir well. Stir in the paprika, dill, and pasta.

🍃 Lightly grease an 8-inch baking pan or coat it with nonstick spray. Pour the mixture into the pan and bake until firm and golden brown, about 45 minutes.

[PER SERVING (USING LOW-FAT SOUR CREAM): CAL. 345 / FAT 6.7 G / PROTEIN 23 G / CARB. 47 G / CHOL. 8.8 MG / SODIUM 329 MG]

SERVING SUGGESTIONS
Serve Mushroom Noodle Pudding with Tangy Spinach-Yogurt Soup (page 48) or Braised Chicken Breasts Tapenade (page 169), and Strawberry Cheesecake Ice Cream (page 229).

Quick Creamy Pasta

Serves 1

The only rule that applies to preparing pasta and eggs is: *Don't overcook the pasta.* Otherwise, fix this fast bury-your-face-in-the-bowl comfort food according to impulse.

15 minutes from start to finish, more or less depending on ingredients

 This is meant to be a spur of the moment meal.

Basic formula for each serving

1 teaspoon salt
4 ounces dried long pasta, such as linguine, spaghetti, or capellini
1 large egg, lightly beaten
3 tablespoons low-fat cottage cheese
1 tablespoon nonfat milk
1 tablespoon grated or shredded sharp cheese, such as cheddar, Parmesan, or romano
¼ teaspoon grated fresh garlic
2 tablespoons minced onion or scallion, white part only
Fresh or dried herbs, to taste, such as basil, oregano, tarragon, thyme, and chives
Optional add-ins such as chickpeas, sun dried tomatoes, olives, pine nuts (also see Variations)

*b*ring an abundant amount of water to a boil over high heat in a large pot (check package for water-to-pasta guidelines or see page 111). When it reaches a boil, add the salt and pasta. Boil until chewy, but cooked through. Time will vary according to thickness, so watch closely and sample often.

🍃 Meanwhile, in a large glass or earthenware mixing bowl, combine the egg, cottage cheese, milk, cheese, garlic, onion, herbs, and any of the optional add-ins you'd like.

🍃 Drain the pasta and toss back into the cooking pot, stirring constantly; add the egg mixture. Place over medium-low heat and stir until the pasta is coated with a smooth, creamy sauce.

To finish off the pasta in the microwave

🍃 Stir drained pasta and egg mixture together briskly with a wooden spoon. Put uncovered in the microwave, and cook at full strength for one minute. Remove and stir again. The pasta is done if it's coated with a smooth, creamy sauce. If the sauce is still runny, return it to the oven, and cook at full strength at 30 second intervals until it's done.

Variations

Omit the optional add-ins and add cheddar cheese, cilantro, and kidney beans or feta cheese, oregano, and dill or Parmesan cheese, basil, capers, and sun-dried tomatoes.

[PER SERVING (WITH PARMESAN CHEESE): CAL. 537 / FAT 8.5 G / PROTEIN 30.9 G / CARB. 83.4 G / CHOL. 281 MG / SODIUM 1133 MG] % RDA: 29 IRON; 24 CALCIUM.

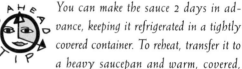

Linguine with Mussels and Shrimp

Serves 4

Mussels are quick to take on flavor; just show them a sauce and they pick up the seasoning.

Make sure the mussels you buy are good and plump. Prying the puny ones out of their shells can drive you nuts and disappoint you in the end with flavor as slight as their size.

1 hour from start to finish

You can make the sauce 2 days in advance, keeping it refrigerated in a tightly covered container. To reheat, transfer it to a heavy saucepan and warm, covered, over medium-low heat, stirring often.

1 cup dry white wine

1 white onion, quartered

1 bay leaf

2 pounds mussels in their shells, scrubbed and debearded (see box, page 122)

2 anchovy fillets, rinsed and patted dry

1 tablespoon extra virgin olive oil

1 yellow or white onion, chopped

4 garlic cloves, crushed and minced

½ cup minced fresh parsley

¼ cup minced fresh basil

Pinch dried red pepper flakes

5 fresh tomatoes (about 1½ pounds), peeled, seeded, and chopped, or one 16-ounce box or can imported Italian tomatoes

2 teaspoons capers, rinsed

1 pound fresh medium shrimp, shelled and deveined (see box, page 122)

10 ounces dried linguine

*i*n a large heavy saucepan, combine the wine, onion, and bay leaf and bring them to a boil over medium-high heat. Add the mussels, cover, turn down the heat to medium-low, and let them steam until they open, about 8 minutes. Using a large slotted spoon, transfer the mussels to a large bowl. Discard the cooking liquid, throw away any mussels that haven't opened, and leave the rest to cool.

Mince the anchovies. Heat the olive oil in a large skillet. Add the onion, garlic, parsley, and basil, and sauté on low heat, stirring often, until the onion is limp and translucent, about 10 minutes.

Stir the pepper flakes, tomatoes, anchovies, and capers into the onions. Let the

HOW TO CLEAN MUSSELS
❶ ❷ ❸

Clean mussels just before cooking; once they've been debearded they will start to spoil.

❶ Fill a large bowl with cool water and soak the mussels, turning them over with your hands, and scrubbing at the dirt on the shells with a hard-bristled brush. Discard any unopened mussels.

❷ Rinse, change the water, and repeat if necessary, until the grit's all gone.

❸ Tug on the beard, the coarse string sticking out of the shell. It should pull away easily.

HOW TO CLEAN SHRIMP
❶ ❷ ❸

❶ Peel off the shell.

❷ Stick the tip of a small sharp knife into the head end of the shirmp, and slice a shallow indentation along the top toward the tail.

❸ Pull out the stringy black vein and rinse the shrimp under cool water.

mixture simmer, uncovered, stirring occasionally, for 10 minutes.

Meanwhile, take all but 8 of the mussels out of their shells, and throw away the shells. (You'll use the mussels in the shells as a garnish.) Set all of the mussels aside, and stir the shrimp into the sauce.

Bring a large pot of water to a boil and cook the linguine according to the package directions.

While the linguine's cooking, stir the mussels into the sauce, and keep simmering over low heat, just until the mussels are heated through.

Drain the linguine in a colander, and transfer the sauce into the pot you've used to cook the pasta. Add the linguine and toss well with a large wooden fork and spoon. Transfer to a serving bowl and serve at once, garnished with the whole mussels.

[PER SERVING: CAL. 584.2 / FAT 8.8 G / PROTEIN 50.6 G / CARB. 69.3 G / CHOL. 207.2 MG / SODIUM 1,336.7 MG*] *VALUE GIVEN IS BEFORE SALTING. % RDA: 25.9 VIT. A; 30.8 VIT. C; 62.9 IRON.

Carrot and Spinach Lasagna with Lemon Sauce

Serves 6

I tend to be suspicious of lasagna, which often comes as a pile of ingredients whose identities are all too conveniently masked by sauce and cheese.

This one has nothing to hide. It takes more time and attention than the more familiar tomato and mozzarella lasagna, but it compensates with incomparably vivid flavors, and spectacular colors, too.

1 hour to assemble

45 minutes to bake

You can make just the filling or the whole dish, except for the sauce, 2 days in advance. To reheat, cover with foil and warm at 300° F. for about 20 minutes.

½ cup dried apricots

1 pound spinach, washed and stemmed

8 carrots, peeled and sliced very thin

½ cup fresh orange juice

1 bay leaf

2 cups part-skim ricotta cheese

1½ cups grated imported Parmesan cheese or grated Gruyère cheese

Pinch ground nutmeg

1 tablespoon extra virgin olive oil

1 small white onion, minced

1 large egg, lightly beaten

½ pound fresh lasagna noodles (found in the refrigerator section), or thin dried lasagna noodles that need no parboiling (it will say this on the box)

Lemon Sauce

1 tablespoon unsalted butter

1 tablespoon all-purpose flour

2 cups low-fat or nonfat milk

1 teaspoon finely grated lemon zest

Pinch ground nutmeg

Put the apricots in a saucepan and add enough water to cover by several inches. Bring to a gentle simmer, cover, and continue to simmer, over medium-low heat, until the apricots are very soft, about 40 minutes.

Meanwhile, chop the spinach coarsely and place it in a large saucepan with about 2 tablespoons of water. Cover and steam it over low heat until it's turned bright green, about 4 minutes.

In a large saucepan combine the carrots, orange juice, and bay leaf. Add water to cover and bring to a boil over high heat. Turn the heat down to medium, and simmer until the carrots are cooked through and very soft, 15 to 20 minutes. Drain off the remaining liquid, discard the bay leaf, and puree the carrots in a food processor or blender.

In a large mixing bowl, stir together the carrot puree, half the ricotta, half the Parmesan or Gruyère, and a pinch of nutmeg.

Drain the apricots and puree them in a food processor or blender. Stir them into the carrot mixture, and set it aside.

Heat the olive oil in a small skillet. Sauté the onion over medium heat until it's soft and translucent, about 7 minutes.

Transfer the onion to another large mixing bowl. Add the spinach, egg, and the remaining ricotta and Parmesan or Gruyère.

Heat the oven to 400°F. Cook the lasagna noodles according to the package directions. Place 1 layer of noodles on the bottom of an 8-inch square baking pan. Spread the carrot mixture on top.

Top the carrot layer with another layer of pasta, and spread the spinach mixture over that. Top with another layer of pasta. Cover with foil and bake for 45 minutes.

Meanwhile, make the Lemon Sauce by melting the butter in a saucepan over low heat and stirring in the flour. Keep stirring until the butter and flour turn light gold in color, about 3 minutes.

Stirring steadily, pour in the milk. Bring the sauce to a boil over medium-high heat, lower the heat to medium, and stir until it thickens, about 10 minutes. Add the lemon zest, and stir well to blend.

Let the lasagna sit for 10 minutes before slicing. Serve pieces topped with a generous spoonful of hot Lemon Sauce.

[PER SERVING: CAL. 571.2 / FAT 17.7 G* / PROTEIN 32.1 G / CARB. 68.9 G / CHOL. 93.8 MG / SODIUM 1,026.9 MG] *LASAGNA MADE WITH PART-SKIM RICOTTA. FOR FEWER CALORIES, LESS TOTAL FAT, AND CHOLESTEROL, SWITCH TO NONFAT. SAUCE MADE WITH NONFAT MILK. % RDA: 336.4 VIT. A; 55.5 VIT. C; 26.2 IRON; 69.2 CALCIUM.

Gnocchi

Serves 4 to 6

Gnocchi are a type of pasta, softer and more absorbent than the spaghettis and noodles we know by that name. Among pleasures, the sensation of eating good gnocchi is unique; each one sops up sauce, then releases it as you chew.

1 hour from start to finish

You can make the gnocchi up to 2 days in advance, keeping them refrigerated and covered until ready to cook.

3 large russet potatoes (about 1½ pounds), preferably organic
1 large egg, beaten
1½ cups semolina flour

ake the potatoes, either in a conventional oven or microwave (see page 97).

Remove the skin, put the potatoes in a bowl, and mash them together with the egg using a potato masher or the back of a large wooden spoon. Mash in the flour, ½ cup at a time, tapering off as the dough becomes stiff. Stop adding flour once the dough is smooth and firm enough to hold its shape.

Dust your hands and a flat work surface with flour, and tear off ⅓ of the dough. Roll it into a rope about ½ inch thick. Cut the rope into 1-inch pieces. Repeat until you've used all the dough. You can use the gnocchi at once, or refrigerate them, tightly covered, for up to 2 days.

🍃 To prepare the gnocchi, cook the desired sauce, such as Light(er) Béchamel Sauce with Parmesan (see below) or Perfect Tomato Sauce, Too (see page 112). When the sauce is ready and you're about to serve, bring a large pot of water to a boil over medium-high heat. Add the gnocchi, and boil until they rise to the surface, about 2 minutes. Drain them thoroughly in a colander, distribute among serving bowls, and pour the sauce on top. Serve immediately.

[PER SERVING: CAL. 254.5 / FAT 1.2 G* / PROTEIN 6.4 G / CARB. 54.2 G / CHOL. 45.7 MG / SODIUM 22.2 MG*] *VALUE GIVEN IS BEFORE SALTING.

Light(er) Béchamel Sauce with Parmesan

Makes 2 cups

Béchamel doesn't have to be rich to taste rich, as you'll see.

15 minutes from start to finish

This sauce is best made just before serving.

2 cups low-fat or nonfat milk
1 tablespoon unsalted butter
2 tablespoons flour
Pinch ground nutmeg
½ cup grated imported Parmesan cheese

cald the milk in a heavy saucepan over medium heat. Keep it warm over very low heat.

🍃 Melt the butter in a separate saucepan over low heat. When it's

HOW TO SCALD
❶ ❷ ❸

"Scald" is a good old-fashioned word that's all but gone the way of making cocoa from scratch on the stove top (a process that calls for scalding). It means heating milk slowly over medium-low heat, until it's just below the boiling point. "Below" is the critical word here because milk never hits boiling without boiling over.

❶ Place the milk in a heavy saucepan (enamel is best).
❷ Turn the heat to medium-low, and stay close by with your eye on it.
❸ As soon as the level of the milk starts to rise—indicating that it's about to break into a boil—take the pan off the heat.

bubbling, add the flour and whisk until it forms a golden paste, about 3 to 4 minutes.

🍃 Whisking constantly, add the hot milk in a steady stream. Bring the milk to a gentle simmer and continue to whisk until the sauce thickens, about 10 minutes.

🍃 Whisk in the nutmeg and the cheese, and serve at once.

To make the sauce in a microwave

🍃 Put the butter in a large Pyrex bowl, and melt on high for 30 seconds. Whisk in the flour, and cook at high for another 30 seconds. Whisk again, then cook for 30 seconds more.

🍃 Whisk in the milk, and cook at high for 1 minute. Whisk again, then return the sauce to the oven, whisking and cooking at 1-minute intervals until the sauce is thick and smooth, 4 to 5 minutes, depending on your microwave oven.

🌿 Stir in the nutmeg and cheese, and serve.

[PER SERVING: CAL. 86.8 / FAT 4 G* / PROTEIN 6.3 G / CARB. 6.1 G / CHOL. 12.2 MG / SODIUM 166.6 MG**] *MADE WITH NONFAT MILK. **VALUE GIVEN IS BEFORE SALTING.

Gnocchi with Sun-Dried Tomatoes (and Chicken)

Serves 6

You'll find that the sun-dried tomatoes burst like sparklers in the mild cheese sauce, which can be made with sliced chicken breast or without it.

20 minutes to prepare, once the bechamel sauce and gnocchi are made

 You can make the sauce, up to the point where you add the béchamel, as many as 3 days in advance, keeping it refrigerated in a tightly covered container. When you're ready to serve, transfer the sun-dried tomato mixture, with chicken, if included, to a heavy saucepan, cover, and warm over medium-low heat. Meanwhile, make the bechamel, and proceed with the recipe.

1 tablespoon unsalted butter
1 yellow or white onion, chopped
½ cup minced fresh parsley
6 sun-dried tomatoes (dry packed), minced
½ pound boneless chicken breast, thinly sliced (optional)
¼ cup dry white wine
1 recipe Light(er) Béchamel Sauce with Parmesan (see page 125)

1 recipe Gnocchi (see page 124), uncooked, or 1½ pounds store-bought gnocchi (available at Italian bakeries and specialty shops), uncooked

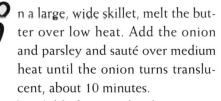n a large, wide skillet, melt the butter over low heat. Add the onion and parsley and sauté over medium heat until the onion turns translucent, about 10 minutes.

🍂 Add the sun-dried tomatoes and the chicken, if using, and sauté, stirring often until the chicken colors, about 2 minutes.

🌿 Add the wine and keep stirring over medium heat until most of it evaporates and the chicken is cooked through, about 4 to 5 minutes more.

🍂 Cook the gnocchi as directed on page 124.

🌿 Add the chicken or tomato mixture to the hot bechamel sauce and mix well. Spoon generously over the gnocchi, and serve at once.

[PER SERVING FOR GNOCCHI WITH SUN-DRIED TOMATOES: CAL. 307 / FAT 4 G / PROTEIN 8 G / CARB. 58 G / CHOL. 53 MG / SODIUM 76 MG]

[PER SERVING FOR GNOCCHI WITH SUN-DRIED TOMATOES (AND CHICKEN): CAL. 350 / FAT 5 G / PROTEIN 16.5 G / CARB. 58 G / CHOL. 75.1 MG / SODIUM 108 MG] % RDA: 50 VIT. C; 21 IRON.

SERVING SUGGESTIONS
Serve these Gnocchi with Sun-Dried Tomatoes (and Chicken) with Mediterranean Eggplant and Peppers (page 81) or Chilled Tomato Timbales in Tender Spinach Casing (page 89).

Gnocchi with Leeks and Ricotta

Serves 4 to 6

A lively, clean-tasting sauce makes this dish uncommonly light.

45 minutes to prepare if the gnocchi are already made

 These gnocchi are best made just before serving.

½ tablespoon unsalted butter

½ tablespoon extra virgin olive oil

1 large leek, white part only, cleaned and coarsely chopped

2 carrots, peeled and chopped

4 celery stalks, without the leaves, coarsely chopped

1 cup vegetable broth, either homemade (see page 44) or canned

1 recipe Gnocchi (see page 124), uncooked, or 1½ pounds store-bought gnocchi (available at Italian bakeries and specialty shops), uncooked

2 cups part-skim ricotta cheese

Minced fresh chives

*i*n a large skillet, heat together the butter and oil until the butter has melted. Sauté the leek, carrots, and celery over medium-low heat. Add ½ cup of the broth and continue to sauté, adding more as it's absorbed, until the leek becomes very soft, about 25 minutes.

Bring a large pot of water to a boil over medium-high heat. Add the salt and when the water returns to a boil, add the gnocchi and cook until they rise to the surface.

Remove the gnocchi with a slotted spoon,

SERVING SUGGESTIONS
Serve Gnocchi with Leeks and Ricotta with Cold Sweet Potato Soup (page 61), Roasted Red Pepper Terrine (page 88), or a tossed salad (page 64).

distributing them evenly among serving bowls. Place the ricotta in a mixing bowl and add 3 tablespoons of the gnocchi cooking water to it. Whisk it until it's a thick, smooth sauce. (It won't be creamy smooth, but it should be even textured.)

Whisk the ricotta into the leek mixture and pour it in even portions over the gnocchi. Sprinkle each serving with chives.

[PER SERVING: CAL. 361.9 / FAT 2.3 G* / PROTEIN 18.3 G / CARB. 63.2 G / CHOL. 48.4 MG / SODIUM 552.5 MG**] *MADE WITH PART-SKIM RICOTTA. FOR LESS TOTAL FAT AND CHOLESTEROL, SWITCH TO NONFAT. **VALUE GIVEN IS BEFORE SALTING. % RDA: 81.1 VIT. A; 47.8 VIT. C; 21.1 IRON; 50.4 CALCIUM.

Basic Risotto

Serves 4 to 6

There's no scientific basis for this, but I believe that once you've made risotto you'll feel savvier, more confident, and better able to take on the world than ever before. The reason is the perception that this dish is incredibly difficult to make, a myth perpetrated by (I can't prove this either) expensive restaurants with a stake in dissuading clients from cooking well at home. If you're convinced that making risotto is a major challenge, you're bound to feel pleased with yourself when you find you can do it.

In fact what you will have discovered is that risotto is easy, and that you can make it whenever you have rice, broth, butter, cheese, and 50 minutes or so on hand.

50 minutes from start to finish

 You can make the broth well in advance (see page 46 or 44 for broth storage). The risotto is best made just before serving.

4 cups chicken broth or strong vegetable broth, either homemade (page 44 or 46) or canned
1 tablespoon unsalted butter (see Note)
1 shallot, minced
1 cup arborio rice
2 tablespoons white wine
Generous pinch powdered saffron, dissolved in 1 tablespoon hot water
⅓ cup grated imported Parmesan cheese
1 tablespoon heavy cream or yogurt cheese (see box, page 133)
Salt and freshly ground pepper to taste

*i*n a stockpot or large saucepan, bring the broth to a gentle simmer over low heat.

🍃 Melt the butter in a heavy saucepan over medium-low heat. Sauté the shallot until soft, about 7 minutes. Add the rice and sauté until it's glistening and well coated with the shallot, about 3 minutes.

🍃 Raise the heat to medium and add the wine. Stir until it evaporates, about 2 minutes. Using a ladle, add about 1 cup hot broth. Stir constantly until the broth has been absorbed. Add another ladleful of broth and keep stirring until it's been absorbed.

🍃 Continue the process, adding broth ½ cup at a time and stirring in this way until the kernels are plump and no longer chalk white in the center. This should take 25 to 30 minutes altogether. The rice is *almost* done when the kernels are still separate but starting to bind, and there are pools of broth on the surface. It's *done* when the liquid has been absorbed, and the kernels are bound in what looks like very ricey, yet somewhat creamy, rice pudding.

🍃 Add the saffron in its soaking liquid and the Parmesan cheese. Stir well to combine, making sure almost all the liquid has been absorbed. Turn off the heat.

🍃 Stir in the Neufchâtel or yogurt cheese, and season with salt and pepper. Serve right away.

[PER SERVING: CAL. 173.1 / FAT 3.9 G* / PROTEIN 6.1 G / CARB. 26.3 G / CHOL. 10.9 MG / SODIUM 195.5 MG**] *MADE WITH HEAVY CREAM. **VALUE GIVEN IS BEFORE SALTING.

Carrot-Ginger Risotto

Serves 4 to 6

Living in Milan's Chinatown, I used to get some strange ideas. Some were even good.

For this dish, the plan was to take Chinese flavors that normally go *over* rice, and cook them *into* the rice instead. The tastes permeate the grains, not merely cover them. Delicious through and through.

30 minutes for the broth

40 minutes to cook once the broth is made

 You can make the broth up to 5 days in advance (see page 46 or 44 for broth storage). The risotto is best made just before serving.

4 cups vegetable or chicken broth, either homemade (see page 44 or 46) or canned

One 2-inch piece ginger, peeled and very thinly sliced, plus1 teaspoon finely grated fresh ginger

2 scallions, chopped, green and white parts kept separate

½ cup orange juice, preferably fresh

1 tablespoon unsalted butter

1 carrot, peeled and diced

1 tablespoon finely grated orange zest

1 cup arborio rice

2 tablespoons mirin (sweet rice wine for cooking, available at Asian specialty shops) or white wine

1 tablespoon heavy cream or yogurt cheese (see box, page 133)

Put the vegetable or chicken broth, sliced ginger, scallion greens, and orange juice into a saucepan. Cover and bring to a boil over medium-high heat, turn down the heat to medium-low, and simmer gently for 30 minutes. Strain it through a fine sieve, discard the ginger and scallions, then pour the broth back into the saucepan, and return it to a simmer.

🍤 In a separate saucepan, melt the butter over medium-low heat, and sauté the whites of the scallions, carrot, grated ginger, and orange zest until the scallions are soft and limp, about 7 minutes. Add the rice and stir until it's well coated with the seasonings and glistening, about 3 minutes.

🖊 Add the Mirin or white wine and stir vigorously until it evaporates, about 1 minute.

🍤 Using a ladle, add about 1 cup hot broth. Stir constantly over medium heat until the broth has been absorbed. Add another ladle-

ful of broth and keep stirring until it's been absorbed.

🍃 Continue the process, adding broth ½ cup at a time and stirring in this way until the kernels are plump and no longer chalk white in the center. This should take 25 to 30 minutes altogether. The rice is *almost* done when the kernels are still separate but starting to bind, and there are pools of broth on the surface. It's *done* when the liquid has been absorbed, and the kernels are bound in what looks like very ricey, yet somewhat creamy, rice pudding.

🍃 When the risotto is very nearly done, add the heavy cream or yogurt cheese and stir well to blend. Serve at once.

[PER SERVING: CAL. 165.7 / FAT 3.0 G* / PROTEIN 5.2 G / CARB. 27.2 G / CHOL. 9 MG / SODIUM 178 MG] *MADE WITH HEAVY CREAM.

SERVING SUGGESTIONS
Serve Carrot-Ginger Risotto with Asian Snow Pea and Mussel Salad (page 75), Chicken Breasts (or Pressed Tofu) with Sweet Mustard Glaze (page 176), or Poached Fish (page 190).

Lemony Risotto

Serves 4 to 6

Lemon provides such a strong sensation, it's often hard to appreciate its taste. But here Parmesan acts as a buffer, tempering the tartness so you can savor the deep, lovely lemon flavor.

30 minutes for the broth
40 minutes for the risotto

 You can make the broth up to 5 days in advance and store it tightly covered in the refrigerator. The risotto is best made just before serving.

1 lemon
3 cups vegetable or chicken broth, either homemade (see page 44 or 46) or canned
1 large leek, white and green part, cleaned and chopped
1 bay leaf
1 tablespoon unsalted butter
2 shallots, minced
2 tablespoons minced fresh parsley
1 cup arborio rice
2 tablespoons dry white wine
⅓ cup grated imported Parmesan cheese

alve and juice the lemon and remove the zest with a vegetable peeler. Leave half the zest in strips and mince the rest. Set aside the juice and the minced zest.

Place the strips of zest in a saucepan with the broth, leek, and bay leaf. Bring to a boil over medium-high heat, then cover and simmer gently over low heat for 30 minutes.

Strain the broth through a sieve, discard the leek and bay leaf, and pour it back into the saucepan. Cover and bring it back to a gentle simmer over low heat.

Meanwhile, in a separate saucepan melt the butter. Sauté the shallots, parsley, and minced lemon zest over medium-low heat until the shallots are soft, about 10 minutes. Add the rice and stir until it's coated with the seasonings and glistening, about 3 minutes. Add the white wine and lemon juice, turn up the heat, and stir until it's just about evaporated, about 2 minutes. Lower the heat.

Using a ladle, add about 1 cup hot broth. Stir constantly over medium heat until the broth has been absorbed. Add another ladleful of broth and keep stirring until it's been absorbed.

Continue the process, adding broth ½ cup at a time and stirring in this way, until the kernels are plump and no longer chalk white in the center. This should take 25 to 30 minutes altogether. The rice is *almost* done when the kernels are still separate but starting to bind and there are pools of broth on the surface. It's *done* when the liquid has been absorbed, and the kernels are bound in what

looks like very ricey, yet somewhat creamy, rice pudding.

When the risotto is nearly done, stir in 2 tablespoons more broth, along with the Parmesan cheese, and stir well until all of the liquid has been absorbed, about 3 to 4 minutes. Serve right away.

[PER SERVING: CAL. 179.5 / FAT 3.4 G / PROTEIN 6.1 G / CARB. 29.8 G / CHOL. 9 MG / SODIUM 190.1 MG]

SERVING SUGGESTIONS
Serve Lemony Risotto with Chicken Roasted with Garlic (page 181) or Monkfish with Mushrooms and Lentils (page 194).

Beet Risotto

Serves 4 to 6

Brilliant color and a sweet burst of beet in every bite.

30 minutes for the broth

40 minutes once the broth is made

 You can make the beet broth up to 4 days in advance, keeping the broth and the remaining cooked beet well wrapped and refrigerated until ready to use. The risotto is best made just before serving.

2 medium beets, trimmed

1 bay leaf

1 tablespoon unsalted butter

1 small onion, chopped

1 tablespoon orange zest

1 cup arborio rice

2 tablespoons raspberry vinegar or lemon
    vinegar (see pages 235–36)

Pinch sugar

1 tablespoon low-fat sour cream or yogurt
    cheese (see box, page 133)

Put the beets and bay leaf in a saucepan and add 4 cups of water. Bring to a boil over medium-high heat, then lower the heat and simmer, covered, over medium heat, until the beets are cooked through, about 40 minutes, depending on size.

Remove the beets with a slotted spoon, then strain the cooking water and discard the bay leaf. Pour the cooking water back into the saucepan. Slip the skins off the beets.

Chop 1 of the beets and set aside.

In a food processor puree the other beet and stir into the strained broth. Cover the broth and keep it at a gentle simmer over low heat.

In another large, heavy saucepan, melt the butter. Add the onion and orange zest, and sauté over medium heat until the onion is soft and translucent, about 7 minutes. Add the chopped beet, and stir well. Add the rice and stir until it's well coated with the seasonings and glistening, about 2 minutes.

Add the vinegar and stir until it evaporates, about 2 minutes.

Using a ladle, add about 1 cup hot broth. Stir constantly over medium heat until the broth has been absorbed. Add another ladleful of broth and keep stirring until it's been absorbed.

Continue the process, adding broth ½ cup at a time and stirring in this way until the kernels are plump and no longer chalk white in the center. This should take 25 to 30 minutes altogether. The rice is *almost* done when the kernels are still separate but starting to bind, and there are pools of broth on the surface. It's *done* when the liquid has been absorbed, and the kernels are bound in what looks like very ricey, yet somewhat creamy, rice pudding.

When the risotto is done, stir in the sugar, heavy cream or yogurt cheese, and stir well to blend. Serve at once.

[PER SERVING: CAL. 157.2 / FAT 3 G* / PROTEIN 2.4 G / CARB. 29.1 G / CHOL. 9.0 MG / SODIUM 11.3 MG] *MADE WITH LOW-FAT SOUR CREAM.

Pumpkin Risotto

Serves 4 to 6

This dish may change the way you look at pumpkins. Instead of potential jack-o'-lanterns, you'll see steaming bowls of creamy rice, rich, spicy, and pleasingly sweet.

50 minutes from start to finish

You can make the broth far in advance, keeping it frozen or refrigerated until ready to use (see page 44 or 46 for broth storage). The risotto is best made just before serving.

3 cups vegetable or chicken broth, either homemade (see page 44 or 46) or canned
1½ tablespoons unsalted butter
1 white or yellow onion, minced
½ cup minced fresh parsley
1 cup diced fresh pumpkin
1 cup arborio rice
2 tablespoons dry white wine
½ cup grated imported Parmesan cheese
Pinch ground nutmeg
1 tablespoon heavy cream or yogurt cheese (see box, right)

ring the broth to a simmer, covered, in a saucepan over medium-low heat.

❧ Melt the butter in a large heavy saucepan over medium-low heat. Add the onion and parsley and sauté until the onion is soft and translucent, about 7 minutes.

✎ Add the pumpkin and sauté until it's well coated with the onion and parsley. Add the rice and stir until it's coated with the seasonings and glistening, about 2 minutes.

❧ Add the wine and stir until the liquid evaporates, about 3 minutes.

✎ Using a ladle, add about 1 cup hot broth. Stir constantly over medium heat until the broth has been absorbed. Add another ladleful of broth and keep stirring until it's been absorbed.

❧ Continue the process, adding broth ½ cup at a time and stirring in this way until the kernels are plump and no longer chalk white

HOW TO MAKE YOGURT CHEESE
❶ ❷ ❸

To make a nonfat substitute for cream cheese, crème fraîche, or heavy cream, drain the moisture from nonfat yogurt as follows (start at least 6 hours before you'll need it):

❶ Line a strainer or fine colander with a coffee filter or a piece of cheesecloth and prop it up so it will drain into a glass or bowl.

❷ Pour the yogurt into the filter. Put it in the refrigerator and let it drain for 6 hours or overnight.

❸ Scoop the cheese out of the filter and use it as a spread in place of cream cheese or in recipes in place of heavy cream or crème fraîche. Covered and refrigerated, it keeps for 3 days.

in the center. This should take 25 to 30 minutes altogether. The rice is *almost* done when the kernels are still separate but starting to bind, and there are pools of broth on the surface. It's *done* when the liquid has been absorbed, and the kernels are bound in what looks like very ricey, yet somewhat creamy, rice pudding.

🍃 When the risotto is very nearly done, add 2 more tablespoons of broth, the Parmesan, and the nutmeg. Stir until the broth has been absorbed and the cheese blended throughout.

🍃 Add the cream or yogurt cheese, and stir well to blend. Serve at once.

[PER SERVING: CAL. 206 / FAT 5.9 G* / PROTEIN 7.2 G / CARB. 28.7 G / CHOL. 17.1 MG / SODIUM 231.8 MG] *MADE WITH HEAVY CREAM.

Summer Garden Risotto (with Scallops)

Serves 4 to 6

Making the most of what risotto does best, this recipe concentrates summer's signature flavors into one wonderful dish.

50 minutes from start to finish

 You can make the Roast Garlic Pesto while the rice is cooking. And you can make the broth up to 5 days in advance, longer if it's frozen (see page 46 or 44 for broth storage). The risotto is best made just before serving.

3 cups chicken broth or strong vegetable broth, either homemade (see page 46 or 44) or canned
1 tablespoon extra virgin olive oil

1 shallot, minced
2 ripe tomatoes, peeled, seeded, and chopped
1 cup arborio rice
2 tablespoons white wine
½ pound bay scallops (optional)
1 recipe Roast Garlic Pesto (see page 139)

i n a stockpot or large saucepan, bring the broth to a gentle simmer over low heat.

🍃 Heat the oil in a large heavy saucepan. Over medium-low heat, sauté the shallot until soft, about 7 minutes. Add the tomatoes and continue to cook until they break down into soft pulp, about 7 minutes more.

🍃 Add the rice and stir until it glistens and is well coated with the tomatoes, about 2 minutes.

🍃 Add the wine and stir until it evaporates, about 2 minutes. Using a ladle, add about 1 cup hot broth. Stir constantly over medium heat until the broth has been absorbed. Add another ladleful of broth and keep stirring until it's been absorbed, too.

🍃 Continue the process, adding broth ½ cup at a time and stirring in this way until the kernels are plump and no longer chalk white in the center. This should take 25 to 30 minutes altogether. The rice is *almost* done when the kernels are still separate but starting to bind, and there are pools of broth on the surface. It's *done* when the liquid has been absorbed, and the kernels are bound in what looks like very ricey, yet somewhat creamy, rice pudding. If you're using scallops, add them now, and continue stirring until they're cooked, about 3 minutes.

🍃 Add the Roast Garlic Pesto and stir thoroughly. Turn off the heat. Serve right away.

[PER SERVING FOR SUMMER GARDEN RISOTTO: CAL. 196.5 / FAT 3.3 G* / PROTEIN 8.5 G / CARB. 30.2 G / CHOL. 2.7 MG / SODIUM 195.1 MG**] *MADE WITH PART-SKIM RICOTTA. FOR LESS TOTAL FAT AND CHOLESTEROL, SWITCH TO NONFAT. **BEFORE SALTING. % RDA: 22.1 VIT. C.

[PER SERVING FOR SUMMER GARDEN RISOTTO (WITH SCALLOPS): CAL. 229.3 / FAT 3.4 G* / PROTEIN 15.1 G / CARB. 31.2 G / CHOL. 15.3 MG / SODIUM 255.6 MG**] *MADE WITH PART-SKIM RICOTTA. FOR LESS TOTAL FAT AND CHOLESTEROL, SWITCH TO NONFAT. **BEFORE SALTING. % RDA: 22.1 VIT. C.

SERVING SUGGESTIONS
Serve Summer Garden Risotto (with Scallops) with a tossed salad (spage 64), Aromatic Leek and Potato Soup (page 50), or Grilled Assorted Vegetables (page 143).

Risotto with Mussels

Serves 4 to 6

Call this mussels squared. You steam them in broth, then use the broth to cook the rice, stirring in the shelled mussels and saffron at the end. The rice is thick with the sweet, tender mollusks, and each kernel plump with a flavor that's almost too good to bear.

1 hour from start to finish

You can make the mussels and broth 2 days in advance, keeping them refrigerated, well wrapped, until ready to use. The risotto is best made just before serving.

2 cups water
½ cup dry white wine
2 white or yellow onions, quartered
4 garlic cloves, thinly sliced
4 pounds fresh mussels in their shells, scrubbed and debearded (see box, page 122)
1½ cups bottled clam broth
1 tablespoon unsalted butter
1 shallot, minced
1 cup arborio rice
Generous pinch powdered saffron, dissolved in 1 tablespoon hot water
1 tablespoon Neufchâtel or yogurt cheese (see box, page 133; optional)

*i*n a stockpot, combine the water, wine, onions, and garlic. Bring to a boil over medium-high heat.

🍃 Add the mussels; cover and steam until they open, about 7

minutes. Remove them with a slotted spoon, shaking as much liquid as possible back into the stockpot. Discard any mussels that haven't opened.

✻ When the mussels are cool enough to handle, take them out of the shells, discarding the shells and setting the mussels aside.

✻ Strain the mussel cooking liquid and return it to the stockpot. Stir in the clam broth and bring the mixture to a boil over medium-high heat. Lower the heat, keeping the broth at a gentle simmer.

✻ Melt the butter in a large heavy saucepan. Sauté the shallot over medium heat until soft, about 10 minutes. Add the rice and sauté until it's coated with shallot and glistening, about 3 minutes.

✻ Using a ladle, add about 1 cup hot broth. Stir constantly over medium heat until the broth has been absorbed. Add another ladleful of broth and keep stirring until it's been absorbed.

✻ Continue the process, adding broth ½ cup at a time and stirring in this way until the kernels are plump and no longer chalk white in the center. This should take 25 to 30 minutes altogether. The rice is *almost* done when the kernels are still separate but starting to bind, and there are pools of broth on the surface. It's *done* when the liquid has been absorbed, and the kernels are bound in what looks like very ricey, yet somewhat creamy, rice pudding.

✻ When the risotto is very nearly done, add the saffron in its soaking liquid and stir well to combine. Turn off the heat.

✻ Stir in the Neufchâtel or yogurt cheese if desired and the mussels, stirring well to distribute them evenly. Serve at once.

[PER SERVING: CAL. 258.0 / FAT 4.7 G / PROTEIN 2.6 G / CARB. 33.2 G / CHOL. 35.3 MG / SODIUM 333.5 MG] % RDA: 29.3 IRON.

SERVING SUGGESTIONS
Serve Risotto with Mussels with Silken Vegetable Soup (page 52), Carrot and Apricot Terrine (page 87), or a tossed salad (page 64).

Risotto with Shrimp

Serves 4 to 6

This may seem no more than a slight variation on Risotto with Mussels (see page 135). But risotto is so sensitive to flavor, when you change the principal ingredient, you get an altogether different dish.

1 hour from start to finish

 You can make the shrimp and broth 2 days in advance, keeping them refrigerated, well wrapped, until ready to use. The risotto is best made just before serving.

2 cups water
½ cup dry white wine
2 white or yellow onions, quartered
4 garlic cloves, sliced

2 pounds fresh unshelled medium shrimp

1 cup bottled clam broth

1 tablespoon unsalted butter

2 shallots, minced

¼ cup minced fresh parsley, plus additional for garnish

1 cup arborio rice

Generous pinch powdered saffron, dissolved in 1 tablespoon hot water

1 tablespoon Neufchâtel or yogurt cheese (see box, page 133; optional)

Salt and freshly ground pepper to taste

*i*n a large saucepan or stockpot, combine the water, wine, onions, and garlic. Bring to a boil over medium-high heat.

🍃 Add the shrimp in their shells, cover, and steam until they turn pink, about 3 to 5 minutes. Remove the shrimp with a slotted spoon, shaking as much liquid as possible back into the stockpot.

🌿 When the shrimp are cool enough to handle, take them out of the shells, discarding the shells. Devein the shrimp and set them aside.

🍃 Strain the cooking liquid and return it to the stockpot. Stir in the clam broth and bring the mixture to a boil over medium-high heat. Lower the heat, keeping the broth at a gentle simmer.

🌿 Melt the butter in a large heavy saucepan. Sauté the shallots and the ¼ cup of parsley until the shallots have softened, about 10 minutes. Add the rice and sauté until it's well coated with the shallots and glistening, about 3 minutes.

🍃 Using a ladle, add about 1 cup hot broth. Stir constantly over medium heat until the broth has been absorbed. Add another ladleful of broth and keep stirring until it's been absorbed.

🌿 Continue the process, adding broth ½ cup at a time and stirring in this way until the kernels are plump and no longer chalk white in the center. This should take 25 to 30 minutes altogether. The rice is *almost* done when the kernels are still separate but starting to bind, and there are pools of broth on the surface. It's *done* when the liquid has been absorbed, and the kernels are bound in what looks like very ricey, yet somewhat creamy rice pudding.

🍃 When the risotto is very nearly done, add the saffron in its soaking liquid and stir well to blend with the rice. Turn off the heat.

🌿 Stir in the Neufchâtel or yogurt cheese, if using, and the shrimp, stirring to distribute evenly. Season with salt and pepper. Serve at once, garnished with the additional minced parsley.

[PER SERVING: CAL. 347.2 / FAT 6.2 G / PROTEIN 36.2 G / CARB. 32.3 G / CHOL. 241.6 MG / SODIUM 285.9 MG] % RDA: 29.6 IRON.

SERVING SUGGESTIONS

Serve Risotto with Shrimp with Chilled Cucumber Soup (page 60), Grilled Assorted Vegetables (page 143), or Spicy Black Beans with Fresh Plums (spage 157).

Focacce

Makes 4 focaccia

Focaccia is pizza dough that's been brushed with olive oil and sprinkled with herbs and just about anything else. In some parts of Italy it's eaten for breakfast. But in Milan, bakeries put out fresh batches at noon and at five. Few things ran on schedule in that city, but I could have set my watch by the crowds that swelled outside the bakery on my corner waiting to pounce on the *focacce* when they came out still steaming and smelling of yeast.

20 minutes to prepare
1½ to 2 hours to rise
15 minutes to bake

 You can make the dough 2 days in advance, keeping it refrigerated in a tightly covered plastic container (I use a clean 32-ounce yogurt tub). You can keep baked focacce, wrapped in foil and refrigerated, for 2 to 3 days. Reheat in a 300° F. oven, or eat them cold.

1 package (2½ teaspoons) dry active yeast

2 teaspoons sugar

1 cup warm water

2 tablespoons extra virgin olive oil, approximately

1 teaspoon salt

3 cups unbleached all-purpose or bread flour, plus extra for kneading

Cornmeal

Coarse salt

P ut the yeast in a large earthenware bowl (see Note). Stir in the sugar and water. Set it aside until bubbles appear on the surface, about 5 minutes.

Stir in 1 tablespoon of the olive oil, the teaspoon of salt, and 1 cup of the flour. Mix well. Stir in the rest of the flour ½ cup at a time until the dough is firm enough to knead.

Turn the dough out onto a lightly floured surface and knead for about 10 minutes, dusting it lightly with flour whenever it gets too sticky, until it's smooth and elastic. Pat it into a ball.

Rub a large clean bowl with a teaspoon of the olive oil, and roll the dough in the bowl to coat the surface.

Cover the bowl with a towel and set it aside in a warm, draft-free place to rise until doubled, about 1 to 1½ hours.

Heat the oven to 500° F. Punch the dough down and divide it into 4 pieces of equal size. Shape each piece into a round about 4 inches in diameter and ½ inch thick. Sprinkle a baking sheet or baking stone with cornmeal, and place the rounds on top. Prick the surface of each round in several places with a fork. Cover with a light kitchen towel and let rest for 25 to 30 minutes, until slightly puffy.

✎ Brush the rounds with the remaining olive oil and sprinkle them evenly with the coarse salt, adding one of the following toppings, if desired. Bake on the lowest rack in the oven until browned, about 15 minutes.

Note: You can make the dough in the work bowl of a food processor, processing after each addition of flour until you have a dough that's soft but not sticky. Knead in the machine until the dough is smooth and forms a ball on its own, about 1 minute. Oil a mixing bowl and set the dough inside to rise as directed above. Proceed with the recipe as written.

Variations

Just before baking, sprinkle the *Focacce* with:
Grated imported Parmesan cheese
Fresh rosemary
Minced fresh basil and minced sun-dried tomatoes
Minced fresh oregano or crumbled dried oregano
Thinly slivered marinated olives

For Pizzas

Instead of brushing the dough with oil, slather it with Perfect Tomato Sauce (see page 112) or Perfect Tomato Sauce, Too (see page 113). Sprinkle with grated imported Parmesan, shredded mozzarella, minced fresh basil, and crumbled dried oregano, and bake as above.

[PER SERVING:* CAL. 207.2 / FAT 3.5 G / PROTEIN 5.2 G / CARB. 36 G / CHOL. 0 / SODIUM 268.1 MG] *EXCLUDES TOPPINGS.

Roast Garlic Pesto

Makes a little more than ½ cup

Raw garlic would overpower this dish. Roasting makes it mild.

6 garlic cloves, unpeeled
¼ cup minced fresh basil
¼ cup grated imported Parmesan cheese
½ cup nonfat or part-skim ricotta cheese

*h*eat the oven to 425°F.
🍃 Wrap the garlic cloves in aluminum foil and place them on a baking sheet in the oven until they become very soft, about 25 minutes. Unwrap them and let them cool at room temperature.
✎ Squeeze the pulp out of the garlic cloves and into the work bowl of a compact food processor or a blender fitted with a small container. Add the rest of the ingredients and process into a thick paste.

[PER SERVING: CAL. 54 / FAT 2 G / PROTEIN 4 G / CARB. 4 G / CHOL. 8.7 MG / SODIUM 85 MG]

vegetable main dishes

· · · · · ·

Grilled Assorted Vegetables ✽ Grilled or Broiled Pressed Tofu ✽ Savory French Toast Sandwich ✽ Baked Eggplant and Radicchio Sandwich ✽ Vegetable-Tofu Stir-Fry (with Chicken) ✽ Potato Frittata ✽ Cheese and Potato Pierogin ✽ Individual Potato Tortas ✽ Vegetable Ragu ✽ Wonderful Warm Winter Slaw ✽ Chickpea Curry ✽ Spicy Black Beans with Fresh Plums ✽ Sweet Corncakes with Mixed Pestos or Crab Filling Mayonnaise ✽ Broccoli Pesto ✽ Cilantro Pesto ✽ Mushrooms and Bean Curd (and Scallops) in Thai Peanut-Coconut Curry Sauce ✽ Savory Carrot Pie ✽ Savory Mushroom Pie ✽ Dough for Savory Pie

The difference between vegetables and dinner is not arbitrary. *Technically*, it's a matter of balancing nutrients. An adequate vegetable entrée has a source of protein, such as legumes or bean curd and a grain to complete it, such as rice. *Gastronomically* (that is, more important), it's a matter of balancing flavors and textures. **For Example:**
• Lentils, chickpeas, and pintos are just beans on their own. But with rice (carbohydrate and proteins that "complete" the proteins in the legumes), cheese (protein and calcium), and tomatoes (vitamin C, which helps release the iron in the legumes), they're dinner . . . not just because the nutrients come into balance, but because the flavors and textures do, too. • Mushrooms with broccoli (vitamins and fiber) is just a side dish, but stir-fried with bean curd (protein) and served with peanut sauce (more protein) and pita bread (carbohydrate), it's dinner. The textures balance each other—soft mushrooms/crisp broccoli, smooth tofu/bulky noodles, and the flavors do the same: the rich peanut sauce tames the sharp seasoning. • And a potato is only that, until you add eggs (protein), for instance, and a light cheese sauce (more protein and

calcium). This nourishing dish is balanced for flavor, too; potatoes are so mild that even a subtle sauce has punch by contrast.

To convert a meat dish to a vegetarian dish, first, choose a dish that calls for a lot of vegetables. Then:

• Compensate for flavor. Substitute a strong vegetable broth—not water—for chicken or beef broth in the original recipe. If the recipe calls for sautéing onions, garlic, leeks, and such, cook them over very low heat for twice as long, until they virtually melt. (They taste richer that way.) Finally, increase the amount of herbs and spices by half (for example, if the recipe calls for 1 tablespoon of ground cumin, add 1½ tablespoons). • Compensate for texture. Firm mushrooms and chunks of eggplant can stand in for meat or poultry. (Be careful not to overcook them or they'll be mushy.) Tempeh and pressed tofu can fill in for meat as well, providing both protein and texture. Coarse bulgur wheat and chopped cooked beans can mimic ground beef in taco filling and pasta sauces. • Compensate for nutrients. If you're replacing meat with eggplant, mushrooms, or bulgur, add beans, tofu or tempeh, hard-cooked eggs, or cheese to supply protein and vital minerals.

The following dishes can be made with poultry or fish, or without it:

- Couscous with Vegetables (and Fish) (see page 197)
- Chili with Seafood or Beans (see page 204)
- Fresh Tomatoes and Feta Cheese with Shrimp or Chickpeas (see page 203)
- Cabbage Filled with Spinach, Basmati Rice, and Fresh Salmon or Spicy Lentil Puree (see page 199)
- Rice Salad with Mango and Chickpeas (with or without Chicken) (see page 77)
- Gnocchi with Sun-Dried Tomatoes (and Chicken) (see page 126)

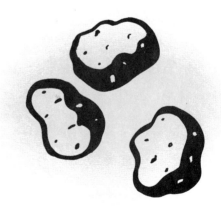

COMING TO TERMS

There are two phrases that are often used as if they mean the same thing, when, in fact, there is a critical difference between them. Ignoring the difference can cause confusion and disappointment. I'm thinking of "as good as" and "just like."

A vegetarian version of a dish can taste easily as good as (or better than) the version with meat. But it won't taste the same.

Example of correct usage:

True: Chili with beans tastes as good as chili with seafood.

False: Chili with beans tastes just like chili with seafood.

Grilled Assorted Vegetables

Serves 4

I don't cook vegetables on the grill for convenience (it requires too much prep work for that) but for flavors and textures I can't achieve any other way.

About 2 hours total, depending on the number and type of vegetables you grill, the condiments you choose, and the time it takes to prepare the coals

 You can make any of the marinades and condiments up to 5 days in advance, storing them tightly covered in the refrigerator.

Assorted vegetables of your choice (see below for suggestions)

Marinade, such as any of the oil and vinegar dressings (see page 65) or Sweet Mustard Glaze (see page 176)

Optional: one of the pestos (see page 160 or 161)

Any one or a number of relishes (see page 106 or 107)

Pita bread and Basic Tahini Dressing (see page 71)

Special equipment: wooden skewers (see Note)

Soak the wooden skewers in water to cover for at least 30 minutes. Prepare the coals for grilling (see box, right). While the coals are heating, blanch those vegetables that must be pre-cooked. (Check list, page 144.)

In a large ceramic mixing bowl, toss them with the marinade and skewer them, or skewer the vegetables first and brush them with the glaze.

HOW TO GET A GRILL GOING
❶ ❷ ❸

For this method you'll need solid fire starter, a gummy substance resembling cork, that is available wherever lighter fluid and charcoal are sold. It is nontoxic and unlikely to flare.

❶ Spread charcoal in a single layer across the charcoal grate on your grill.

❷ Pile the charcoal into a pyramid in the center, and place 2-inch pieces of solid starter among the coals. Light the starter.

❸ When the flames have died down, use a poker or a metal spatula with a plastic handle to spread them back into a single layer. The coals are ready when they're glowing (not flaring) and covered with white ash.

Note: For a smoked flavor, soak a heaping handful of mesquite wood chips in water for 30 minutes. Throw the wet chips on the hot coals, just before you cook.

Put all vegetables of one kind on a skewer (cherry tomatoes on 1 skewer, mushrooms on another, and so on) so they'll cook evenly. Some vegetables will be ready before others, and you'll want to take them off the grill so they won't burn while the rest are still cooking. Place the skewers on the grill and cover. Check after 3 minutes, and turn over those that have browned. Brush them with additional marinade or glaze, cover, and cook until lightly browned, but not charred, turning as needed.

If you'd like, when the vegetables are very nearly done, dot them with one of the pestos and continue grilling, covered, until it bubbles, about 1 to 2 minutes.

Serve grilled vegetables with any one or a combination of relishes.

Or put them in pita pockets and serve with tahini dressing.

Blanch the vegetables below for the times indicated in parentheses. (The blanching times are approximate.)

To blanch, bring a large saucepan of water to a boil over medium-high heat. Meanwhile, fill a large bowl with water and ice.

Blanching one type at a time, plunge the vegetable into the boiling water and leave it for the amount of time given, or until you can just pierce it with the point of a sharp knife.

Scoop it out with a slotted spoon and plunge it into the iced water to stop the cooking, about 30 seconds. With the slotted spoon transfer it to a plate covered with absorbent paper towel. Then either toss the vegetable in a bowl with marinade, or skewer it, and proceed with the recipe.

These vegetables must be blanched

Artichokes, trimmed and quartered if large, just trimmed if baby (4 minutes)

Beets, quartered (4 minutes), then slip off peel

Firm mushrooms, such as cremini, portobello, white button, washed (3 minutes)

Leeks (white part only), washed, cut into 1-inch cylinders (3 minutes). The leek may fall apart, but you can skewer it in layers of ½-inch thickness.

New potatoes, scrubbed, whole (4 minutes)

Onions, peeled and quartered (3 minutes). The onion will fall apart, but you can skewer it by piercing it in layers of ½-inch thickness.

Red potatoes, scrubbed and quartered (4 minutes)

Zucchini and summer squash, cut into 1-inch-thick slices (1 minute)

HOW TO STEAM OR BLANCH VEGETABLES IN THE MICROWAVE
❶ ❷ ❸

❶ Pour water into a microwave-safe dish to the depth of I inch.

❷ Add one type of vegetable and cover the dish (you can use plastic wrap).

❸ Microwave at the highest setting. How long it takes will depend on the strength of your oven, what you're cooking, and how much there is of it. Broccoli can take as few as 4 minutes, or as many as 6, asparagus from 3 to as many as 5, cauliflower 5 to 7 minutes, and snow peas 30 seconds to I minute.

Safety warning: Be very careful not to hold your face directly over any dish you remove from the microwave. The steam that will escape when you lift the cover or peel back the plastic wrap can scald you.

These vegetables don't need blanching

Bell peppers, seeded and sliced into thick strips

Cherry tomatoes

Japanese eggplant, unpeeled, cut into 1-inch rounds

Pressed tofu, cut into ½-inch cubes. (If you can't find pressed tofu, you can make it yourself. See box, below.)

Soft mushrooms, such as shiitake or oyster

Note: Use skewers made of wood rather than metal because metal heats up and cooks the vegetables from the inside before they have a chance to brown.

[PER SERVING: CAL. 303.8 / FAT 6.5 G / PROTEIN 4.4 G / CARB. 55.9 G / CHOL. 0 / SODIUM 603.5 MG] % RDA: 71.7 VIT. C.

Grilled or Broiled Pressed Tofu

Serves 4

Here's how to prepare tofu as a vegetarian alternative to Tandoori Spice Marinade for Chicken (see page 177) or for grilling with the Chicken Breasts with Sweet Mustard Glaze (see page 176).

Pressed tofu, homemade (see box, left) or store-bought

1 recipe Tandoori Spice Marinade (see page 177) or Sweet Mustard Glaze (see page 176)

1 recipe relish of your choice (see page 106 or 107)

 eat the grill (see page 143) or the broiler.

🍃 Spread the marinade or glaze on the tofu, then grill or broil the tofu until it's heated all the way through, about 4 to 6 minutes on each side.

SERVING SUGGESTIONS
Serve Grilled or Broiled Pressed Tofu with Nectarine Relish (page 107) or Red Cabbage and Onion Relish (page 106).

HOW TO PRESS TOFU
❶ ❷ ❸

If you can't find pressed tofu, it's easy to make your own.

❶ Put several layers of absorbent paper towel inside a baking pan or wide bowl.

❷ Put a 1-pound block of firm or extra-firm tofu on top and put another few layers of paper towel over it.

❸ Weigh it down with something very heavy, such as a cast-iron pot or a pile of ceramic plates. Refrigerate overnight.

Savory French Toast Sandwich

Makes 1 sandwich

For all I admire about the French way with food, there are some things I just don't get. The *croque monsieur,* for one, a soggy panfried ham sandwich, or the *croque madame,* which is the same awful thing with an egg on top. The problem isn't the concept, but the fact that they're only served in cafés, which are, by nature, unable to make them well, since someone must keep an eye on a sandwich of this kind, to see that it stays crisp. But most cafés are too busy to post a vigil at the stove.

However, if you're willing to tend to it, you can make a sandwich based on the *croque monsieur/madame* principle that will taste much better than any you might have in France.

20 minutes from start to finish

 This sandwich is best made just before serving or it will be soggy.

1 large egg, lightly beaten

⅓ cup low-fat or nonfat milk

½ teaspoon grated lemon zest

2 slices unbleached white or whole wheat
   sandwich bread

4 sun-dried tomatoes (dry packed), chopped

¼ cup shredded Monterey Jack, Muenster, or
   provolone cheese

*i*n a wide bowl, whisk together the egg, milk, and lemon zest.

🍃 On one slice of bread, evenly distribute the sun-dried tomatoes and the cheese, and place the second piece of bread on top.

🍃 Dip the sandwich into the egg and milk mixture, making sure to soak both sides.

🍃 Heat a nonstick skillet on the stove, and place the sandwich in the center. Cook over low heat, checking often to make sure it doesn't stick, until the bottom is golden brown, about 6 minutes. Turn it over with a spatula and brown the other side, about 4 minutes more. Serve right away, with soup or a tossed salad.

[PER SERVING: CAL. 458.8 / FAT 14.1 G / PROTEIN 15.5 G / CARB. 65.1 G / CHOL. 16 MG / SODIUM 471.2 MG]   % RDA: 41.9 VIT. C; 26 CALCIUM.

SERVING SUGGESTIONS
Serve Savory French Toast Sandwich with a tossed salad (page 64), Mediterranean Eggplant and Peppers (page 81), or Baba Ganoush (page 71).

Baked Eggplant and Radicchio Sandwich

Makes 1 sandwich

Radicchio, sharp and a bit bitter when raw, becomes mild and so savory when cooked that dishes that call for it, such as this simple sandwich, need no further seasoning.

20 *minutes from start to finish*

 This sandwich is best made just before serving or will be soggy.

1 Japanese eggplant
1 teaspoon extra virgin olive oil
1 cup shredded radicchio
1 long sandwich roll
¼ cup shredded part-skim mozzarella cheese

 eat the oven to 425°F. Peel the eggplant and slice it lengthwise into 4 strips. Place them on a nonstick or lightly oiled baking sheet and bake for 15 minutes, until tender.

Meanwhile, heat the oil in a small skillet. Add the radicchio, and sauté over medium-

SERVING SUGGESTIONS
Serve the Baked Eggplant and Radicchio Sandwich with Chunky Lentil Soup with Parmesan (page 56), Artichoke Soup (page 47), or Warm Confetti Salad (page 68).

low heat until it wilts, about 5 minutes. Turn off the heat.

Split the sandwich roll and layer the eggplant, radicchio, and cheese inside.

[PER SERVING: CAL. 325 / FAT 12 G / PROTEIN 16 G / CARB. 33 G / CHOL. 24 MG / SODIUM 518 MG] VALUES WILL VARY DEPENDING UPON THE KIND OF ROLL YOU USE.

Vegetable-Tofu Stir-Fry (with Chicken)

Serves 6

Stir-frying is supposed to be easy. Ha! How on earth are you supposed to get all those different ingredients to cook evenly?

I'll tell you how *I* do it. I cheat. Instead of stir-frying the vegetables, I blanch them on the stove or in the microwave, one type at a time, tossing them all at once into the wok only to heat them through and season them with the sauce I've got going in there. In this way I don't overcook the broccoli or snow peas while waiting for the carrots to be done.

30 minutes to prepare the vegetables

10 minutes to cook

 Stir-fries are best made just before serving.

1 tablespoon soy sauce

1 tablespoon dry sherry

1 pound extra-firm tofu, diced

1 pound boneless skinless chicken breast, thinly
    sliced (optional)

1 pound assorted steamed vegetables, thinly
    sliced, such as broccoli, cabbage, shiitake or
    portobello mushrooms, zucchini, carrots,
    bamboo shoots, snow peas, spinach

2 tablespoons vegetable or chicken broth,
    homemade (see page 44 or 46) or canned

2 teaspoons arrowroot or cornstarch (see Note)

1 tablespoon peanut oil (unrefined if you can
    find it) or light sesame oil

2 large garlic cloves, grated

One 2-inch piece fresh ginger, peeled and
    grated

2 tablespoons minced scallions, white part only

¼ cup plus 1 tablespoon hoisin sauce (available
    at Asian markets or specialty stores)

6 cups cooked white or brown rice

i n a large bowl, stir together the soy
sauce and sherry. Add the tofu and
chicken, if using, and set aside.

🐟 Put an inch of water in a wok,
cover it, and bring it to a boil over
medium-high heat. Put the vegetables in the
wok 1 type at a time, steaming until just
cooked through. The cooking time will depend on the kind of vegetable, but count on
about 3 minutes for carrots, 2 to 3 minutes for

zucchini, 3 to 4 minutes for broccoli and cabbage. You don't have to steam snow peas or
mushrooms. As each vegetable is done, use a
slotted spoon to transfer it to a large bowl.
Change the water if it gets muddy colored.
You can also blanch the vegetables in the microwave (see box, page 144).

🐟 Combine the broth and arrowroot or
cornstarch in a small bowl. Empty the water
from the wok and heat the wok over high
heat until it starts to smoke. Add the oil, then
the garlic, ginger, and scallions, stirring

HOW TO STEAM FRESH VEGETABLES
❶ ❷ ❸

You'll need a basket steamer, a collapsible
aluminum basket available at housewares
stores or wherever you can get basic kitchen
utensils.

❶ Pour water into a large saucepan to the
depth of about 2 inches.

❷ Put the vegetables into the basket
steamer, and lower the steamer into the
water.

❸ Cover the pot and simmer over medium-
low heat until the vegetables are just cooked
through.

Note: The cooking time will depend on the
type of vegetable and the size of the pieces.
Generally, broccoli florets will be done in 3–4
minutes, asparagus tips in 3–4 minutes, cauliflower florets in 7–9 minutes, snap sugar
peas in 1 minute or less.

briskly for 1 minute to flavor the oil. Add the tofu and chicken, if used, and toss well until each is cooked through, about 4 minutes. If either the tofu or chicken starts to stick, add a tablespoon of the sherry–soy sauce marinade to the wok.

🍃 With a slotted spoon, transfer the chicken and tofu to a large plate. Pour all of the vegetables into the wok and toss well, adding hoisin sauce, and stirring for 1 minute. Toss the chicken or tofu back into the wok.

🍃 Stir the arrowroot or cornstarch mixture again and add it to the wok. Continue stirring until everything's coated with a light, glossy sauce, about 1 minute more. Serve immediately with the rice.

Note: Arrowroot flour is a thickener that comes from a tropical tuber. I prefer it to cornstarch, which tends to turn gummy.

[PER SERVING FOR VEGETABLE-TOFU STIR-FRY (WITH CHICKEN): CAL. 273.9 / FAT 9.6 G / PROTEIN 29.1 G / CARB. 15.4 G / CHOL. 43.8 MG / SODIUM 447.3 MG] % RDA: 117.9 VIT. C; 51.8 IRON; 20 CALCIUM.

[PER SERVING FOR VEGETABLE-TOFU STIR-FRY: CAL. 188.6 / FAT 8 G / PROTEIN 12 G / CARB. 15.4 G / CHOL. TR. / SODIUM 347.2 MG] % RDA: 117.9 VIT. C; 48.8 IRON; 20 CALCIUM.

Grating garlic and ginger on the fine mesh of a cheese grater releases more flavor than chopping, mincing, or crushing. For easy cleanup, place a sheet of parchment paper over the teeth before you grate. When you peel the paper away, the shavings will fall into a neat pile, ready to be tossed into your dish, and the grater will be clean. Throw the used parchment away.

Potato Frittata

Serves 2

Add a thick slice of bread and some tossed salad greens, and this quick, simple dish is the perfect supper on a damp, chilly night.

30 minutes from start to finish

 You can make this frittata up to 2 days in advance and serve it cold or reheat it wrapped in foil for 10 minutes in a 325°F. oven until warm through.

½ pound (about 4) low-starch (red boiling) potatoes, thinly sliced
3 large eggs, beaten
¼ cup evaporated skim milk
⅓ cup shredded cheddar or Gruyère cheese
Pinch crumbled dry oregano
Salt and freshly ground black pepper to taste

Steam the potatoes until just cooked through, about 8 minutes (see page 148).

🍃 Meanwhile, heat the broiler.

🍃 When the potatoes have cooked, distribute them evenly on the bottom of an 8-inch nonstick ovenproof (make sure it doesn't have a plastic handle) omelet pan, lightly greased or coated with nonstick spray.

🍃 Beat together the eggs, evaporated milk, cheddar cheese, oregano, and salt and pepper in a mixing bowl. Heat the omelet pan over medium heat, and pour the egg mixture over the potatoes. Cook, stirring occasionally with a fork to keep the eggs from cooking too fast on the bottom, about 7 minutes. When the eggs have nearly set, lift the eggs on one side and tilt the pan so any uncooked egg runs down to cook underneath. Continue cooking until firm, about 3 minutes more. Turn off the heat. Place the pan under the broiler to brown, about 1 minute.

🖋 Place a large plate over the omelet pan, and invert the frittata onto the plate. Let sit for 5 minutes before slicing and serving.

[PER SERVING: CAL. 351 / FAT 5.7 G / PROTEIN 19.6 G / CARB. 54 G / CHOL. 21 MG / SODIUM 328 MG] % RDA: 37 CALCIUM.

SERVING SUGGESTIONS

Serve Potato Frittata with A Tossed Salad for All Seasons (page 64), Mediterranean Eggplant and Peppers (page 81), or Tomato-Posole Soup (page 51).

Cheese and Potato Pierogin

Serves 4

Potatoes extend the cheese in these delicious filled dumplings, making them creamy without adding fat. The sweet and crunchy cabbage topping complements by contrast.

2 hours from start to finish

 You can prepare the filling, dough, and/or topping up to 3 days in advance, keeping them tightly covered and refrigerated.

4 medium-size medium starchy potatoes, such as Yukon Gold or Yellow Finn
½ cup cottage cheese
⅓ cup shredded Monterey Jack or Muenster cheese
½ teaspoon whole cumin seeds (optional)
1½ cups all-purpose flour
½ cup semolina flour
¼ teaspoon salt
1 large egg, beaten
2 teaspoons unsalted butter or canola oil
2 cups thinly sliced onion
1 cup grated carrot
3 cups shredded green or red cabbage
Pinch crumbled dried basil
Pinch crumbled dried oregano
Salt and freshly ground pepper to taste
Plain yogurt or sour cream (optional)

 irst prepare the filling (you can do this up to 3 days in advance):

🖋 Bake the potatoes (see page 97 for alternate methods). When they're cool enough to handle, scoop out the pulp and place in a large mixing bowl. Mash the potatoes, beating in the cottage cheese, cheese, and the cumin, if used. Refrigerate, covered, until you're ready to fill the pierogin.

🌿 In a mixing bowl, combine the all-purpose and semolina flours and salt, stirring with a long-tined fork to blend. Stir in the egg, and mix, using your hands or the back of a wooden spoon, until you have a stiff, smooth dough. Wrap in wax paper and refrigerate until firm enough to roll, about an hour.

🍃 Divide the dough into two equal portions, and on a lightly floured surface, roll out one portion to a thickness of about ¼ inch. Using a biscuit cutter or the rim of a wineglass cut out rounds about 3 inches in diameter.

🌿 Place a generous tablespoon of filling in the lower portion of each round. Fold the upper portion of dough over to enclose the filling, and press along the rim to seal. Repeat, pressing together the scraps of dough and rolling them out again. Repeat with the second half of the dough, until all the filling is used.

🍃 Bring a large pot of water to a boil over high heat. Add the pierogin four or five at a time and boil until they rise to the surface. Let them continue to boil five minutes longer. Remove with a slotted spoon and let drain on paper towels.

🌿 Meanwhile, prepare the cabbage and onions.

🍃 Heat the butter or oil over medium heat in a large covered skillet. Add the onions, carrots, cabbage, basil, and oregano, and sauté, stirring often, until the vegetables soften, about 7 minutes. Season with salt and pepper to taste. Add 2 tablespoons of water, stir, cover, and let steam until the vegetables are limp, about 10 minutes.

🌿 Place the pierogin in the pan with the cabbage-onion mixture, and stir to coat with the vegetables and heat throughout. Serve right away, topped with a dollop of yogurt or sour cream.

[PER SERVING (WITHOUT SOUR CREAM OR YOGURT TO SERVE): CAL. 438 / FAT 8.2 G / PROTEIN 16 G / CARB. 72.5 G / CHOL. 63.2 MG / SODIUM 303.5 MG] % RDA: 58 VIT. A; 73 VIT. C; 24 IRON; 21 CALCIUM.

Individual Potato Tortas

Serves 4

This dish is delicious hot or cold. Sturdy and compact, it's perfect for picnics. The recipe is long, but the result is a one-dish meal, needing only bread and a crisp salad on the side.

1 hour to prepare
40 minutes to bake

 You can make the sauce—up to the point at which you add the Parmesan cheese—3 days in advance, keeping it refrigerated in a tightly covered container. To proceed with the recipe, transfer the sauce to a heavy covered saucepan and warm slowly over medium-low heat.

Or you can make the entire dish up to 3 days in advance. Serve chilled, or reheat by placing it in a 300° F. oven, wrapped loosely in foil, for about 20 minutes.

6 large russet potatoes, scrubbed
2 large eggs, beaten
1 cup shredded part-skim mozzarella cheese
2 tablespoons unsalted butter
1 small white onion, diced

2 garlic cloves, crushed and minced

2 teaspoons crumbled dried oregano

2 teaspoons crumbled dried basil

1 teaspoon whole fennel seed

½ cup canned or boxed tomatoes, ideally an
    imported Italian brand, such as Pomi

2 pounds fresh mushrooms of at least 2 types,
    such as white button, oyster, or portobello,
    cleaned and quartered

¼ cup white wine

1 tablespoon all-purpose flour

1 cup low-fat or nonfat milk

Freshly ground pepper to taste

1 cup grated imported Parmesan cheese

eat the oven to 425°F. Bake the potatoes for 50 minutes to an hour, scoop out the insides, and mash them in a mixing bowl. Leave the oven on. You can also bake the potatoes in a microwave (see page 97).

🍃 Mash the eggs into the potatoes, then stir in the mozzarella cheese so that it's well distributed throughout. Set aside.

🌿 In a large skillet, melt 1 tablespoon of the butter and sauté the onion, garlic, oregano, basil, and fennel seed over medium heat until the onion is soft and translucent, about 7 minutes. Meanwhile, puree the tomatoes in a food processor.

🍃 Add the mushrooms and continue cooking, stirring constantly, until the mushrooms start to release liquid, about 4 minutes.

🌿 Add the wine and cook, stirring, for 2 more minutes, until the wine evaporates. Be careful not to cook too long or the mixture will become watery.

🍃 With a slotted spoon, transfer the mixture to a large mixing bowl. Stir the tomato puree in with the mushrooms and mix well. Set aside. Pour off the remaining liquid.

🍃 In the same skillet, melt the remaining tablespoon of butter. Add the flour and whisk constantly over low heat until the mixture becomes bubbly and golden, about 3 minutes.

🌿 Whisking constantly, pour in the milk. Raise the heat to medium and continue stirring until the sauce thickens, about 10 min-

---

NO ONE EVER ASKS ME ABOUT MY TRIUMPHS . . .

They always want to hear about disasters, about the exploding soufflés, the imploding cakes, and the time I served clams to an unwitting friend whose subsequent hospital stay reminded me she was allergic to shellfish. One of my worst calamities concerned gnocchi. I'd invited some new friends to dinner and made gnocchi in a delicate manner I'd recently perfected. Just when I'd put them in to boil, a friend phoned to tell me she'd gotten engaged that afternoon. I held on for the critical details—40 minutes of them. By the time I remembered dinner, it was too late. The gnocchi had blown to bits. Not having learned my lesson with the first course, I talked too long at the table, and by the time I remembered the snapper in the oven, it was better forgotten.

I've made gnocchi plenty of times since then (see page 124), but when I don't want to take any chances, I make potato torta, which is as chewy and cheesy as good gnocchi, but without the risk.

utes. Stir in the mushroom mixture, then stir in the Parmesan cheese. Season with pepper. Place about 3 tablespoons of sauce in the bottom of four 2-cup-capacity ovenproof serving bowls or small Pyrex bowls (see Note).

❧ For each serving take a handful of the potato mixture (using about ⅛ of the mixure) and make a patty the diameter of the bowl, and place it inside, over the layer of sauce. Ladle more sauce over the potato layer, then make another patty to place on top. Finish with a ladleful of sauce. Repeat for each bowl. Or you can layer the ingredients in an 8-inch deep-dish pie plate.

🌿 Bake for 40 minutes, until the sauce is bubbly. Let the tortas rest for 5 minutes before serving.

Note: I recommend oven-to-table porcelain bowls. They may seem expendable until you own them, when you may find they come in handy for soup, hot cereal, baked apples, bread pudding, and more.

[PER SERVING: CAL. 510.8 / FAT 15.3 G* / PROTEIN 25.5 G / CARB. 63.5 G / CHOL. 135 MG / SODIUM 572.5 MG**] *MADE WITH NON-FAT MILK AND PART-SKIM MOZZARELLA. **VALUE GIVEN IS BEFORE SALTING. % RDA: 74.2 VIT. C; 29.7 IRON; 52.9 CALCIUM.

Vegetable Ragu

Serves 4

A favorite hearty "meal in minutes," roughly forty-five from start to finish. Serve it over rice or a dense pasta, such as perciatelli, rigatoni, or ziti.

45 minutes from start to finish

 You can make this dish up to 3 days in advance and serve it cold or hot. To reheat the ragu, transfer it to a heavy saucepan and set it, covered, over medium-low heat, stirring often until warmed through, about 20 minutes.

4 Japanese eggplants, peeled and cut into slices ½ inch thick
1 tablespoon extra virgin olive oil
1 large white onion, chopped
2 garlic cloves, crushed and minced
½ cup minced fresh basil
½ cup minced fresh parsley
1 tablespoon balsamic vinegar
2 zucchini, finely diced
4 large unpeeled tomatoes, cored and chopped
2 cups cooked white beans, drained (rinsed if canned)
Salt and freshly ground pepper to taste
4 hard-boiled eggs, chopped (optional)

 eat the oven to 425° F. Place the eggplant slices on a nonstick or lightly oiled baking sheet, and bake until tender, about 12 minutes. When they're cool enough to handle, chop them coarsely.

🌿 Meanwhile, in a large skillet, heat the olive oil. Add the onion, garlic, basil, and parsley and sauté over medium heat until the onion is soft and translucent, about 7 minutes. Add the vinegar and cook, stirring, for 2 minutes more, until most of the vinegar evaporates.

🦋 Add the zucchini, eggplant, and tomatoes. Turn the heat down to medium-low and cook, stirring occasionally, for 15 minutes. The sauce should be chunky, and the ingredients cooked through.

🦋 Stir in the white beans and season with salt and pepper. If you'd like, garnish each portion with a quarter of the chopped eggs just before serving.

[PER SERVING*: CAL. 398.8 / FAT 3.7 G / PROTEIN 13.5 G / CARB. 77 G / CHOL. 0 / SODIUM 54.5 MG**] *MADE WITHOUT HARD-BOILED EGGS. **VALUE GIVEN IS BEFORE SALTING. % RDA: 31.8 VIT. A; 114.6 VIT. C; 44.4 IRON.

Wonderful Warm Winter Slaw

Serves 4

This dish targets every conceivable craving and hits each spot with something hearty (mushrooms), creamy (cheese sauce), crunchy (cabbage), sweet (beets), and sharp (dill). Steamed brown rice makes it a meal and adds body without blunting the flavors.

1 hour 20 minutes from start to finish

 This dish is best made just before serving.

1½ tablespoons unsalted butter

1 large white or yellow onion, thinly sliced

1 teaspoon salt

2 tablespoons minced fresh dill, or 2 teaspoons crumbled dried dill

1 pound mixed fresh mushrooms, such as button, oyster, and portobello, cleaned and sliced

2 cups chopped red cabbage (see box, page 148)

2 cups cauliflower florets (see box, page 148)

1 tablespoon all-purpose flour

1 cup warm low-fat or nonfat milk

1 teaspoon dry mustard

1 cup grated sharp cheddar cheese

1 medium beet, cooked, peeled and chopped (see box, below)

Steamed brown rice, preferably Wehani brand

HOW TO COOK A BEET
❶ ❷ ❸

Regardless of whether you bake, boil, or microwave beets, you'll retain more nutrients if you leave the peel on in the process. Baking allows the fewest nutrients to be lost.

❶ Cut off the stem and leaves.

❷ Gently scrub the surface to remove grit.

❸ Wrap tightly in foil and bake at 400° F. until tender (about 1½ to 2 hours, depending on size). Or, plunge them into boiling water, cover, lower the heat, and simmer until tender, about 40 minutes. Slide the peel off.

*i*n a large skillet melt ½ tablespoon of the butter in a large skillet. Add the onion, salt, and dill, and sauté gently over low heat, stirring often, until the onion is limp and tender, about 20 minutes.

🌿 Add the mushrooms to the skillet. Continue cooking over low heat, stirring often, until they're just cooked through, about 10 minutes more. Be sure to keep the heat very low, or the mix will become watery. The moment the mushrooms are cooked, turn off the heat.

🌿 Steam the cabbage until it's tender but not mushy, about 12 minutes. Transfer it to a colander and let it drain.

🌿 Steam the cauliflower until just cooked through, 8 to 10 minutes. Set aside.

🌿 In a medium saucepan, melt the remaining 1 tablespoon butter. As soon as it starts to sizzle, whisk in the flour, and cook over low heat, whisking constantly, until the mixture is bubbly and golden, about 3 minutes.

🌿 Raise the heat to medium, add the milk, and keep whisking until the mixture is smooth and thick, about 10 minutes. Turn off the heat.

🌿 Add the mustard and cheese, and beat swiftly until smooth.

🌿 Transfer the mushroom mixture, cabbage, cauliflower, and beet to a large mixing bowl. Toss well. Pour the cheese sauce on top, and toss again to coat the vegetables thoroughly. Serve at once, with brown rice.

[PER SERVING: CAL. 355.5 / FAT 12.7 G* / PROTEIN 15.5 G / CARB. 42.2 G / CHOL. 31 MG / SODIUM 240 MG**] *MADE WITH NONFAT MILK AND WHOLE-MILK CHEDDAR CHEESE. ** VALUE GIVEN IS BEFORE SALTING. % RDA: 95.4 VIT. C; 34.3 CALCIUM.

HOW TO PEEL A TOMATO
❶ ❷ ❸

Most recipes call for peeled tomatoes. Here's how it's done:

❶ Bring a large pot of water to a boil.

❷ Add the whole tomatoes, and wait for the water to return to a boil.

❸ Count 20 seconds, then immediately remove the tomatoes with a slotted spoon. Let them rest until they're cool enough to handle. Cut out the stem at the top and strip off the skin.

Note: The seeds are bitter, so get rid of as many as you can without losing the pulp.

Chickpea Curry

Serves 4

There are no rules where curry's concerned. I rarely make it the same way twice, relying on my nose more than measuring spoons to determine how much to add of this or that. The aroma I aim for is hard to describe. The most meaningful way to put it is to say it makes me hungry.

This version is meatless, but you can toss in a cup or two of shredded poached chicken with the lemon juice at the end. Serve it with rice, ideally jasmine or basmati.

40 minutes to make

10 minutes to rest

 You can make this curry up to 3 days in advance, and serve it cold or hot. To reheat the curry transfer it to a heavy covered saucepan and warm it slowly over medium-low heat, stirring often.

3-inch chunk fresh ginger, peeled

6 large garlic cloves

1 tablespoon unsalted butter or canola oil

1 large white or yellow onion, chopped

½ cup minced fresh cilantro

1 tablespoon Madras-style curry powder

1 tablespoon ground cumin

2 teaspoons ground coriander

2 teaspoons ground turmeric

Pinch cayenne pepper

4 large tomatoes (about 1 pound), peeled, seeded, and chopped

1 Granny Smith apple, peeled, cored, diced

3 cups cooked chickpeas, drained (rinsed if canned)

1 tablespoon fresh lemon juice

¼ cup raisins

2 tablespoons unsweetened shredded coconut

1 cup plain low-fat or nonfat yogurt, plus more to taste

inely grate the ginger and garlic with a cheese grater. Heat the butter or oil in a medium skillet, and sauté the ginger, garlic, onion, cilantro, curry powder, cumin, coriander, turmeric, and cayenne pepper over medium-low heat, until the onion is soft and translucent, about 10 minutes.

Stir in the tomatoes, apple, and chickpeas, and cook over low heat, covered, stirring occasionally, until the tomatoes have cooked down into a pulpy stew, about 20 minutes. Add the lemon juice, raisins, and coconut, and simmer, uncovered, stirring occasionally, for 5 minutes, just to thicken and blend.

Turn off the heat, stir in the yogurt, cover, and let it rest for 10 minutes before serving.

[PER SERVING: CAL. 278.8 / FAT 6.7 G / PROTEIN 9.8 G / CARB. 43.2 G / CHOL. 0.8 MG / SODIUM 200.1 MG*] *VALUE IS GIVEN BEFORE SALTING. % RDA: 39.9 VIT. C; 20 IRON.

Spicy Black Beans with Fresh Plums

Serves 4

I feel a bit guilty when I cook with fruit, as if I'm trying to double up on dessert. Well, maybe so. But it's a self-justifying transgression and a nutritious one as well, as you'll discover when you try this luscious lunch or supper dish. It's also one of my favorite condiments for grilled vegetables, chicken, or fish.

60 minutes from start to finish

This dish can be made up to 3 days in advance, stored well wrapped in the refrigerator, then served hot or cold. To reheat, transfer to a heavy saucepan and warm slowly over medium-low heat.

4 sweet plums, such as black friars or Santa Rosa

½ tablespoon unsalted butter or canola oil

1 large white or yellow onion, chopped

1 large red pepper, cored, seeded, and diced

1 large yellow pepper, cored, seeded, and diced

2 garlic cloves, crushed and minced

2 whole cloves

2 teaspoons ground cumin

1 teaspoon crumbled dried oregano

Pinch cayenne pepper

½ cup minced fresh cilantro

2 teaspoons fresh lemon juice

1 teaspoon light honey

2 cups cooked black beans, well drained (rinsed if canned)

Salt to taste

3 cups cooked white rice (optional)

ring a large pot of water to a boil. Add the plums and boil for 1 minute to loosen the skin. Remove the plums with a slotted spoon and set them aside to cool.

🦐 Melt the butter or heat the oil in a large skillet. Add the onion, red and yellow peppers, garlic, cloves, cumin, oregano, cayenne pepper, and cilantro. Sauté over medium heat, stirring often, until the onion is soft and translucent, about 7 minutes.

🍃 Peel the plums, remove the pits, and coarsely chop the pulp.

🦐 Stir the lemon juice, honey, and plum pulp into the onion mixture. Add the beans, stir, and cover. Turn the heat down to low and continue to cook until the peppers are soft, stirring often to prevent sticking, about 30 minutes. Season with salt and serve warm, over rice if desired, at room temperature or well chilled.

[PER SERVING: CAL. 211.4 / FAT 2.5 G / PROTEIN 8 G / CARB. 38.6 G / CHOL. 0 / SODIUM 5.6 MG*] *VALUE GIVEN IS BEFORE SALTING. % RDA: 30.7 VIT A; 183.8 VIT. C.

SERVING SUGGESTIONS
Serve Spicy Black Beans with Fresh Plums chilled as a salad or as a side dish with Poached Chicken Breasts or Artichokes with Artichoke Stuffing (page 172) or Poached Fish (page 190).

Sweet Corncakes with Mixed Pestos or Crab Filling

Makes 4 to 8 cakes

There's no heavy coating or deep frying to defeat the delicate taste of corn in this strictly seasonal supper dish.

1 hour from start to finish

 You can make the pesto or the crabmeat filling up to 3 days in advance, keeping each refrigerated in a tightly covered container. You can make the corncakes the day before, wrap them in foil, and serve cold or reheat—still in the foil—in a 300° F. oven for 15 to 20 minutes.

3 ears fresh corn

2 large eggs

1½ tablespoons all-purpose flour

Pinch sugar

Pinch ground cumin (omit if making crabcakes)

Pinch salt

1 recipe Cilantro Pesto (see page 161) or 1 recipe Broccoli Pesto (see page 160)

Garnishes (optional)

Sour cream

Yogurt cheese (see box, page 133)

Salsa

1 recipe Crab Filling with garnishes (recipes follow; optional)

Bring a large pot of water to a rolling boil over high heat and plunge the corn into it. Cover, and when the water returns to a boil, turn off the heat. Let the corn sit for 5 minutes.

Using tongs, lift out the corn and rinse with cold water to cool. Scrape the kernels off the cob, and put them into the work bowl of a food processor. Add the eggs and flour, and process in short pulses until the mixture is still coarse in texture but even in color and well combined. Stir in the sugar, cumin if making plain corncakes, and salt.

Rub a little olive oil over the surface of a heavy nonstick pan or griddle, and heat until a bit of batter dropped on the surface bubbles in the center and browns on the bottom.

If making plain corncakes, pour 3 tablespoons of batter into the pan or onto the griddle. When bubbles form on the surface and the bottom has browned, about 3 to 4 minutes, flip it over (using a nonmetallic spatula) to brown the other side, about 3 to 4 minutes more. Transfer to a plate and cover with foil to keep warm, and repeat until you've used up all the batter. Serve each corncake spread with one of the pestos and/or garnished with sour cream, yogurt cheese and salsa, if you'd like.

If making crabcakes, pour 3 tablespoons of batter into the pan or onto the griddle, and when bubbles form on the side and the bottom is lightly browned, about 4 minutes, place a generous spoonful of Crab Filling in the center.

Cover the filling with another 3 tablespoons of corn batter. Using a nonmetallic spatula, carefully flip the corncake to cook the other side until brown, about another 4 minutes. Transfer the corncake to a plate and cover with foil to keep warm. Serve the crabcakes garnished with sour cream, yogurt cheese, alfalfa sprouts, cherry tomatoes, and/or slivers of ripe avocado.

Crab Filling (optional)

Makes about ⅔ cup

1 tablespoon homemade mayonnaise (see
    below) or your favorite commercial brand
1 tablespoon minced scallions, white part only
1 teaspoon capers, rinsed and drained
1 tablespoon minced fresh chives
½ pound lump crabmeat, picked over to
    remove shells

Garnishes (optional)

Sour cream
Yogurt cheese (see box, page 133)
Alfalfa sprouts
Cherry tomatoes
Ripe avocado

🐚 In a bowl, combine the mayonnaise, scallion, capers, chives, and crabmeat. Stir well
with a fork to blend the ingredients evenly.
Refrigerate until ready to use.

[PER SERVING FOR SWEET CORNCAKES WITH MIXED PESTOS: CAL.
114.3 / FAT 3.4 G / PROTEIN 4.7 G / CARB. 15.9 G / CHOL. 137 MG /
SODIUM 177.6 MG*] *VALUE GIVEN IS BEFORE SALTING.

[PER SERVING FOR SWEET CORNCAKES WITH CRAB FILLING: CAL.
81.8 / FAT 3.7 G / PROTEIN 11.7 G / CARB. 0.2 G / CHOL. 81.1 MG /
SODIUM 272 MG*] *VALUE IS GIVEN BEFORE SALTING.

RAW EGG ADVISORY

As much as I love this mayonnaise, and would
resist writing anything that might discourage
you from making it, I have to mention that
it's risky to eat foods that contain raw eggs.
Eggs can carry salmonella bacteria, which
cause a particularly unpleasant, potentially
lethal, kind of food poisoning. Most health au-
thorities recommend avoiding uncooked eggs
altogether. But I take my chances now and
then, minimizing the risk as much as possible
by choosing very fresh eggs without cracks or
fissures.

Mayonnaise

Makes about ⅓ cup

Defenders of fresh mayonnaise must
be prepared to answer the following
objections, that (a) it's too complicated, and (b) it's too fattening.

So . . . (a) it's easy, saving time for
you in the end by stretching plain and
simple dishes into something much,
much more.

And (b) it's not fattening *if* you use
it sparingly on light foods such as
salad greens, Poached Fish (see page
190), Sweet Corncakes with Mixed
Pestos or Crab Filling (see page 158),
or steamed or Grilled Assorted Vegetables (see page 143).

10 minutes from start to finish

Refrigerated in a covered container, fresh mayonnaise will keep for up to a week.

2 large egg yolks
1 tablespoon fresh lemon juice
1 teaspoon Dijon mustard
½ teaspoon minced fresh garlic
Few sprigs fresh Italian parsley
⅓ cup extra virgin olive oil
Pinch cayenne pepper
Salt to taste

*I*n a small bowl, blend together the egg yolks, lemon juice, mustard, garlic, and parsley with an electric mixer until well combined, or you can use a food processor.

🌿 Keeping the mixer running smoothly, add the oil in a slow, steady stream. The mixture should become thick and glossy.

🌿 Season with cayenne pepper and salt.

[PER SERVING: CAL. 128.7 / FAT 13.2 G / PROTEIN 1 G / CARB. 0.4 G / CHOL. 90.7 MG / SODIUM 12.7 MG*] *VALUE GIVEN IS BEFORE SALTING.

HOW TO MAKE PESTO ICE CUBES
❶ ❷ ❸

❶ Spoon 2 tablespoons of pesto into each compartment of an ice-cube tray.

❷ Freeze until solid.

❸ Add, still frozen, to soups, sauces, or very hot pasta or risotto, stirring until it melts completely, and disperses throughout the dish.

Broccoli Pesto

Makes 1 cup

You may find that even dedicated broccoli detractors will enjoy the green when you serve it this way.

30 minutes from start to finish

You can make this pesto up to 4 days in advance, keeping it refrigerated in a tightly covered container. You can keep it frozen for up to 3 months.

1 cup broccoli florets
¼ cup grated imported Parmesan cheese
¼ cup grated sharp cheddar cheese
Tiny pinch mace

*S*team the broccoli (see page 148 for directions). Refrigerate to cool, about 15 minutes.

🌿 In a food processor or blender, make a dense paste by blending the broccoli, Parmesan, and cheddar. Add the mace and process again to distribute it throughout the pesto.

[PER SERVING: CAL. 32.2 / FAT 1 G / PROTEIN 4.2 G / CARB. 0.9 G / CHOL. 2.7 MG / SODIUM 85.3 MG]

SERVING SUGGESTIONS
Serve Broccoli Pesto with Sweet Corncakes with Mixed Pestos or Crab Filling (page 158), Grilled Assorted Vegetables (page 143), or Barbecued or Broiled Turkey Burgers with All the Fixin's (page 184).

Cilantro Pesto

Makes about ⅔ cup

For cilantro lovers only, a fusillade of flavor.

30 minutes from start to finish

You can make this pesto up to 4 days in advance, keeping it refrigerated in a tightly covered container. You can keep it frozen for up to 3 months.

1 cup minced fresh cilantro
¼ cup grated imported Parmesan cheese
½ garlic clove, grated
½ cup nonfat or part-skim ricotta cheese
1 teaspoon fresh lemon juice
½ jalapeño pepper, roasted, peeled, and seeded
   (follow instruction for roasting bell peppers,
   see box, page 88; optional)

ombine all of the ingredients in the bowl of a food processor or blender. Process to make a smooth, dense paste.

SERVING SUGGESTIONS
Serve Cilantro Pesto with Sweet Corncakes with Mixed Pestos or Crab Filling (page 158), Grilled Assorted Vegetables (page 143), or Barbecued or Broiled Turkey Burgers with All the Fixin's (page 184).

PESTO CUBES
When they were painting thumbs green, I must have had mine in my mouth. I was the one who failed third-grade science because I couldn't get a potato to sprout. There are advantages to being unable to sustain plant life. I've never had to weed my garden because I know better than to plant one to begin with. But there are drawbacks, too, primarily the fact that I have to buy fresh herbs, often paying extortionate prices for things my gifted friends can grow on their windowsills. Consequently, I try to get as much use as possible out of the herbs I buy.

Freezing pesto in ice-cube trays is one of my favorite ways to extend the shelf life of fresh herbs. This way, you can use the fresh basil you bought in late August to season the minestrone you make around New Year's. You can use 1 or 2 cubes at a time, saving the rest for later.

Mushrooms and Bean Curd (and Scallops) in Thai Peanut-Coconut Curry Sauce

Serves 4 to 6

Seeking more spice in life? Look no further.

40 minutes from start to finish

 You can make the broth well in advance (see page 44 or 46 for broth storage), or use canned. You can make the peanut sauce (all of the steps are done in the food processor) up to 5 days in advance, keeping it refrigerated in a covered container.

½ cup vegetable or chicken broth, either homemade (see page 44 or 46) or canned

2 shallots, sliced

4 garlic cloves, minced

1 cup mixed fresh mushrooms (such as shiitake, portobello, and oyster) washed

1½ cups broccoli florets

1 tablespoon grated fresh ginger

¼ cup minced fresh cilantro

¼ cup minced fresh basil

2 tablespoons peanut butter

½ tablespoon soy sauce

¼ cup coconut milk (available where Thai and Cuban foods are sold; also see pages 235–36)

1 tablespoon cider vinegar

1 jalapeño pepper, roasted, peeled, and seeded (follow instructions for roasting bell pepper, see box, page 88)

1 red pepper, roasted, peeled, and seeded (follow instructions for roasting bell pepper, see box, page 88)

1 tablespoon arrowroot or cornstarch

14 ounces extra-firm tofu cut into ½-inch cubes, or 1 pound bay scallops, rinsed

3 cups cooked white, basmati, or brown rice

2 tablespoons minced scallions, white part only

our ¼ cup of the broth into a large, wide skillet and bring to a simmer over medium-high heat.

🦐 Add the shallots and 2 of the garlic cloves, turn the heat down to medium-low, and simmer, stirring often, until the vegetables soften, about 7 minutes. Add the mushrooms and continue cooking, stirring briskly, until they color and soften, about 4 minutes. Add more broth 1 or 2 tablespoons at a time to keep the ingredients from sticking. Turn off the heat.

🍃 Meanwhile, steam the broccoli (see page 148).

🦐 In a food processor or blender, combine the rest of the garlic, the ginger, cilantro, basil, peanut butter, soy sauce, coconut milk, vinegar, and peppers. Process until smooth.

🍃 Transfer the mixture to the skillet with the mushrooms, and stir well. In a small bowl, mix together the arrowroot or cornstarch and the remaining broth and add it to the skillet. Bring to a simmer over medium-high heat, stirring constantly until the mixture thickens. Add the tofu, if using, cover, and lower the heat to medium-low.

🦐 If you're using scallops, add them to the skillet and stir until they color and cook through, about 3 to 4 minutes. Add the broccoli and toss well to coat with the sauce.

🍃 Serve immediately over rice and garnished with minced scallions.

[PER SERVING FOR MUSHROOMS AND BEAN CURD IN THAI PEANUT-COCONUT CURRY SAUCE: CAL. 433.7 / FAT 15.7 G / PROTEIN 23 G / CARB. 47.7 G / CHOL. TR. / SODIUM 258.8 MG] % RDA: 75.6 VIT. C; 79.4 IRON; 28 CALCIUM.

[PER SERVING FOR MUSHROOMS AND BEAN CURD (AND SCALLOPS) IN THAI PEANUT-COCONUT CURRY SAUCE: CAL. 367.2 / FAT 7.5 G / PROTEIN 27.4 G / CARB. 45.4 G / CHOL. 37.8 MG / SODIUM 425.1 MG] % RDA: 24.9 VIT. A; 75.2 VIT. C.

Savory Carrot Pie

Serves 4

This filling is so sweet, your guests may think you've goofed and served dessert for dinner. But the savory crust and the Parmesan come through to correct that impression. It's also phenomenally nutritious (see values below).

3 hours from start to finish, including the time it takes for the dough to rise and bake

You can make the dough up to 4 days in advance, keeping it refrigerated wrapped in wax paper. You can make the filling up to 2 days in advance, keeping it refrigerated in a tightly covered container. You can make the whole pie and keep refrigerated, tightly wrapped, for up to 3 days, or frozen for up to 3 months. To defrost and reheat, wrap in foil and place in a 325°F. oven for 25 to 35 minutes until warmed through.

1 recipe Dough for Savory Pie (see page 165)
¾ pound (6 to 7 medium) carrots, peeled and sliced
2 bay leaves
2 teaspoons grated fresh ginger
1 cup fresh orange juice
2 cups water (or to cover)

½ teaspoon ground cinnamon
Pinch ground nutmeg
Pinch dry marjoram, crumbled
1 large egg, lightly beaten
1 cup part-skim ricotta cheese
½ cup grated imported Parmesan cheese

repare the Dough for Savory Pie. Heat the oven to 400°F. In a large saucepan, combine the carrots, bay leaves, ginger, orange juice, and water to cover. Bring to a boil over medium-high heat, cover, turn the heat down to medium, and simmer until the carrots are mushy, about 20 minutes. Alternatively, place the same ingredients in a deep microwaveable bowl, cover, and microwave at full power until the carrots are mushy, 10 to 15 minutes, depending on the strength of your oven.

Pick out the bay leaves. Using a slotted spoon, transfer the carrots to the work bowl of your food proccessor. Puree in pulses so it doesn't become watery. Add the cinnamon, nutmeg, and marjoram and proccess briefly to blend. Transfer to a large mixing bowl, and stir in the egg, ricotta cheese, and Parmesan cheese until thoroughly combined.

Roll out the dough on a 12-inch square piece of parchment paper into a round 10 inches in diameter. Pile the filling in the center and spread it out leaving a 2-inch margin all around. Bring the dough up around the sides as if you were going to encase the filling, but leaving a "window" 6 inches in diameter at the top. Crimp the dough around the sides to hold it in place. Transfer to a baking sheet or preheated baking stone, and bake until the crust is deep golden, and the filling is set, about 40 minutes. If the crust browns before the filling has set, cover with foil, lower the heat to 300°F. and bake about 10 minutes more.

[PER SERVING: CAL. 388 / FAT 6.1 G / PROTEIN 24 G / CARB. 57.5 G / CHOL. 145 MG / SODIUM 868 MG] % RDA: 256 VIT. A; 64 VIT. C; 18 IRON; 52 CALCIUM.

SERVING SUGGESTIONS
Serve Savory Carrot Pie with Wheat Berry Soup (page 53), Tangy Spinach-Yogurt Soup (page 48), or Grilled Assorted Vegetables (page 143), and Fresh Fruit Compote (page 230).

Savory Mushroom Pie

Serves 4

This is one of the most time-efficient dishes I know. The filling doesn't take long to make, and it's delicious for days afterward. You might want to double the pie recipe and freeze one for later, since it reheats to perfection in a microwave or conventional oven.

3 hours from start to finish, including the time it takes for the dough to rise and bake

 You can make the dough up to 4 days in advance, keeping it refrigerated, tightly wrapped in wax paper. You can make the filling up to 2 days in advance, keeping it refrigerated in a tightly covered container. You can make

the whole pie and keep refrigerated, tightly wrapped, for up to 3 days, or frozen for up to 3 months. To defrost and reheat, wrap in foil and place in a 325°F. oven for 25 to 35 minutes.

1 recipe Dough for Savory Pie (see page 165)
2 teaspoons canola oil
1 small onion, sliced
4 scallions, white part only, sliced
1 leek, white part only, cleaned and sliced
1 teaspoon grated fresh ginger
1 tablespoon white wine vinegar
2 cups cleaned and sliced firm mushrooms, such as button, cremini, or portobello
½ pound tofu
½ cup sour cream, low-fat or nonfat if you'd like

*P*repare the Dough for Savory Pie. Heat the oven to 400°F. Heat the oil in a skillet over medium-high heat. Add the onion, scallion, leek, and ginger, and sauté over medium-heat until the vegetables are limp, about 10 minutes. Add the vinegar and stir until it evaporates, about 3 minutes.

Add the mushrooms and sauté until they start to give up liquid, about 4 minutes. Remove from the heat.

In a food processor or blender, combine the tofu and sour cream and process until smooth. Turn into a large mixing bowl then transfer the mushroom mixture into the bowl using a slotted spoon and stir to blend.

Roll out the dough on a 12-inch square piece of parchment paper into a round 10 inches in diameter. Pile the filling in the center, and spread it out leaving a 2-inch margin all around. Bring the dough up around the sides as if you were going to encase the filling, but leaving a 6-inch diameter "window" at the top. Crimp the dough around the sides to hold it in place. Transfer to a baking sheet or preheated baking stone, and bake until the crust is deep golden and the filling is set, about 40 minutes. If the crust browns before the filling has set, cover with foil, lower the heat to 300° F., and bake about 10 minutes more.

[PER SERVING (USING NONFAT SOUR CREAM): CAL. 358 / FAT 8.2 G / PROTEIN 21 G / CARB. 49 G / CHOL. 69 MG / SODIUM 615 MG] % RDA: 48 IRON; 21 CALCIUM.

SERVING SUGGESTIONS
Serve Savory Mushroom Pie with Artichoke Soup (page 47) or Baked Stuffed Turnips (page 93).

Dough for Savory Pie

Makes enough dough for 1 pie (4 servings)
This dough makes a crust that's not quite like pizza, not quite like pastry. It's firmer than the former, more pliant than the latter, and as good as either one.

1 hour 40 minutes, including time for the dough to rise and bake
You can keep the dough refrigerated wrapped tightly in plastic wrap, for up to 3 days. Bring to room temperature before using, also allowing it to rise.

1 teaspoon dry active yeast
⅓ cup tepid water
½ teaspoon dry malt or sugar
¾ cup all-purpose flour
¾ cup whole wheat pastry flour
1 teaspoon salt
1 large egg, lightly beaten
3 tablespoons nonfat sour cream

*i*n a small mixing bowl, stir together the yeast and water. Let sit until frothy, about 10 minutes.

In a large bowl, combine the dry malt or sugar, all-purpose and pastry flours, and salt. Make a well in the center, and add the egg, sour cream, and yeast mixture. Stir to make a soft dough. Turn out onto a lightly floured surface and knead briefly until smooth.

Clean the larger mixing bowl, and return the dough to it. Cover with plastic wrap or a light towel and place in a warm spot until doubled, about 45 minutes. Use the dough for Savory Carrot Pie (see page 163) or Savory Mushroom Pie (see page 164).

[PER SERVING: CAL. 208 / FAT 5 G / PROTEIN 9 G / CARB. 385 G / CHOL. 68.5 MG / SODIUM 565.2 MG]

poultry

· · · · · ·

Braised Chicken Breasts Tapenade ✺ Tea Steamed Chicken or Bean Curd with Vegetables ✍ Poached Chicken Breasts or Artichokes with Artichoke Stuffing ✺ Chicken and Mushrooms (A Classic Comfort Dish) ✺ Chicken Breasts (or Pressed Tofu) with Sweet Mustard Glaze ✍ Tandoori Spice Marinade for Chicken (or Pressed Tofu) ✺ Chicken Stewed with Fennel, Tomatoes, and Saffron ✍ Chicken and Lentil Stew ✺ Chicken Legs Filled with Sweet Shredded Cabbage ✍ Chicken Roasted with Garlic ✺ Grilled Fajita Salad (with Turkey) ✍ Barbecued or Broiled Turkey Burgers with All the Fixin's ✺ Not-So-Sloppy Joes ✍ Almost Vegetarian Holiday Dinner ✺ Rice Stuffing with Pine Nuts and Dried Cherries ✍ Roast Turkey

Poultry is full of potential. It can turn stewed vegetables, simple pasta dishes, and tossed salads into something more nourishing and substantial. It can be made to mimic other meats, ground to act like hamburger (see Barbecued or Broiled Turkey Burgers with All the Fixin's, page 184) or stewed like beef (see Chicken Stewed with Fennel, Tomatoes, and Saffron, page 178). But then poultry is splendid as poultry, too, roasted with garlic (see page 181), stuffed with shredded cabbage and dried cherries (see page 180), and poached with artichokes and herbs (see page 172).

Buying Poultry

- Read the expiration date on the label. Poultry goes bad quickly, so buy the pack with the date that's furthest ahead.
- Look at the color. Don't buy it if the meat is yellowing or the skin is sallow.
- Sniff through the packing. If a sour aroma permeates the plastic wrap, it's bad.
- Organically fed free-range poultry costs more than poultry raised in coops, but having had more exercise and more wholesome food, it may taste better, too. If you can't find free-range poultry where you shop, ask the meat-counter manager to order it for you.

How Poultry Can Resolve One of the Great Dilemmas of Our Day . . .

What if you're planning to serve poultry, then find out that some of your guests don't eat meat of any kind? The simplest solution is to roast a chicken or turkey and serve it with several substantial side dishes, for example Sweet Potato Pancakes (see page 102), Gingered Leek and Fennel Flans (see page 90), and Baked Stuffed Turnips (see page 93). Roasting involves little effort and attention, and you can make the side dishes in advance. When it's time to serve, carve the roast chicken or turkey and pile the meat on a separate platter with the side dishes set out around it so that your guests can help themselves to whatever they'd like.

What About the Skin?

- *On* for roasting, grilling, or broiling. The skin keeps the meat moist without adding fat in the process.
- *Off* for simmering, stewing, and poaching. Fat from the skin can drip into the cooking liquid, which, if served as a sauce, will add fat to each portion.
- *Off* for eating. Without the skin, a chicken breast has less than half the fat it has with the skin.

Four Critical Safety Tips

Poultry is peculiarly hospitable to the kind of bacteria that can turn a pleasant meal into a brutal (possibly lethal) bout with food poisoning.

Here are four critical safety tips to avoid contamination:

1. Don't defrost poultry at room temperature. Transfer frozen poultry from the freezer to the refrigerator, placing it in a large pan so it won't drip.

2. Always mop up any liquid that seeps from raw poultry and wash thoroughly the area the raw poultry touched, as well as all utensils you've used to prepare the poultry.

3. Don't let cooked poultry cool at room temperature. If you're not serving it right away, wrap it and refrigerate it as soon as it's done.

4. Always store stuffing and poultry separately. Remove all of the stuffing from a bird before storing. Never stuff a bird until just before you cook it.

Some additional precautions you may wish to take are the following:

- Take the meat out of the store package as soon as you get it home and rewrap it.
- If it's a whole chicken or turkey, take out the giblets and wrap them separately in plastic or foil. Freeze them or throw them out if you're not planning to use them within a day or two.
- Rinse the poultry thoroughly, pat dry, and wrap loosely in plastic or foil.
- Refrigerate it if you'll be using it within 3 days.
- For longer storage, wash the poultry, dry it, seal in airtight wrapping, and freeze. A "ziplock" bag is ideal for this purpose.

Braised Chicken Breasts Tapenade

Serves 3 to 4

Tapenade is an olive and anchovy puree that is served as a spread and condiment in the south of France. It's very strong on its own, but balanced with sweet ripe tomatoes, it's a delicious, summery seasoning for chicken.

20 minutes to prepare

30 minutes to cook

 You can make the tapenade up to a week in advance, keeping it refrigerated in a tightly covered container. The cooked chicken is also very good cold and will keep for 2 days, well wrapped, in the refrigerator.

6 sun-dried tomatoes (dry packed), finely minced

1 anchovy fillet, rinsed, patted dry, and minced

1 teaspoon capers, minced

8 Niçoise-style black olives, pitted

1 teaspoon extra virgin olive oil

1 tablespoon fresh lemon juice

2 whole chicken breasts, split

3 large ripe tomatoes, peeled, seeded, and diced, or one 16-ounce box or can tomatoes, seeded and diced

¼ cup torn fresh basil leaves

Anchovies are inconspicuous but influential. Generally, they're used sparingly, only as a seasoning. The heavy briny flavor has the effect of steadying lighter flavors so you can taste them. To sample how this works, try Perfect Tomato Sauce (see page 112).

Used not so sparingly, they're a rich, pungent salty treat that can turn a simple dish into an addictive substance. To sample this effect, try Pissaladière-Inspired Potato Tarts (see page 97).

I prefer salt-packed anchovies, because they're more versatile, without the flavoring they get when they're packed in oil. Yet oil-packed anchovies are easier to find, and they work very well. Whichever you use, be sure to rinse them thoroughly in several changes of water, and pat them dry before adding them to your dish.

 eat the oven to 425°F.

🍃 In a compact food processor, or a blender fitted with a small container, combine the sun-dried tomatoes, anchovy, capers, olives, olive oil, and lemon juice. Process the mixture in short spurts until a rough paste forms.

🍃 Using your fingers, spread the paste on the chicken, lifting the skin to rub it underneath rather than on top.

🍃 Place the tomatoes and basil in a baking pan. Add the chicken, and spoon some of the tomato mixture on top. Cover the pan with foil and place it in the oven.

🍃 The chicken is done when clear juices run from the breasts when pierced with a knife, about 30 minutes.

[PER SERVING: CAL. 231.8 / FAT 6.3 G / PROTEIN 36.8 G / CARB. 5.2 G / CHOL. 92.1 MG / SODIUM 446.7 MG] % RDA: 35 VIT. C.

Tea Steamed Chicken or Bean Curd with Vegetables

Serves 2

Smoky dark tea, a common seasoning in some parts of China, balances the sweeter flavors of ginger and fruit juice in this versatile dish. The longer you marinate the chicken or tofu and vegetables, the sharper and more satisfying the contrast.

1 hour to overnight to marinate
1 hour to cook

 You can prepare the marinade up to 3 days in advance, keeping it tightly covered and refrigerated. You can marinate the chicken or tofu overnight, keeping it covered and refrigerated.

For the Marinade
1 tablespoon black bean sauce (available in Asian specialty shops and by mail order; see pages 235–36)
1 teaspoon soy sauce, low-sodium if desired
2 tablespoons fresh orange or pineapple juice
2 cloves garlic, grated
2 tablespoons grated fresh ginger
2 tablespoons minced fresh cilantro
1 scallion, white part and ½ inch of the green, minced

For the Chicken or Bean Curd and Vegetables
1 boneless skinless chicken breast (about ¾ pound), split, or ¾ pound firm tofu, cubed
1 pound mixed vegetables, such as snow peas, asparagus, broccoli, spinach, shiitake or oyster mushrooms, cut into bite-sized pieces if necessary

For the Tea Broth

1½ tablespoons loose dark smoky tea, such as
   Lapsang Souchong (see Note)

2 scallions, white part and 1 inch of the green,
   sliced

1 tablespoon grated fresh ginger

2 garlic cloves, crushed

2 teaspoons Chinese five spice powder
   (available in Asian specialty shops or by mail
   order; see pages 235–36)

1 tablespoon cornstarch or arrowroot

3 cups cooked rice

*i*n a mixing bowl, combine all of the ingredients for the marinade. Transfer to a deep glass or earthenware baking dish. Add the chicken or tofu and vegetables, and turn to coat. Cover with plastic wrap and refrigerate for at least 1 hour, and up to 12 hours, turning occasionally.

To make the broth combine the tea, scallions, ginger, garlic, and five spice powder in a deep saucepan or a wok. Place a rack in the pan, and add water up to an inch below the rack. If the tines of the rack are spaced widely apart, place tin foil over the rack so the food doesn't fall through. Bring to a boil over medium high heat. Place the chicken or tofu on the rack, cover, lower the heat to medium, and steam until the meat is no longer pink when pierced with a knife, 30 to 40 minutes, depending on thickness; or until the tofu is thoroughly infused with flavor, about 25 to 30 minutes.

Transfer the meat or tofu to a plate and cover with tin foil to keep warm. Place the vegetables on the rack, cover and steam until crisp-tender, 4 to 7 minutes, depending on size. Transfer them to the plate with the chicken.

Using a fine sieve strain the broth into a small saucepan. In a small bowl, stir the cornstarch or arrowroot into three tablespoons of water, then stir this mixture into the saucepan. Heat over medium-high, stirring constantly until it thickens, about 7 minutes. Pour over chicken and vegetables and serve over rice.

Note: My favorite tea for this broth comes from The Republic of Tea, available in specialty shops and by mail order (see pages 235–36).

[PER SERVING (WITH CHICKEN): CAL. 162 / FAT 2.8 G / PROTEIN 30 G / CARB. 3.7 G / CHOL. 73 MG / SODIUM 217 MG]

[PER SERVING (WITH BEAN CURD): CAL. 160 / FAT 7.2 G / PROTEIN 14 G / CARB. 7.8 G / CHOL. 0 / SODIUM 167 MG]

Serves 6

The traditional northern Italian recipe for chicken with artichokes calls for more oil than I like to use, and I took the dust-dry results of my efforts to modify it as the collective vengeance of generations of Milanese cooks who resented what I was trying to do. I was about to give up when I saw a recipe in an Italian cooking magazine for boneless chicken breasts stuffed with vegetables, recommending they be poached. I gave it one more shot. Borrowing this idea, I filled the breasts with plump baby artichokes that I had steamed, then sautéed. To my delight, the dish was even better than the one I'd set out to duplicate.

1 hour to prepare

20 minutes to cook

You can make the filling up to 3 days in advance, keeping it refrigerated in a covered container. You can make the stuffed artichokes up to 3 days ahead, too. Serve them cold, or reheat them by transferring to a baking dish. Add 2 tablespoons of water, cover with foil, and place in a 300° F. oven until warmed through, about 20 minutes.

1 lemon

5 baby artichokes, stems trimmed and tough outer leaves removed, or one 10-ounce box fresh-frozen artichoke hearts

2 tablespoons extra virgin olive oil

3 garlic cloves, minced

2 celery stalks, diced (roughly 1 cup)

¼ cup minced fresh parsley

1 tablespoon crumbled dried oregano

¼ cup dry white wine

1¼ cups chicken or vegetable broth, either homemade (see page 46 or 44) or canned

3 large whole chicken breasts, boned, skinned, and split or 4 large artichokes, stems trimmmed, tough outer leaves removed, and pointed tips cut off

*h*eat the oven to 425° F. Squeeze the juice from the lemon into a large glass or earthenware bowl. Grate half the zest into a separate bowl, and discard the rest. Place the baby artichokes in the bowl with the lemon juice, and add cold water to cover.

Heat the olive oil in a large skillet. Sauté the garlic, celery, parsley, oregano, and lemon zest over medium heat until the garlic and celery are very tender, about 10 minutes. Turn off the heat.

🍃 Transfer half a cup of the artichoke soaking water to a large nonreactive saucepan and bring it to a boil over medium-high heat. Meanwhile, drain the rest of the water from the artichokes, cut them into quarters, and scrape out the fuzzy choke. Place them in the boiling water, turn the heat down to medium-low, cover the saucepan, and let the artichokes steam until they're soft, about 7 minutes.

🍃 Transfer the artichokes to the skillet with the celery mixture and cook over medium heat, adding equal amounts of wine and chicken or vegetable broth to prevent sticking, about 2 tablespoons each at a time. Cover, turn the heat down to low, and keep cooking until the artichokes are mushy, about 20 minutes. Be sure to check often, adding just enough wine and broth as necessary to keep them from sticking to the pan. (If you use up the wine, continue to add broth, if necessary.) When the artichokes have just about cooked down into a puree, turn off the heat. Stop here if you are going to use the filling to stuff whole artichokes after the chicken breasts.

🍃 Place 3 chicken breast halves, if using, on a cutting board. Put ⅓ of the artichoke filling onto the center of each, and spread it with the back of a spoon, leaving a ¼-inch border around the edges. Cover each with the remaining breast halves, sandwiching the filling.

🍃 Place a baking rack inside a deep ovenproof dish. Pour in the remaining broth. Carefully place the chicken breasts on the rack, cover the pan with foil, and bake for about 20 minutes. The chicken is done when the meat is tender all the way through, and clear liquid, rather than pink, runs from it when you pierce the center with a knife. The top and bottom pieces should fuse, encasing the filling.

🍃 To serve, cut the breasts in half widthwise and give each person half. Spoon some of the poaching liquid on top.

HOW TO COOK AN ARTICHOKE
❶ ❷ ❸

Stovetop

❶ Lay the artichoke on its side on a flat surface. Using a heavy knife, cut off the top inch.

❷ Cut away the bottom stem so the artichoke can stand upright.

❸ Stand the artichokes in a nonreactive pan, squirt with fresh lemon juice, and add 3 inches of water. Cover, bring to a boil, then lower the heat and simmer until the artichokes are tender, about 20 minutes, checking the water level as it evaporates to avoid burning.

Microwave

❶ Stand the artichokes in a microwaveable baking dish, squirt them with lemon juice, and add 3 inches of water.

❷ Cover tightly with plastic wrap and microwave on high for 4 minutes.

❸ Turn the dish around halfway, and microwave on high again, for another 4 minutes. If they are not yet tender, turn the dish halfway again and repeat at 1-minute intervals until you can pierce the bottoms easily with a paring knife.

For Stuffed Artichokes

Serves 4

🍃 Cook the whole artichokes (see box, page 173).

🍂 When the artichokes are cool enough to handle, push back the inner leaves so that you can see the fuzzy "choke" at the inside base. Using a paring knife, scrape away as much of it as possible.

🍃 Fill the artichokes evenly with the stuffing. Pour the remaining broth into a baking pan, add the artichokes upright, and cover with foil.

🍂 Bake for 20 minutes, and serve immediately. Or refrigerate and serve chilled.

[PER SERVING FOR POACHED CHICKEN BREASTS WITH ARTICHOKE STUFFING: CAL. 372.7 / FAT 9.6 G / PROTEIN 59.1 G / CARB. 8.2 G / CHOL. 146 MG / SODIUM 247.7 MG*] *VALUE GIVEN IS BEFORE SALTING.

[PER SERVING FOR ARTICHOKES WITH ARTICHOKE STUFFING: CAL. 124.1 / FAT 4.4 G / PROTEIN 3.3 G / CARB. 15.7 G / CHOL. 0 / SODIUM 174.4 MG*] *VALUE GIVEN IS BEFORE SALTING. % RDA: 22.7 VIT. C.

SERVING SUGGESTIONS

Serve Poached Chicken Breasts with Artichoke Stuffing with Gingered Leek and Fennel Flans (page 90), Carrot-Ginger Risotto (page 129), or Mushroom Barley (page 102). Serve Artichokes with Artichoke Stuffing with Vegetable Ragu (page 153) or Lemony Risotto (page 130).

Chicken and Mushrooms (A Classic Comfort Dish)

Serves 4

Like trends in fashion, food fads have no grace periods, and to serve what's "out" is to be considered tacky and therefore to be avoided, even if it means living with a shelf load of cajun hot sauce or whatever until it's back "in" again.

Not that everything comes back. For instance I'm sure we'll never witness another craze for cooking with canned cream of mushroom soup, the extra-virgin olive oil of its day. In a way it's a shame, because some of the things you could make with it were really pretty good.

This updated classic is as comforting as the cream of mushroom casseroles I remember from childhood, and much more nourishing, since it's made without the hydrolized oil, stabilizers, and such that many condensed soups contain. It's a quick, convenient dish that's equally good over rice and pasta.

50 minutes from start to finish

 You can make this dish up to 3 days in advance. Keep refrigerated and reheat over medium-low heat, stirring often.

2 teaspoons canola oil or unsalted butter

2 yellow onions, thinly sliced

2 scallions, white part only, sliced

2 tablespoons white wine or 1 tablespoon white wine vinegar

1 pound boneless skinless chicken breast, thinly
   sliced
8 ounces cleaned and sliced firm mushrooms,
   such as cremini, white button, or
   portobello
2 teaspoons crumbled dried dill
2 teaspoons crumbled dried oregano
 Pinch crushed red pepper (optional)
1 cup Light Mushroom Broth or chicken broth
   (see page 47 or 46), divided
1 tablespoon arrowroot or cornstarch
½ cup evaporated skim milk
¼ cup sour cream, low-fat or nonfat if desired
2 tablespoons grated imported Parmesan
   cheese

*i*n a large skillet, heat the canola oil over medium-high heat. When hot, add the onion and scallions, turn down the heat to medium, and sauté until soft and limp, about 8 minutes. Add the wine or vinegar, and stir until it evaporates, about 3 minutes.

🌿 Toss in the chicken, and stirring quickly brown it on all sides, about 3 to 4 minutes. Transfer the chicken to a plate, cover loosely with foil and set aside.

🍃 Add the mushrooms, dill, oregano, and pepper if used, to the skillet and stir until the mushrooms start to give up liquid, about 6 minutes. Add half of the broth and bring to a simmer. Meanwhile, in a small bowl whisk the arrowroot or cornstarch into the remaining ½ cup broth. Stir into the skillet along with the evaporated skim milk. Stir constantly until the sauce thickens and reduces by about a quarter, about 6 minutes. Add the chicken and stir until cooked through, about

3 to 4 more minutes. Turn off the heat, stir in the sour cream and Parmesan, and serve over rice or pasta.

[PER SERVING (USING LOW-FAT SOUR CREAM): CAL. 262 / FAT 5.7 G / PROTEIN 35.5 G / CARB. 16 G / CHOL. 0 / SODIUM 167 MG]

SERVING SUGGESTIONS
Serve Chicken and Mushrooms with Artichoke Soup (page 47) or Focacce (page 138), and Banana Cake (page 224).

Chicken Breasts (or Pressed Tofu) with Sweet Mustard Glaze

Serves 3 to 4

Broiled or grilled, this glazed chicken tastes hearty and bold. You can use the glaze for Grilled Assorted Vegetables, too (see page 143).

20 minutes to prepare
10 minutes to cook

You can make the glaze up to a week in advance, keeping it refrigerated in a tightly covered container. The cooked chicken is also very good cold, and will keep for 2 days in the refrigerator.

¼ cup chicken or vegetable broth, homemade (see page 46 or 44) or canned

1 large shallot, thinly sliced

1 garlic clove, minced

1 tablespoon tomato paste

2 tablespoons honey

1 tablespoon Dijon mustard

Pinch dried tarragon or thyme

1 tablespoon fresh orange juice

2 tablespoons balsamic vinegar

Freshly ground pepper to taste

2 whole chicken breasts, split, or 1 recipe (1 pound) pressed tofu, homemade (see box, page 145) or store-bought

*h*eat the broiler, or light your grill so you'll be able to cook over very hot coals (see page 143).

🍃 In a small saucepan bring the broth to a gentle simmer over medium heat. Add the shallot and garlic, turn down the heat to medium-low, and simmer, uncovered, stirring often, until the vegetables soften, about 7 minutes.

🍃 Add the tomato paste, honey, mustard, tarragon or thyme, orange juice, vinegar, and pepper, stirring until the mixture thickens into a dense paste, about 4 minutes.

🍃 Remove the glaze from the heat and let it cool slightly, about 5 minutes.

🍃 Using a pastry brush, slather the glaze on the chicken breasts, if using, lifting the skin to brush it underneath rather than on top.

🍃 Place the chicken under the broiler skin side up or on the grill skin side down. If grilling, cover it with the grill lid or foil. Turn the breasts over after 4 to 6 minutes if broiling, and 8 minutes if grilling, and cook until clear juice runs from the breast when you pierce it with a knife, about 4 to 8 minutes more.

🍃 Cook the tofu as directed (see box, page 145). Brush the glaze on the tofu to coat it well.

[PER SERVING FOR CHICKEN BREASTS WITH SWEET MUSTARD GLAZE: CAL. 187.7 / FAT 3.4 G / PROTEIN 28.8 G / CARB. 9.4 G / CHOL. 73 MG / SODIUM 184 MG*] *VALUE GIVEN IS BEFORE SALTING.

[PER SERVING FOR PRESSED TOFU WITH SWEET MUSTARD GLAZE: CAL. 210.5 / FAT 9.2 G / PROTEIN 15.9 G / CARB. 14.4 G / CHOL. 0 / SODIUM 136.3 MG*] *VALUE GIVEN IS BEFORE SALTING. % RDA: 67.2 IRON; 23.5 CALCIUM.

Tandoori Spice Marinade for Chicken (or Pressed Tofu)

Serves 3 to 4

This mild marinade makes tender, tasty chicken, with almost no help from you. Just mix it up in the morning, add the chicken, cover, and refrigerate; then throw it on the grill or under the broiler when you get home that night.

10 minutes to prepare

3 hours to marinate

 You can marinate the chicken up to 12 hours in advance, keeping it refrigerated and well wrapped, and turning the pieces from time to time.

2 cloves garlic

One 2-inch piece fresh ginger, peeled and sliced

½ teaspoon lemon zest

Juice from ½ lime

¼ cup cilantro leaves

1 tablespoon curry powder (see Note)

1 teaspoon ground cumin

⅔ cup plain low-fat or nonfat yogurt

Pinch cayenne pepper

1 teaspoon salt

2 whole chicken breasts, split or 1 recipe (1 pound) pressed tofu, homemade (see box, page 145), or store-bought, thickly sliced

*i*n a compact food processor or a blender fitted with a small container, combine the garlic, ginger, lemon zest, lime juice, cilantro, curry powder, and cumin. Process the mixture until everything is finely minced and well combined.

Add the yogurt and process again.

Transfer the mixture to a glass bowl and stir in the cayenne and the salt. Add the chicken breasts or pressed tofu, and turn over to coat them well with the marinade.

Cover with plastic and chill at least 3 hours, turning the breasts or tofu occasionally.

Heat the broiler or light your grill so you'll be cooking over very hot coals (see page 143).

Place the chicken under the broiler skin side up or on the grill skin side down. If grilling, cover it with the grill lid or foil. Turn the breasts over after 4 to 6 minutes if broiling, and 8 minutes if grilling, and cook until clear juice runs from the breast when you pierce it with a knife, about 4 to 8 minutes more.

To cook the pressed tofu, see box, page 145.

Note: Curry powder is a blend of a number of spices, and different manufacturers use different spices in varying proportions. Taste around to find one you like best. You'll also find that Tandoori Spice works just as well as curry powder in marinades of this kind.

[PER SERVING FOR TANDOORI SPICE MARINADE FOR CHICKEN: CAL. 171.7 / FAT 2.7 G* / PROTEIN 31.5 G / CARB. 4.3 G / CHOL. 74.4 MG / SODIUM 639.2 MG**] *MADE WITH NONFAT YOGURT. **VALUE GIVEN IS BEFORE SALTING.

[PER SERVING FOR TANDOORI SPICE MARINADE FOR PRESSED TOFU: CAL. 194.6 / FAT 8.6 G / PROTEIN 18.5 G / CARB. 9.3 G / CHOL. 1.4 MG / SODIUM 591 MG*] *VALUE GIVEN IS BEFORE SALTING. % RDA: 66.1 IRON; 35.1 CALCIUM.

Chicken Stewed with Fennel, Tomatoes, and Saffron

Serves 4 to 6

If you're planning to serve this to guests, you might want to pad your entryway in case they swoon as they catch their first whiff of what's cooking at your place.

Please don't be misled by the long list of ingredients; this dish isn't difficult. You just put everything in a bowl to marinate overnight, transfer it to the stove, and let it stew.

20 minutes to prepare

Marinate 8 hours overnight

45 minutes to cook

 This is a do-ahead dish, because it must be marinated overnight. You can stew it up to 2 days in advance, then serve it cold or warm it slowly, in a covered heavy skillet, over medium-low heat, for about 20 minutes.

1½ tablespoons extra virgin olive oil

8 large fresh tomatoes (about 2 pounds), peeled, seeded, and chopped, or two 16-ounce boxes or cans imported Italian tomatoes, drained and chopped

1 cup hearty red wine, such as a Burgundy

2 large white or yellow onions, thinly sliced

2 large fennel bulbs, including the leafy fronds, coarsely chopped

4 garlic cloves, crushed and minced

½ cup minced fresh parsley

2 teaspoons fennel seed

2 bay leaves

Generous pinch powdered saffron

2 teaspoons finely grated orange zest

2 teaspoons salt

Freshly ground pepper to taste

2 cups (about 1 pound) tiny new potatoes

4 chicken legs with thighs attached, skinned

*P*ut all of the ingredients except the chicken in a large glass bowl, and mix well. Add the chicken and stir again until it's thoroughly coated with the marinade. Cover and refrigerate at least 8 hours, or overnight, stirring occasionally if possible.
※ Using a large slotted spoon, take the chicken out of the bowl and pour the marinade into a large pot. Cover and bring to a simmer. Let it simmer, covered, over medium heat, stirring occasionally, until you can pierce the potatoes with a knife and the tomatoes have cooked down into sauce, about 20 minutes.
🍃 Put the chicken in the pot, cover, and continue simmering until the meat is falling off the bone, about 45 minutes. Check often to make sure the chicken doesn't overcook.
※ Serve in big soup bowls with lots of crusty bread and a big salad on the side.

[PER SERVING: CAL. 453.6 / FAT 12.4 G / PROTEIN 32.1 G / CARB. 40.3 G / CHOL. 90 MG / SODIUM 170.2 MG*] *VALUE GIVEN IS BEFORE SALTING. % RDA: 100.9 VIT. C; 22.3 IRON.

Perhaps because they've always been cheap and plentiful, lentils have been held in contempt for much of history. The low point in their popularity may have come during the reign of Caligula, when the Emperor snatched an obelisk from Egypt and had it packed in lentils for the journey to Rome.

Chicken and Lentil Stew

Serves 4

When people talk about good home cooking, they often mean something solid and soothing, like this stewed chicken seasoned with lentils.

20 minutes to prepare

2 hours to cook

This dish tastes delicious the day after it's been made, and will keep tightly covered in the refrigerator for up to 4 days. It keeps well frozen for up to 3 months.

1 tablespoon extra virgin olive oil

2 cups chopped onion

2 cups chopped, cleaned leek (white part only)

2 cups chopped celery

2 cups chopped carrot

3 garlic cloves, crushed and minced

1 tablespoon crumbled dried oregano

1 teaspoon crumbled dried thyme

2 teaspoons ground cinnamon

2 whole cloves

1 tablespoon tomato paste

½ cup red wine

1 cup lentils, rinsed and picked over

3 cups chicken or vegetable broth, homemade (see page 46 or 44), or canned

1 cup chopped peeled, drained tomatoes, canned or fresh (see box, page 155)

One 2½ pound chicken

*h*eat the oven to 425° F.

Heat the olive oil in a deep ovenproof casserole or dutch oven over medium-high heat. Add the onion, leek, celery, carrot, garlic, oregano, thyme, cinnamon, and cloves, reduce the heat to medium, and sauté until the vegetables are soft, about 15 minutes.

Add the tomato paste and wine, and stir to blend. Stir in the lentils, broth, and tomatoes. Turn up the heat to medium-high, and bring to a simmer. Add the chicken and spoon the vegetables over it. Cover the casserole off the heat. Put the casserole in the oven and let it bake, spoon-basting (spooning the vegetables and juices over the chicken) every 15 minutes, until the meat falls easily away from the bone, about 2 hours. Cut the chicken into pieces and serve with rice.

[PER SERVING: CAL. 603 / FAT 24 G / PROTEIN 61 G / CARB. 30.2 G / CHOL. 142 MG / SODIUM 273 MG] % RDA: 50 VIT. A; 49 VIT. C; 36 IRON.

SERVING SUGGESTIONS
Serve Chicken and Lentil Stew with Eggplant Pancakes (page 82) and Chocolate Bundt Cakes (page 226).

Chicken Legs Filled with Sweet Shredded Cabbage

Serves 4

Just call this a treat: the most tender part of the chicken filled with a stuffing that's crunchy and sweet.

For a vegetarian dish, serve the stuffing on Sweet Potato Pancakes (see page 102).

40 minutes to prepare
1 hour to bake

 You can make the filling up to 3 days in advance, keeping it refrigerated in a covered container. You can also make the tomato sauce well ahead of time, and keep it frozen (see page 113).

Stuffing

1 tablespoon unsalted butter or canola oil

2 large white or yellow onions, minced

2 carrots, peeled and minced

2 celery stalks, including leaves, diced, or 1 small fennel bulb, including fronds, diced

2 cups shredded green cabbage

¼ cup pine nuts

¼ cup dried cherries or raisins

4 large chicken legs with thighs attached, skinned

1 recipe Perfect Tomato Sauce, Too (see page 113) (see Note)

1 tablespoon low-fat sour cream or yogurt cheese (see box, page 133)

or the stuffing, in a large skillet, melt the butter or heat the oil. Sauté the onions, carrots, celery or fennel, and cabbage over medium-low heat, stirring occasionally, until everything is soft and limp, about 25 minutes. Turn off the heat.

🍃 Transfer the mixture to a large mixing bowl and stir in the pine nuts and dried cherries.

🍂 Heat the oven to 425°F. Lay the pieces of chicken on a cutting board so that the meatiest parts of the thighs are facing up and the leg bones are pointing down. Cut a deep slit into the meat along the top—the ridge that joins the leg and thigh—creating a cavity.

🍃 Fill each cavity with an equal amount of stuffing.

🍂 Wrap each chicken leg tightly in aluminum foil. Place inside a baking pan and add an inch of water to the pan.

🍃 Bake for an hour, until clear liquid (rather than pink) runs from the chicken when you pierce it with a knife. About 10 minutes before the chicken is done, heat the tomato sauce gently over low heat. Just before serving, stir the sour cream or yogurt cheese into the tomato sauce. Unwrap the legs and spoon the sauce over the chicken. Serve immediately. *Note:* For a delicious cold dish, omit the sauce, and scoop the stuffing out of the legs as soon as they're baked. Wrap the legs and stuffing separately and refrigerate. When they're well chilled, either restuff the chicken legs or serve the stuffing on the side.

[PER SERVING: CAL. 354.4 / FAT 15.7 G / PROTEIN 32.1 G / CARB. 20.9 G / CHOL. 103.5 MG / SODIUM 119.8 MG*] *VALUE GIVEN IS BEFORE SALTING. % RDA: 108.1 VIT. A; 51.8 VIT. C.

Chicken Roasted with Garlic

Serves 4

Every recipe for this dish leads off with assurance that forty cloves of garlic are not too many, that roasted whole they mellow out, and that the overall effect is delicious. I wish I could think of a more original introduction, but that critical information belongs up front.

Although my opening's standard, my recipe is not. It calls for roasting the chicken under a dough of flour and yogurt. The dough bakes while it seals in the aromatic juices. In the end you have moist, sensationally seasoned meat and crisp garlicky toast to go with it. It also looks spectacular and smells like the gardens of paradise.

40 minutes to prepare

1½ hours to roast, approximately

This dish is best made just before serving. To refrigerate the leftovers, take the meat off the bones, wrap it well, and refrigerate for up to 2 days.

2 sprigs fresh rosemary

One 4-pound roasting chicken (reserve the giblets for broth if you'd like, see page 46)

30 to 40 garlic cloves, unpeeled

1 cup minced fresh Italian parsley

1 tablespoon grated lemon zest

2 tablespoons extra virgin olive oil

⅔ cup all-purpose flour

1 teaspoon baking powder

½ teaspoon salt

¼ cup low-fat or nonfat plain yogurt, approximately

eat the oven to 350°F. Put the sprigs of rosemary in the chicken cavity. Place the chicken on a rack in a roasting pan just large enough to hold it. Refrigerate.

Peel one of the garlic cloves, mince it finely, and mix it in a small bowl with the parsley and the lemon zest.

Heat the olive oil in a large skillet and sauté the parsley mixture along with the whole garlic cloves over low heat until the minced garlic begins to color, about 4 minutes. Turn off the heat.

Make the dough for the crust. Place the flour in a large mixing bowl and add the baking powder and salt. Stir well to blend. With a wooden spoon, stir in the yogurt. Knead with your hands to make a dough that's soft, but stiff enough to handle. You may have to add more flour or yogurt to get the right consistency. You can also mix the dough in a food processor; put the ingredients into the work bowl and process, adding more flour or yogurt if necessary, until the dough is firm enough to handle, but soft enough to roll.

🌿 Lightly flour a work surface and roll out the dough into an oblong large enough to drape over the chicken.

🍃 Spoon the sautéed unpeeled garlic cloves over the chicken, and put some inside the cavity. With kitchen twine, bind the legs together in front, closing the cavity. Place the dough over the chicken, and press it to seal in the garlic. Don't worry about distributing the garlic evenly. There will be enough of it to season the chicken no matter how lopsided it lands. Also, the dough will harden and shrink during the roasting, so don't be surprised to see it ride up on the chicken as it cooks.

🌿 Roast for about 1½ hours. Test it by poking a sharp knife just under one of the wings. When the juices run clear, it's done. Lift off the crust and break it into small pieces for serving. Let the chicken sit for 5 to 10 minutes before carving and serve with the garlic cloves, which can be squeezed out and mashed at the table.

[PER SERVING*: CAL. 559.4 / FAT 19.8 G / PROTEIN 63.7 G / CARB. 26.1 G / CHOL. 169 MG / SODIUM 568.1 MG**] *INCLUDES THE BAKED CRUST, BUT NOT THE CHICKEN SKIN. **VALUE GIVEN IS BEFORE SALTING. % RDA: 35 VIT. C; 31.3 IRON.

SERVING SUGGESTIONS
Serve Chicken Roasted with Garlic with Wholly Wholesome Mashed Potatoes (page 99), Red Potatoes in Saffron Marinade (page 101), or Braised Onions with Sweet Rice Stuffing (page 94).

Grilled Fajita Salad (with Turkey)

Serves 4

Fans of Southwest seasonings take notice: this may be one of the best salads you've ever tried. Throw some well-soaked mesquite chips on the coals just before grilling, and you'll boost the flavor by several degrees.

1 hour to marinate

30 minutes to prepare and cook, once the grill is ready

 You can make the beans up to a week in advance and store them, tightly covered, in the refrigerator. You can marinate the turkey overnight, keeping it refrigerated, or you can grill it up to 2 days ahead.

Juice of 2 limes

1 small garlic clove, peeled, crushed, and minced

2 tablespoons minced fresh cilantro

Pinch ground cumin

Pinch chili powder

Pinch salt

Pinch cayenne pepper

¾ pound turkey cutlets, cut into 1-inch-thick strips

1 red onion, quartered

1 red pepper, cored, seeded, and cut into 2-inch chunks

1 green pepper, cored, seeded, and cut into 2-inch chunks

12 cherry tomatoes

2 cups corn kernels, fresh or frozen

2 cups finely shredded green cabbage

2 cups cooked white or brown rice

2 cups cooked kidney beans, drained (rinsed if canned)

1 cup shredded cheddar cheese

2 jalapeño peppers, roasted, peeled, seeded, and minced (follow instructions for roasting bell peppers, see box, page 88)

$^1/_4$ cup green salsa

$^1/_2$ cup low-fat sour cream or plain low-fat or nonfat yogurt

Oil-free tortilla chips

Flour tortillas (optional)

Special equipment: wooden skewers

Combine the lime juice, garlic, cilantro, cumin, chili powder, salt, and cayenne in a glass or ceramic bowl. Add the turkey, onion, red and green peppers, and cherry tomatoes, toss to mix well, then cover with plastic wrap, and let marinate, refrigerated, for at least an hour.

Bring 1 inch of water to a boil over medium-high heat in a small saucepan. Add the corn kernels, cover, lower the heat to medium-low, and simmer for 4 minutes, or until cooked through. Remove from the heat and drain the water from the pan. Cool.

Meanwhile, prepare your grill (see page 143) or heat your broiler. Soak the skewers in water to cover for 30 minutes.

When the fire is ready, thread the onions, peppers, and tomatoes on skewers, putting each type of vegetable on a separate skewer. Place them on the grill, cover, and cook until they start to char (about 6 minutes, depending on the type of vegetable and the grill temperature). If you're using a broiler, cook 1½ inches from the heat. You'll have to rotate

the skewers more often because the vegetables will cook quickly.

Rotate the skewers as the vegetables start to char, and add the turkey slices to the grill or place under the broiler. Cover, and grill until the meat has browned, about 3 minutes (possibly less if broiling). Cover again, and grill until the turkey juices run clear when the meat is pierced with a sharp knife, about 4 to 6 minutes longer.

Remove everything from the grill or the broiler.

To serve, place an equal portion of cabbage, rice, and beans on 4 plates, and sprinkle with the cheese. Top with an equal amount of grilled vegetables and turkey.

In a bowl, stir together the jalapeño peppers, green salsa, and sour cream or yogurt until well blended, and drizzle it over the salad. Garnish each serving with the tortilla chips. Serve with warmed flour tortillas, if desired.

[PER SERVING: CAL. 535.1 / FAT 12.9 G* / PROTEIN 38.2 G / CARB. 62.7 G / CHOL. 70 MG / SODIUM 578.1 MG**] *MADE WITH WHOLE-MILK CHEDDAR CHEESE. **VALUE GIVEN IS BEFORE SALTING. % RDA: 33.6 VIT. A; 165.6 VIT. C; 29.5 IRON; 40.5 CALCIUM.

Barbecued or Broiled Turkey Burgers with All the Fixin's

Serves 4

Turkey burgers can be tricky because they tend to dry out *fast*. The simplest, most effective solution is to mix egg whites with the ground meat. This makes it moist without adding fat. Also, the meat itself is bland, which is why I always season my burgers with herbs and pile the condiments on top.

10 minutes to prepare

10 minutes to cook

 Turkey burgers are best made just before serving, or they become dry.

1 pound ground turkey breast (see Note)

1 large egg white

1 garlic clove, grated

Pinch dried oregano

Pinch dried thyme

Pinch salt

Pita bread or whole wheat hamburger buns

Prepare a charcoal grill for cooking (see page 143) or heat your broiler.

In a large mixing bowl, use your hands to combine the ground turkey, egg white, garlic, oregano, thyme, and salt.

Shape the meat into 4 patties, about 1 inch thick. Place on the grill and cover, or put under the broiler.

After 5 minutes, turn the burgers over to brown the other side. After 4 more minutes, stick a sharp knife into one of the burgers. If the juice runs clear, it's done. If the juice is still pink, give it another minute or 2 and test again

Serve in pita pockets or on hamburger buns, with your favorite condiments and garnishes.

Note: Make sure the ground turkey you buy is breast meat, which contains about 1 percent fat, compared with up to 45 percent fat in meat from other parts of the bird.

[PER SERVING*: CAL. 152.1 / FAT 3.6 G / PROTEIN 28.2 G / CARB. 0.1 G / CHOL. 66.6 MG / SODIUM 607.2 MG**] *EXCLUDES CONDIMENTS. **VALUE GIVEN IS BEFORE SALTING.

SERVING SUGGESTIONS
Serve Barbecued or Broiled Turkey Burgers with All the Fixin's with Nectarine Relish (page 107), Red Cabbage and Onion Relish (page 106), Roasted Red Pepper Terrine (page 88), Baba Ganoush (page 71), chopped fresh tomatoes, and alfalfa sprouts.

Not-So-Sloppy Joes

Serves 4

When I was in junior high, my friends and I would speculate on the contents of the sloppy joes served in the school cafeteria. Never mind the specifics; it's enough to say that the rust-colored meat sauce inspired ideas of such a kind that we couldn't bring ourselves to taste them.

Still, there's something appealing about the idea of sloppy joes. A hearty sweet-and-sour stew served over bread makes a wholesome comforting meal, provided the meat is lean, the sauce is fresh, and the bread is the best you can find.

50 minutes from start to finish

 This sauce will keep well tightly covered and refrigerated for up to 4 days, and frozen for 3 months.

2 teaspoons canola oil

1 cup chopped white or yellow onion

2 cloves garlic, minced

²⁄₃ cup chopped carrot

²⁄₃ cup chopped celery

½ cup chopped red pepper

2 tablespoons fresh chopped parsley

2 whole cloves

1 teaspoon ground cinnamon

2 teaspoons crumbled dried oregano

2 teaspoons crumbled dried marjoram

1½ tablespoons red wine vinegar

²⁄₃ pound ground turkey breast

One 28-ounce can no-salt added whole tomatoes, peeled, chopped, and drained

½ teaspoon salt

2 tablespoons currants

Thick sliced whole wheat bread or toasted whole wheat english muffins

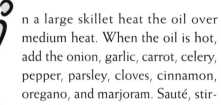

*i*n a large skillet heat the oil over medium heat. When the oil is hot, add the onion, garlic, carrot, celery, pepper, parsley, cloves, cinnamon, oregano, and marjoram. Sauté, stirring often, until the vegetables are soft, about 10 minutes.

Add the vinegar, turn up the heat to medium-high, and stir until most of the liquid has evaporated, about 3 minutes. Turn the heat back down to medium and add the ground turkey. Cook, stirring often, until the meat has browned, about 7 minutes. Stir in the tomatoes, salt, and currants, and let simmer uncovered, stirring occasionally, until the mixture is very thick, about 10 minutes.

Ladle over bread or toasted english muffin and serve hot.

[PER SERVING (FOR SAUCE ONLY): CAL. 218 / FAT 4.2 G / PROTEIN 26 G / CARB. 17 G / CHOL. 53 MG / SODIUM 671 MG] % RDA: 70.5 VIT. A; 101 VIT. C; 16 IRON.

Almost Vegetarian
Holiday Dinner

· · · · · · · ·

Winter Squash Gratin (see page 86)

Mediterranean Eggplant and Peppers (see page 81)

Roast Turkey (see page 187)

Rice Stuffing with Pine Nuts and Dried Cherries
(see right)

Red Cabbage and Onion Relish (see page 106)

Sweet Baked Ricotta with Lemon or Pumpkin
(see page 221)

Holiday dinners have always meant lots of work for those who host them. And while modern cookware and appliances have made it easier in some ways, the fact that people are more particular about what they'll eat has made it more difficult in others.

How far should you go to accommodate your guests' preferences? First, you're hosting a dinner, not running a restaurant. Guests who place special orders (allergies and authentic dietary concerns aside) are too concerned about maintaining their regimen to appreciate the time, trouble, and expense involved in preparing a meal of this kind. If people you've invited reply with a list of foods they won't eat, simply tell them what you're planning to serve, and let them decide whether they want to come share it with you.

At the same time, you invite people with the intention of pleasing them. If you happen to know that some of your guests don't eat

meat, you should plan the meal with this in mind. If you're not able to accommodate them—if their restrictions are quite extreme—the better option for everyone concerned is to invite them on another occasion.

This holiday menu will please part-time vegetarians as well as most vegetarians. Nearly all of the dishes are very low in fat, and all of them are supremely delicious.

Rice Stuffing with Pine Nuts and Dried Cherries

Serves 8 to 10

If you're having vegetarian guests at your holiday meal, set aside a large portion of stuffing to heat in a baking dish instead of inside the turkey. And remember to cook the stuffing with vegetable broth instead of chicken broth. This way the vegetarians at your table, as well as those who'll be having turkey, will be able to enjoy it.

30 minutes to prepare
55 minutes to cook

 You can make the stuffing up to 3 days in advance, keeping it refrigerated in a covered container. But don't stuff the turkey until you're about to cook it. And remove the stuffing from the bird before you store the leftovers, wrapping them separately for refrigerating.

1 tablespoon unsalted butter
2 white or yellow onions, finely chopped
1 tablespoon ground cumin
2 teaspoons ground cinnamon
½ teaspoon ground allspice

¼ cup pine nuts

¼ cup dried cherries or currants

⅔ cup uncooked medium-grain white rice

⅓ cup uncooked wild rice

2 cups chicken or vegetable broth, either
homemade (see page 46 or 44) or canned

*i*n a large saucepan, melt the butter. Sauté the onions, cumin, cinnamon, and allspice over low heat until the onions are so soft they seem to be melting, about 25 minutes.

❧ Add the pine nuts, cherries or currants, and white and wild rice, and stir until the rice is well coated with the other ingredients and glistening, about 2 minutes.

❧ Add the chicken or vegetable broth, and bring it to a gentle boil over medium-low heat. Cover, lower the heat as far as it will go, and let the stuffing steam for 50 minutes. Turn off the heat.

Roast Turkey

Serves 8 to 10

30 minutes to prepare

About 3½ hours to roast (20 minutes for each pound)

4 cups chicken broth, either homemade (see
page 46) or canned, plus more as needed

2 large white or yellow onions, quartered

6 carrots, trimmed, peeled, and cut into 4 pieces
each

1 bunch celery, leaves attached, coarsely
chopped

½ recipe Rice Stuffing with Pine Nuts and
Dried Cherries (see page 186)

One 10-pound turkey, giblets removed

2 tablespoons unsalted butter

Special equipment: baster, cheesecloth, twine,
skewer

*h*eat the oven to 325° F. Pour the chicken broth into a deep roasting pan. Add the onions, carrots, and celery. Bring the mixture to a boil over medium-high heat on top of the stove, reduce the heat to low, and let it simmer 20 minutes.

❧ Meanwhile, stuff the turkey with the rice stuffing. Use a skewer to secure the flap of skin over the cavity. Cross the legs in front of the cavity and tie them together with twine.

❧ Rub the skin evenly with the butter, and drape the cheesecloth on top. Turn off the heat under the roasting pan, and put a roasting rack in the pan.

❧ Place the turkey, breast side up, on the rack, then put the pan on the rack on the lowest rung of the oven. Roast according to the "20 minutes per pound" guideline, basting about every 30 to 40 minutes. As the chicken broth evaporates, replenish with additional broth or water. Remove cheesecloth for final 15 minutes of cooking to allow skin to brown.

❧ Let the turkey sit for 15 minutes (but *no longer*) before carving. Cut the twine, remove the skewer, and scoop the stuffing into a serving bowl to be passed separately.

[PER SERVING: CAL. 160 / FAT 4 G / PROTEIN 4.5 G / CARB. 26 G / CHOL. 4 MG / SODIUM 93.3 MG*] *VALUE GIVEN IS BEFORE SALTING.

fish & seafood

· · · · ·

Poached Fish 🍃 Court Bouillon 🍃 Braised Fish with Winter Greens 🍃 Milk Poached Fish with Chive Cream 🍃 Monkfish with Mushrooms and Lentils 🍃 Broiled Skate with Citrus Glaze 🍃 Couscous with Vegetables (and Fish) 🍃 Cabbage Filled with Spinach, Basmati Rice, and Fresh Salmon or Spicy Lentil Puree 🍃 White Beans and Fresh Tuna 🍃 Grilled Niçoise-Style Sandwich 🍃 Fresh Tomatoes and Feta Cheese with Shrimp or Chickpeas 🍃 Chili with Seafood or Beans 🍃 Spinach and Ricotta in Calamari or Cannelloni

Fish is tastiest and most nourishing when it's simply prepared. Consequently, some of the best fish dishes are also the easiest to make. Fish, which has little fat to start, can be made in many wonderful ways without adding much more—if any—to it. Fish and shellfish can be expensive, but they go so well with vegetables, grains, and even some legumes, that you can do a lot with a relatively small amount.

Buying Fresh Fish

SHOP 🌿 Buy fish at a place that does a lot of business. The faster the turnover, the more likely the fish will be fresh. It's better still if there's a knowledgeable staff to steer you toward the best merchandise, and to clean and bone it for you.

LOOK 🌿 Fillets and steaks should be a clear milky color, or a translucent pink with no dark spots. Whole fish should have a natural sheen, and the eyes should be clear and prominent, not cloudy and shrunken. Don't buy fish that's dull and sallow.

TOUCH 🌿 Fish—even the thinnest fillets—should be firm. Poke it with your finger. If it springs right back, it's fresh.

SMELL 🌿 If it smells fishy, consider what that expression has come to mean, and put it back.

The 10-Minute Rule
(Devised by the Canadian Fisheries and Marine Services)

Measure your fish at its thickest point and cook it 10 minutes for every inch. (If your fish is 1 inch thick, cook it for 10 minutes, 1.5 inches, 15 minutes, and so on.)

> **SADLY . . .**
> Shellfish allergies are very common. Ask ahead before you serve shrimp, scallops, mussels, clams, oysters, or squid.

The Better-Safe-Than-Sorry Rule
(Devised by Me)

In the interest of moist, flavorful fish, check it 3 to 4 minutes before the time you estimate it will be done. The fish is done if a knife sinks easily into the thickest part of the fish and some moisture seeps toward the insertion. The color of the flesh at the deepest part should be opaque, not hard white.

Poached Fish

Serves 4 to 6

I could say that I love poached fish and leave it at that. But there's more to my enthusiasm for this dish, and it isn't very nice.

While it's true I love it, it's also true that I have sometimes—okay, many times—invited people to dinner only to spend the hours before their arrival wishing I hadn't. It wasn't ever that I didn't want to see them, but that I didn't have the time or the stamina to prepare a good meal.

That doesn't happen anymore because I'm onto something. I ease myself into the evening, making the aioli, the fondue, and a side dish or two a few days in advance. All I have to do before the guests arrive is poach a fish as follows.

15 minutes to prepare

1 hour 30 minutes to simmer the broth and poach the fish

 You can make the bouillon well in advance, and store it tightly wrapped in the refrigerator, freezing it if it's more than 4 days. You can also make the mayonnaise and the fondue 2 days ahead, keeping them refrigerated in tightly covered containers until ready to use.

You can poach the fish 2 days ahead, storing it tightly wrapped in the refrigerator. If you do, serve it cold.

1 large garlic clove, thinly sliced into wedges

1 whole 4-pound fish, such as salmon or sea bass, cleaned and gutted (ask your fishmonger to do this for you)

1 recipe Court Bouillon (see page 192)

Condiments (any one or any number of the following)

Mayonnaise (see page 159)

Endive and Leek Fondue (see page 105)

Nectarine Relish (see page 107)

Red Cabbage and Onion Relish (see page 106)

*i*nsert the garlic wedges neatly into the fish, distributing the slices evenly.
🍃 Strain the bouillon and pour it into the bottom of a fish poacher or deep flameproof baking dish with a cover. Bring it to a boil on top of the stove over medium-high heat.

🖋 Place the fish on the poacher rack, or a rack that fits inside the baking dish, and lower it into the poaching liquid. Cover and cook over medium-low heat until the fish is done. Cooking time will vary according to the size of the fish. Check the fish after 8 minutes, then every 2 minutes after that.

🍃 Prepare the fish for serving (see box, right). Pass the condiments on the side.

HOW TO SERVE WHOLE FISH
❶ ❷ ❸

❶ Lift the fish out of the cooking liquid and transfer it to a large platter so that it's lying flat on one side. Cut off the head and tail and throw them away.

❷ Peel off the skin and discard it.

❸ Insert a small sharp knife into the tail end of the fish and run it toward the head, slicing all along the center, the blade of the knife running along the bones. The flesh should come away from the bone easily. Lift it away in large neat sections, working with one side at a time, and transfer it to a serving plate.

Court Bouillon

Makes about 2 quarts

Court Bouillon is a simple fish-poaching solution, lightly seasoning the fish as it cooks. It takes time for the water to take on the flavor of the vegetables, so let it simmer for at least an hour before you use it to cook the fish.

2 quarts water

½ cup white wine

1 tablespoon sea salt

1 bouquet garni, containing several sprigs fresh rosemary, 1 teaspoon dried thyme, and several sprigs fresh parsley (see box, page 44)

4 large white or yellow onions, coarsely chopped

6 carrots, peeled and coarsely chopped

1 celery stalk, including leaves, chopped

1 tablespoon *whole* black peppercorns

2 bay leaves

ombine all of the ingredients in a saucepan. Cover.

🍃 Bring to a boil over medium-high heat, then lower the heat and simmer over medium-low heat, covered, for an hour.

🍃 Turn off the heat and let the bouillon steep for another 30 minutes.

🍃 Strain through a fine sieve, and use right away or refrigerate, covered, for up to 4 days.

Braised Fish with Winter Greens

Serves 4

This is one of the best ways to prepare fish steaks. The greens season them with a delicate flavor and also keep them moist. Try it with swordfish, salmon, halibut, or shark, and greens such as spinach, radicchio, arugula, and butter lettuce.

About 40 minutes from start to finish (the time will vary according to the size of the fish steaks)

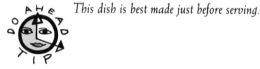 *This dish is best made just before serving.*

2 small garlic cloves, thinly sliced into wedges

Four 8-ounce fish steaks, such as swordfish, salmon, halibut, or shark

1 tablespoon unsalted butter

1 large white or yellow onion, thinly sliced

1 cup minced fresh parsley

1 teaspoon grated lemon zest

3 cups torn mixed greens, such as spinach, radicchio, arugula, or butter lettuce

¼ cup white wine or 2 tablespoons wine vinegar with herbs

nsert the garlic wedges into the fish, distributing the slices evenly among the steaks. Cover the fish and set it aside in the refrigerator. Heat the oven to 425°F.

🍃 Melt the butter in a large skillet. Sauté the onion, parsley, and lemon zest over medium-low heat until the onion is soft and limp, about 10 minutes.

Add the greens and sauté, stirring constantly, until they wilt, about 4 to 6 minutes.

Add the wine or vinegar, raise the heat to medium-high, and continue cooking and stirring until some of it evaporates, about 2 minutes. Turn off the heat.

Spread half the greens in the bottom of a baking pan. Layer the garlic-studded fish steaks on top. Distribute the rest of the greens evenly over the fish, and pour the remaining liquid from the sauté pan around the fish. Cover the baking dish with foil.

Bake until tender and cooked through, 10 to 15 minutes, depending on the thickness of the steaks. Check after 8 minutes, then every 2 minutes after that to be sure you don't overcook them.

To serve, take the garlic slices out of the fish. Place a bed of greens on each plate and lay a steak on top so the greens show around the sides.

[PER SERVING: CAL. 392 / FAT 11. G / PROTEIN 57.7 G / CARB. 10.1 G / CHOL. 85.3 MG / SODIUM 108.6 MG*] *VALUE IS GIVEN BEFORE SALTING. % RDA: 185 VIT. A; 79 VIT. C; 27 IRON.

HOW TO PEEL GARLIC
❶ ❷ ❸

❶ Lay the garlic clove flat on your work surface.

❷ Press down on it with the flat edge of a wide knife, using your palm to press. The garlic clove will crack, freeing the skin.

❸ Peel off the skin and throw it away.

SERVING SUGGESTIONS
Serve Braised Fish with Winter Greens with Baked Stuffed Turnips (page 93).

Milk Poached Fish with Chive Cream

Serves 4

Fish poached in leek infused milk tastes mildly sweet, and the chives add a savory kick. Serve this with potatoes prepared in any fashion, steamed, mashed (see page 99), or au gratin (see page 99).

1 hour 15 minutes from start to finish

 You can prepare the poaching milk up to 3 days in advance, keeping it tightly covered in the refrigerator until ready to use. Reheat the milk gently, taking care not to bring it to a boil.

2 cups milk, nonfat if desired

1 large yellow onion, sliced

1 leek, white part plus 1 inch of the green, washed and sliced

1 bay leaf

¼ teaspoon crumbled dried thyme

1½ pounds firm white fish fillets, such as bass, monkfish, or haddock

1 large egg yolk

2 tablespoons heavy cream

¼ cup minced fresh chives

i n a deep skillet, combine the milk, onion, leek, bay leaf, and thyme. Heat gently over medium-low heat, and let the vegetables and herbs steep in the warm milk until soft, about 15 minutes. Turn off the heat, cover, and let steep 15 minutes longer.

🍃 Add the fish, then gently heat the milk over medium-low heat and poach the fish, taking care not to bring the milk to a boil. When the fish turns white, about halfway through the cooking time, gently turn the fillets with a slotted spoon. Poaching will take 6 to 9 minutes for thick filets such as monkfish, and 3 to 4 for thinner fish such as snapper. When the fish is done—when it's opaque in the center and flaky when pierced with a fork—transfer it with a slotted spatula to a plate covered with paper towel, and cover loosely with foil.

🪶 Pour the milk through a fine sieve into a small saucepan. In a small bowl, whisk together the egg yolk and cream, and add two tablespoons of the hot milk to this mixture. Whisk well, then add 2 tablespoons more. Stir again, then pour the egg yolk mixture into the milk. Cook over low heat, stirring constantly, until the mixture thickens, about 8 minutes. Be careful not to bring to a boil or the sauce will separate.

🍃 Remove the sauce from the heat and stir in the chives. Distribute the fish on serving plates and spoon sauce over each serving.

[PER SERVING (USING NONFAT MILK): CAL. 344 / FAT 8.8 G / PROTEIN 49 G / CARB. 14.8 G / CHOL. 262.1 MG / SODIUM 233 MG]

Serves 4

This is a common combination in some parts of France, a holdover from hard times when few could afford their fill of fish. It's so good you might find it hard to pity the poor peasants who had to make do with it.

1 hour 10 minutes from start to finish

 You can make the lentils 3 days in advance, keeping them refrigerated in a tightly covered container. Remove them from the refrigerator 3 hours before serving, so they can come to room temperature. You can make the sauce up to the point where you add the fish 3 days in advance, keeping it refrigerated in a tightly covered container. To proceed with the recipe, return the sauce to the skillet you used to prepare it, heat slowly, uncovered, over medium-low heat, stirring often, until warmed through.

10 ounces dried porcini mushrooms

2½ cups water

1 whole clove

2 white or yellow onions, 1 quartered and 1 chopped

1 bay leaf

1 cup small uncooked lentils, picked over and rinsed

2 tablespoons unsalted butter

1 leek, white part only, cleaned and chopped

2 large garlic cloves, crushed and minced

1 tablespoon minced fresh sage leaves, or 1 tablespoon crumbled dried sage

1 tablespoon ground cumin

1 teaspoon ground cinnamon

¼ cup minced fresh parsley

½ pound cremini or portobello mushrooms, cleaned and sliced

½ pound mixed other fresh wild mushrooms, such as morels, oyster, or shiitake, cleaned and coarsely chopped

½ cup red wine

Four 8-ounce fresh monkfish fillets, or tuna, halibut, or swordfish steaks

1 tablespoon all-purpose flour

*P*ut the dried porcini in a bowl and pour 1 cup of the water over them. Cover the bowl and set it aside.

🍃 Stick the clove into 1 piece of the quartered onion and put it in a saucepan along with the rest of the quartered onion, the bay leaf, and the lentils. Add the remaining 1½ cups water, bring to a boil over medium-high heat, cover, turn the heat down to low, and simmer for 30 minutes. Turn off the heat and let the mixture sit, covered, while you finish the dish.

🍂 Meanwhile, melt the butter over medium heat in a very large skillet. When it's bubbling, add the chopped onions, leek, garlic, sage, cumin, cinnamon, and parsley. Turn down the heat to medium-low and sauté, stirring often, until the onions and leek are soft and limp, about 10 minutes.

🍃 Add the fresh mushrooms and continue cooking over low heat until they begin to release liquid, about 4 minutes.

🍂 Meanwhile, strain the porcini liquid through a fine sieve or a colander lined with cheesecloth, and reserve the soaking water. Finely dice the porcini and stir them into the skillet.

🍃 Stir in the wine and half of the reserved soaking liquid. Add the fish, cover, and simmer for 4 minutes.

🍂 Using a large spatula, carefully turn the fish over and continue to simmer until it's not quite done. The time will vary according to the thickness of the fillets or steaks. After 4 minutes, pierce the thickest part of the fish with a knife. If the deepest layer inside is still pink, but the rest is opaque, it's ready.

🍃 Lift the fish out of the skillet, transfer it to a large plate, and wrap it in foil, where it will continue to cook. Set it aside.

🍂 Stir the rest of the reserved porcini soaking liquid into the skillet. Sprinkle the flour evenly over the mixture and stir constantly over medium heat until the sauce thickens, about 3 minutes. Turn off the heat.

🍃 Place an even amount of lentils on each of 4 serving plates and top with a piece of fish. Spoon mushroom sauce over each portion, and serve right away.

[PER SERVING: CAL. 523.5 / FAT 11.5 G / PROTEIN 46.2 G / CARB. 51.5 G / CHOL. 68 MG / SODIUM 70.8 MG*] *VALUE IS GIVEN BEFORE SALTING. % RDA: 103 VIT. A; 32 IRON.

SERVING SUGGESTIONS
Serve Monkfish with Mushrooms and Lentils with Braised Onions with Sweet Rice Stuffing (page 94).

butter. Much also goes to Asia where it's fermented for fish sauce, or stir-fried with vegetables.

Simply, skate is a hefty, full-bodied fish with a flavor similar to other "big" white fleshed fish such as snapper or cod, and it can be prepared in similar ways, broiled for one, as in this recipe with a sweet, tangy glaze.

40 minutes to prepare
10 minutes to cook

 You can make the glaze up to 3 days in advance, and store it in the refrigerator in a covered glass container.

1 shallot, minced
1 tablespoon grated fresh ginger
2 large garlic cloves, crushed and minced
1 scallion, white part only, sliced
1 cup fresh orange juice, divided
1 tablespoon tomato paste
½ teaspoon Dijon mustard
1 tablespoon minced fresh cilantro
1 teaspoon honey
1 tablespoon fresh lime or lemon juice
1 teaspoon cider vinegar
¼ teaspoon soy sauce
1½ pounds skinned skate, or firm fish fillets
    such as snapper or cod

*i*n a medium saucepan, place the shallot, ginger, garlic, scallion, and ½ cup of the orange juice. Heat over medium-high heat, stirring often, until the vegetables are soft, and the juice has reduced to become thick and syrupy, about 10 minutes.

🍃 Add the tomato paste and ¼ cup of the

Broiled Skate with Citrus Glaze

Serves 4

Whoever coined the phrase "One man's garbage is another man's treasure," wasn't referring to fish as far as I know. But it's certainly true when it comes to skate, which was priced as a delicacy at my market in Paris, but which my fish seller in Connecticut can't give away. There are few takers here because who knows what to make of it? The fanned, ridged cuts (the wings) don't look like any other fish. Second, it's rarely served in restaurants, so almost no one knows how it should taste. In fact 95 percent of the United States catch is sold abroad, much of it to France where they poach it in Court Bouillon (see page 192) and top it with blackened remaining orange juice, and stir until it's thick again, about 4 minutes. Add the remaining ¼ cup orange juice, mustard, cilantro, honey, lime or lemon juice, cider vinegar, and soy sauce. Turn the heat down to low and stir until reduced to a thick paste, about 7 minutes.

✍ Heat the broiler. Lightly grease or coat with nonstick spray a shallow baking dish. Spread half the glaze over the fish and broil, glaze side up, 2 inches from the heat for 4 minutes. Turn the fish over, spread the remaining glaze on the other side, and return to the broiler for 3 to 4 minutes. Test for doneness by pulling at it with a fork. If the fish is opaque throughout, it's done. If not, return to the broiler and check every minute.

[PER SERVING: CAL. 156 / FAT 1.6 G / PROTEIN 25 G / CARB. 10 G / CHOL. 41 MG / SODIUM 150.5 MG] % RDA: 65 VIT. C.

SERVING SUGGESTIONS
Serve Broiled Skate with Citrus Glaze with Broiled Onions with Sweet Rice Filling (page 94) or Cabbage Cakes (page 83), and Vanilla Cheesecake Ice Cream (page 229).

Couscous is semolina, a high-protein wheat, that's been cooked and dried. But it's also the name of any dish that's served over this grain. The texture of cooked couscous is softer than rice and firmer than Cream of Wheat. Couscous, by itself, is bland until you add sauce or seasoning.

Couscous with Vegetables (and Fish)

Serves 4

I wish all fish tasted like swordfish, which I can't afford very often. As it happens, many of the less costly fish taste like nothing at all. But bland fish don't have to be dull, as you'll discover if you fix them in the following fashion. Don't let the length of the ingredient list put you off; the recipe itself is very simple.

40 minutes to prepare the vegetarian version
1 hour to prepare with fish
30 minutes to cook

 You can make the Fish Polpettini up to 2 days in advance, keeping them refrigerated and well wrapped. You can make the sauce up to 3 days ahead, and refrigerate it tightly covered, cooking the couscous just before serving. To reheat the sauce, transfer to a heavy covered saucepan and set on medium-low heat, stirring often until warmed through, about 15 minutes.

Fish Polpettini (optional)

2 cups torn unbleached white or whole wheat bread, crust removed

½ cup milk

1 pound fresh fish fillets, such as snapper, haddock, or cod

1 large egg, lightly beaten

1 small red onion, minced

1 garlic clove, crushed and finely minced

½ cup minced fresh cilantro

1 tablespoon plus 2 teaspoons ground cumin

Pinch paprika

Pinch salt

Sauce

Generous pinch powdered saffron

1 tablespoon extra virgin olive oil

2 large white or yellow onions, thinly sliced

One 2-inch piece fresh ginger, peeled and finely grated

1 red pepper, cored, seeded, and sliced

1 yellow or orange pepper, cored, seeded, and sliced

1 tablespoon ground cumin

2 teaspoons ground coriander

2 teaspoons ground cinnamon

1 teaspoon paprika

4 large tomatoes (about 1 pound), peeled, seeded, and drained

2 cups tiny new potatoes, scrubbed and halved or quartered, depending on size

1 cup cooked chickpeas, drained, or 2 cups cooked chickpeas if you're making the vegetarian version (rinsed if canned)

¼ cup raisins

1 cup uncooked couscous

1 cup plain low-fat or nonfat yogurt

½ garlic clove, grated

Pinch cayenne pepper

HOW TO MAKE COUSCOUS
❶ ❷ ❸

Always make couscous just before you're going to serve it. If it sits around it gets gummy. If dinner is delayed, fluff the couscous, and add some sauce or butter to keep it from sticking.

❶ For each cup of uncooked couscous, bring 1¼ cups water to a boil. Add a generous pinch of salt.

❷ Stir in the couscous. Cover tightly, turn off the heat, and let sit for 10 minutes.

❸ Lift the lid, fluff with a fork and serve right away.

 o make the Fish Polpettini (skip for the vegetarian version), in a small bowl, soak the bread in the milk for 15 minutes.

🍃 Meanwhile, cut the fish fillets into 2-inch chunks. Either mince them by hand with a sharp heavy knife or put them in a food processor and process in short pulses until the fish is minced but not pureed. Transfer the fish to a large mixing bowl.

🍃 Squeeze the bread dry, and add it to the fish. Stir in the egg, onion, garlic, cilantro, cumin, paprika, and salt. Blend everything together with your hands.

Shape the fish mixture into balls about 1½ inches in diameter. Put them on a plate, cover, and refrigerate. You can do this up to 2 days in advance.

To make the sauce, put the powdered saffron in a small dish and add 2 tablespoons hot water. Set aside to soak.

Heat the oil in a large skillet. Add the onions, ginger, peppers, cumin, coriander, cinnamon, and paprika, and sauté over medium heat, stirring often, until the onions and peppers are soft and limp. Add the tomatoes, potatoes, chickpeas, raisins, and the saffron in its soaking liquid. Cover and let the sauce simmer on medium-low heat for 30 minutes, until the tomatoes cook down into a lumpy sauce, and the potatoes are tender.

Prepare the couscous according to the package directions, or the guidelines at left. Meanwhile, combine the yogurt, garlic, and cayenne in a small serving bowl.

Add the fish balls to the sauce, if including, cover again, and simmer for 3 minutes. Turn the fish over, replace the cover, and cook for 1 more minute. Turn off the heat.

Distribute the couscous on 4 serving plates. Make a well in the center of each portion and fill it with the vegetable mixture, and fish, is using. Pass the yogurt sauce on the side.

[PER SERVING FOR COUSCOUS WITH VEGETABLES: CAL. 442 / FAT 1.8 G / PROTEIN 14.9 G / CARB. 89.6 G / CHOL. 0.9 MG / SODIUM 58.5 MG*] *VALUE GIVEN IS BEFORE SALTING. % RDA: 126 VIT. C; 25.7 IRON.

[PER SERVING FOR COUSCOUS WITH VEGETABLES AND FISH: CAL. 498 / FAT 3.3 G / PROTEIN 31 G / CARB. 84.7 G / CHOL. 74.5 MG / SODIUM 231.2 MG*] *VALUE GIVEN IS BEFORE SALTING. % RDA: 26 VIT. A; 128 VIT. C; 21 IRON; 20 CALCIUM.

Cabbage Filled with Spinach, Basmati Rice, and Fresh Salmon or Spicy Lentil Puree

Serves 4 to 6

No picnic site is so perfect it won't seem lovelier still when you've got something *this* good to eat.

1 hour to prepare if the Lentil Puree is already made
30 minutes to bake
Chill overnight

 This is a do-ahead dish, since it must chill overnight. You can make the lentil filling for the vegetarian version up to 3 days before completing the dish, keeping it refrigerated in a tightly covered container.

1 pound fresh spinach, stemmed and cleaned, or one 10-ounce box frozen spinach
1 head green cabbage, loose outer leaves trimmed away
2 tablespoons unsalted butter
2 large white or yellow onions, thinly sliced
2 garlic cloves, minced
1 cup minced fresh parsley
¼ cup minced fresh chives
¼ cup minced fresh dill, or 2 tablespoons crumbled dried dill
¼ cup dry white wine

Salmon (optional)
2 pounds fresh salmon fillets, skinned
1 tablespoon capers, drained
1 recipe Spicy Lentil Puree (see page 201)
2 cups cooked basmati rice

*i*f you're using fresh spinach, put it in a saucepan with an inch of water. Cover and steam over medium heat until the spinach is cooked, about 3 minutes. Let it cool, squeeze it dry, then set it aside. If you're using frozen spinach, put it in a saucepan, cover, and set over low heat. When the ice starts to melt, turn it over and jab it with a knife to break up the block. Continue to defrost it over low heat, turning often, until it's broken up and frost free. Let it cool, then squeeze out the moisture. Set it aside.

Steam the cabbage in a large pot of boiling water (see page 148 for directions) until you can separate the leaves easily, about 12 to 15 minutes. Peel away 6 large leaves and set them aside. Reserve the rest of the cabbage for another use.

In a large skillet, melt the butter. Sauté the onions, garlic, parsley, chives, and dill over medium-low heat until the onions are very soft and limp, about 20 minutes. Stir often, adding the wine about a tablespoon at a time to prevent sticking.

Heat the oven to 425° F. Lightly butter the bottom and sides of an 8-inch round baking dish or deep-dish pie plate. Lay the cabbage leaves inside so they cover the bottom, overlap at the center, and extend several inches outside the rim.

Spread the spinach evenly over the cabbage. Spread the cooked onion mixture on top.

If using salmon, layer the salmon fillets evenly over the onions. Sprinkle with the capers. Top with the rice.

For the vegetarian version, spread the

Parsley contains vitamins C and A, which are sensitive to heat. To get the benefit of the vitamins, add a few fresh sprigs—finely minced—to the parsley that's been sautéed.

Spicy Lentil Puree over the onions. Top with the rice. For both: the salmon and vegetarian dishes, fold the cabbage leaves over to encase the filling. Cover the pan with aluminum foil.

Bake for 30 minutes. Test doneness by sticking a sharp paring knife through the cabbage. If the salmon is flaky, it's done. Remove and refrigerate immediately. Keep it refrigerated until thoroughly chilled, preferably overnight. Invert onto a serving plate and serve cold.

Spicy Lentil Puree

Makes about 1 1/3 cups

This can also be served as a dip with toasted pita bread, or as a condiment for Poached Fish (see page 190) or chicken (see page 172).

1 tablespoon canola oil or unsalted butter

1 small white onion, minced

1 garlic clove, grated

One 2-inch piece fresh ginger, peeled and grated

1 tablespoon ground cumin

2 teaspoons curry powder

2 teaspoons ground coriander

1 teaspoon ground turmeric

½ teaspoon ground cloves

½ teaspoon ground cinnamon

1 cup uncooked lentils, picked over and rinsed

1½ cups vegetable broth, either homemade (see page 44) or canned, or water

*i*n a large skillet, heat the oil or melt the butter. Sauté the onion, garlic, ginger, cumin, curry powder, coriander, turmeric, cloves, and cinnamon over medium heat until the onion is soft and translucent, about 7 minutes. ❧ Add the lentils and stir well to coat with the spices. Add the vegetable broth or water, bring to a boil, cover, and turn the heat down to low. Steam for 30 minutes, until the lentils are very soft and the liquid has been absorbed. ✑ Transfer the lentils to a food processor or blender and process in short pulses to puree. Be careful not to overprocess or the mixture will be too thin. You can do this step up to 3 days in advance. Refrigerate the puree in a covered container.

[PER SERVING FOR CABBAGE FILLED WITH SPINACH, BASMATI RICE, AND FRESH SALMON: CAL. 466 / FAT 20.2 G / PROTEIN 36.9 G / CARB. 31.6 G / CHOL. 110.7 MG* / SODIUM 172 MG**] *MADE WITH BUTTER. FOR LESS CHOLESTEROL AND SATURATED FAT, USE OIL. TOTAL FAT WILL REMAIN THE SAME. **VALUE GIVEN IS BEFORE SALTING. % RDA: 70 VIT. A; 109 VIT. C; 23 IRON; 23 CALCIUM.

[PER SERVING FOR CABBAGE FILLED WITH SPINACH, BASMATI RICE, AND SPICY LENTIL PUREE: CAL. 271 / FAT 6.7 G / PROTEIN 8.6 G / CARB. 41.2 G / CHOL. 11 MG* / SODIUM 153.4 MG] *MADE WITH BUTTER. FOR LESS CHOLESTEROL AND SATURATED FAT, USE OIL. TOTAL FAT WILL REMAIN THE SAME.

White Beans and Fresh Tuna

Serves 4

I first saw white beans and tuna on a menu in Florence, and the waiter warned me off it, saying that the dish was served cold. I have nothing against cold dishes, and I was curious, so I ordered it anyway.

I haven't ignored a waiter's advice since. It wasn't that the dish was cold, it was that it was awful: tuna canned in oil, mixed with tired white beans and more oil. I've since learned that this dish is a sentimental favorite in Tuscany, a souvenir of the days of heroic struggles against hunger. It's a dish of greater interest to anthropologists than hungry tourists, who go to museums for relics, and restaurants for other reasons.

However, the combination seemed so promising that I went home and made it the way I'd hoped it would be, like this.

30 minutes to prepare
10 minutes to cook

You can make the sauce and the beans up to 3 days in advance and refrigerate them in a tightly covered container. To complete the dish, transfer the sauce with the beans to a heavy saucepan, cover, and warm slowly over medium-low heat, stirring often. Proceed with the recipe from this step. Or you can make this version a cold dish, too. Refrigerate it, covered, as soon as it's done, and let it chill for at least 3 hours. It will keep for 2 days.

1 tablespoon extra virgin olive oil

2 white or yellow onions, thinly sliced

1 garlic clove, crushed and minced

1 large fennel bulb, without the frond, coarsely chopped, or 4 celery stalks, without the leaves, coarsely chopped

1 tablespoon balsamic vinegar

1 cup cooked white beans, drained (rinsed if canned)

4 large tomatoes (about 1 pound), peeled, seeded, and chopped, or one 16-ounce box or can imported tomatoes, drained and chopped

1½ pounds tuna steak, cut into 1-inch cubes

2 cups cooked barley or 1 recipe Mushroom Barley (see page 102)

eat the olive oil in a large skillet, and sauté the onions, garlic, and fennel or celery over medium-low heat until tender and limp, about 20 minutes.
🍃 Heat the oven to 425°F. Add the vinegar to the skillet, turn up the heat, and stir constantly until most of the liquid evaporates, about 1 to 2 minutes.

🍃 Turn the heat down to low and stir in the beans and the tomatoes.

🍃 Place the cubes of tuna in an 8-inch square baking dish, and spread the bean mixture on top. Cover with foil and bake until the fish is just cooked through, about 8 minutes.

🍃 Place the barley or Mushroom Barley in the center of a serving plate. Spoon the fish and sauce evenly around it.

[PER SERVING: CAL. 482 / FAT 11.8 G / PROTEIN 50.5 G / CARB. 42.7 G / CHOL. 64.1 MG / SODIUM 321.8 MG*] *VALUE GIVEN IS BEFORE SALTING. % RDA: 119 VIT. A; 54 VIT. C; 29.5 IRON.

Grilled Niçoise-Style Sandwich

Makes 2 sandwiches

What the French call *pan Bagna* is a sandwich filled with something like salade Niçoise: canned tuna, onion, egg, anchovy, and more. It's fine when it's made in the usual way, but much more interesting when the ingredients are grilled.

30 minutes to assemble from the time your fire is ready
15 minutes to rest

This sandwich is best made just before serving, or it may be soggy.

2 very ripe small tomatoes, quartered

1 small red pepper

Thick slices red onion

2 large sandwich rolls

One 3½-ounce can water-packed tuna, drained

2 hard-boiled eggs

2 anchovy fillets, rinsed, patted dry, and minced

1 teaspoon capers

4 large Greek-style black olives, pitted and
chopped

1 tablespoon extra virgin olive oil

*S*et up a grill with mesquite or charcoal (see page 143), or heat a stove-top grill or the broiler.

🦑 When the heat is very hot, grill or broil the tomatoes, pepper, and onion until they're lightly charred, turning as necessary, 7 to 10 minutes. (They may not be ready at the same time, so take each off the heat as it's done)

🌿 Let the pepper cool, pull off the peel, and slice it into thin strips.

🦑 For each sandwich, slice a roll in half and lay half the pepper strips over the bottom of each. Flake the tuna with a fork and put half the tuna on top of each sandwich. Slice the eggs and layer them over the tuna. Spread the anchovies on top and scatter the capers and olives over that. Cover with the onion slices and the tomato.

🌿 Drizzle the olive oil over everything, then top with the other half of the bun. Set it on a large plate and put another plate on top of them, weighing the plate down with something heavy, such as a cast-iron pot. Leave the sandwiches like that for 15 minutes, so all the juices will run together.

[PER SERVING: CAL. 353 / FAT 14.3 G / PROTEIN 19.1 G / CARB. 35.9 G / CHOL. 20.7 MG / SODIUM 927.2 MG] % RDA: 115 VIT. C; 24 IRON.

Fresh Tomatoes and Feta Cheese with Shrimp or Chickpeas

Serves 4

This delicious dish never fails. Make it when you're tired or uninspired. Or when you're eager to impress someone and just don't want to chance it.

50 minutes from start to finish

 This dish is best made just before serving.

1 tablespoon extra virgin olive oil

1 white or yellow onion, chopped

1 red onion, chopped

2 tablespoons minced fresh oregano, or 1
tablespoon crumbled dried oregano

¼ cup white wine

8 large tomatoes (about 2 pounds), peeled,
seeded, drained, and chopped, or two 16-
ounce cans or boxes imported Italian
tomatoes, drained and chopped

1½ pounds medium shrimp, shelled and
deveined (see box, page 122), or 3 cups
cooked chickpeas, drained (rinsed well if
canned)

4 ounces feta cheese, crumbled

Freshly ground pepper to taste

*h*eat the olive oil in a large skillet. Add the onions and oregano and sauté over medium-low heat until the onions are soft and limp, about 10 minutes. If the onions start to stick, turn down the heat to low and add 1 tablespoon of the wine.

🍃 Stir in the tomatoes and cook over medium heat, uncovered, stirring occasionally, until the tomatoes break down into a pulpy sauce, about 10 minutes.

🍃 Stir in the wine and cook for about 3 minutes, until some of the wine evaporates.

🍃 Add the shrimp or chickpeas with the feta cheese and continue cooking over medium heat, stirring often, until the shrimp have turned pink, about 6 minutes, or until the chickpeas are heated through, about 10 minutes. Turn off the heat, and season with pepper.

🍃 Stir well to distribute the ingredients evenly before serving. Serve with rice, if desired.

[PER SERVING FOR FRESH TOMATOES AND FETA CHEESE WITH SHRIMP: CAL. 384 / FAT 12.5 G / PROTEIN 43.4 G / CARB. 20.5 G / CHOL. 286.5 MG / SODIUM 599 MG] % RDA: 53 VIT. A.; 103 VIT. C; 35 IRON; 27 CALCIUM.

[PER SERVING FOR FRESH TOMATOES AND FETA CHEESE WITH CHICK-PEAS: CAL. 402 / FAT 11.5 G / PROTEIN 16.3 G / CARB. 53.3 G / CHOL. 25 MG / SODIUM 352.7 MG] % RDA: 44 VIT. A.; 105 VIT. C; 31 IRON; 24 CALCIUM.

SERVING SUGGESTIONS
Serve Fresh Tomatoes and Feta Cheese with Shrimp or Chickpeas with Tangy Spinach-Yogurt Soup (page 48) or Mediterranean Eggplant and Peppers (page 81).

Chili with Seafood or Beans

Serves 4

There's only one secret to making sensational chili with seafood, and that's not to take it too seriously. You'd be surprised how well a little chili powder and some good cheddar cheese compensate for less-than-perfect execution.

This recipe is so versatile you can leave the seafood out altogether, using beans instead.

1 hour 10 minutes from start to finish

You can make the sauce for the seafood version up to 3 days in advance, keeping it refrigerated in a tightly covered container. To complete the dish, transfer the sauce to a heavy saucepan, cover, and warm slowly over medium-low heat, stirring often. Proceed with the recipe. You can make the bean version up to 3 days in advance, reheating as directed above.

Sauce

1 tablespoon corn or canola oil
1 red onion, chopped
1 white or yellow onion, chopped
4 garlic cloves, crushed and minced
¼ cup minced fresh cilantro, plus additional for garnish
1 red pepper, roasted, seeded, and sliced (see box, page 88)
1 Anaheim chili pepper, roasted, seeded, and minced (see box, page 88)
1 jalapeño pepper, roasted, seeded, and minced (follow instructions for roasting bell peppers, see box, page 88)
1½ tablespoons chili powder

2 teaspoons ground cumin

2 teaspoons crumbled dried oregano

Cayenne pepper to taste

6 large tomatoes (about 1½ pounds), peeled, seeded, and chopped, or one 16-ounce can or box imported Italian tomatoes, drained and chopped

2 tablespoons green salsa

2 tablespoons white wine

Salt to taste

Seafood (optional)

½ pound medium fresh shrimp, shelled and deveined (see box, page 122)

½ pound bay scallops, rinsed

½ pound fresh or defrosted flash-frozen minced clams, with juice

½ pound firm-flesh fish, such as red snapper, halibut, or monkfish, trimmed and cut into bite-sized chunks

For Vegetarian Chili

3 cups cooked pinto beans, drained (rinsed well if canned)

Garnishes (optional)

1 cup shredded cheddar cheese or mixture shredded cheddar and Monterey Jack

Low-fat sour cream or plain low-fat yogurt

1 ripe avocado, diced

Minced fresh cilantro

Chopped red onion

or the sauce, heat the oil in a wide, deep skillet. Sauté all of the onions, garlic, and cilantro over medium-low heat until the onions are soft and translucent, about 10 minutes.

🍃 Add the red pepper, Anaheim chili, japapeño chili, chili powder, cumin, oregano, and cayenne, and stir well to combine.

🍃 Stir in the tomatoes and the green salsa, and cook over low heat, stirring often, until the tomatoes break down into pulp, about 20 minutes. When the mixture starts to stick to the pan, add the wine and stir vigorously to make a thick sauce.

🍃 Season with salt and/or additional minced fresh cilantro to taste.

🍃 At this stage you can remove the sauce from the heat, let it cool, and store it, well covered, for later use, 3 days refrigerated, up to 3 months frozen. Or you can proceed as follows.

🍃 Stir in the seafood and fish (omit for a vegetarian dish) or the pinto beans. Over medium-low heat, simmer gently, uncovered, stirring constantly, until the fish is cooked or the beans are warmed through, 5 to 7 minutes.

🍃 Serve garnished with a generous portion of cheese, a dollop of sour cream or yogurt, diced avocado, minced cilantro, and/or chopped onion. Or, pass the garnishes on the side.

[PER SERVING FOR CHILI WITH SEAFOOD: CAL. 335 / FAT 6.9 G / PROTEIN 44.4 G / CARB. 21 G / CHOL. 210 MG / SODIUM 704 MG*] *VALUE GIVEN IS BEFORE SALTING. % RDA: 53 VIT. A; 168 VIT. C; 35 IRON.

[PER SERVING FOR CHILI WITH BEANS: CAL. 299 / FAT 4.1 G / PROTEIN 11.6 G / CARB. 51.5 G / CHOL. 0 / SODIUM 191.6 MG*] *VALUE GIVEN IS BEFORE SALTING. % RDA: 44 VIT. A; 173 VIT. C; 30 IRON.

Spinach and Ricotta in Calamari or Cannelloni

Serves 4

A lot of people are squeamish about squid; they're afraid it's going to be slimy or that the tentacles will tickle their throat. But squid is one of the most versatile seafoods, largely because it's so bland you can make it taste any way you'd like.

I like it best as follows, stuffed with spinach, ricotta, and Parmesan cheese and stewed in a tomato sauce seasoned with cumin. The squid sac is a tender casing (provided it's not overcooked) with a mild, sweet taste that comes through despite the bold flavors on either side.

If you'd prefer to eat pasta, you can use the filling for cannelloni instead of squid.

1 hour to prepare
10 minutes to cook

 You can make the filling and the sauce up to 3 days in advance, storing them tightly wrapped in the refrigerator. To complete the dish, proceed with the recipe. When you're ready for the sauce, transfer it to a heavy saucepan, cover, and set over medium-low heat, stirring often until warmed through, about 15 minutes.

Filling

1 pound fresh spinach, washed thoroughly but not dried
1½ cups part-skim ricotta cheese
¾ cup grated imported Parmesan cheese

Pinch ground nutmeg
Pinch dried oregano, crumbled

Sauce

2 tablespoons extra virgin olive oil
2 large white or yellow onions, finely chopped
2 teaspoons ground cumin
1 teaspoon ground cinnamon
½ teaspoon ground allspice
¼ cup dry white wine, or 2 tablespoons white wine vinegar with lemon (see pages 235–36)
4 large tomatoes (about 1 pound), peeled, seeded, and chopped, or one 16-ounce can or box imported Italian tomatoes, drained and finely chopped
Salt to taste

Calamari

12 calamari, roughly 4 inches long, cleaned (see box, page 207)

Cannelloni

8 cannelloni shells
⅓ cup grated imported Parmesan cheese

or the filling, place the damp spinach in a deep saucepan and cover. Place the saucepan over low heat, and steam until the spinach is soft and bright green, about 4 minutes. Turn off the heat, lift the lid, and let it cool.

Stir together the ricotta and Parmesan cheese in a large bowl until thoroughly combined. Add the nutmeg and oregano, and mix well.

When the spinach is cool enough to

HOW TO CLEAN CALAMARI
❶ ❷ ❸

Stand over a sink and:

❶ Hold the body, or sac, in one hand and the head with tentacles in the other. Pull off the head and throw it away.

❷ Feel inside the sac for the "quill," a long flat piece of cartilage resembling plastic. Tug it out, and discard it as well. (Sometimes the quill comes out when you pull off the head, sparing you this step).

❸ With your fingers, press the sac from the narrow end up, as if you were squeezing a tube of toothpaste, then rinse the squid well under cold water, and pat dry.

handle, lift it from the pan and squeeze out as much moisture as you can. Chop it roughly.

🍃 Add the spinach to the cheese mixture, stirring well to distribute it evenly.

🌿 For the sauce, heat the olive oil in a large skillet and sauté the onions over medium-low heat until soft and translucent, about 7 minutes. Stir in the cumin, cinnamon, and allspice, and continue to cook 5 minutes more, stirring to blend.

🍃 Add the wine or vinegar, turn up the heat, and stir until the liquid evaporates, about 3 minutes.

🌿 Turn the heat down to low and add the tomatoes. Continue to cook, stirring occasionally, until the sauce has thickened, about 8 minutes. Add salt to taste.

🌿 For the calamari, using a teaspoon or the flat edge of a butter knife, fill each calamari by feeding the spinach-ricotta filling in through the wide opening at the end. Distribute the filling evenly among the calamari. Seal by threading a toothpick though the open end.

🌿 Place the calamari in the skillet with the sauce and simmer over low heat, turning often to cook uniformly. The calamari are done when they turn white, about 10 minutes. Be careful not to overcook, because squid can become tough.

🍃 For the cannelloni, heat the oven to 425° F. Cook the shells according to package directions, draining them while they're still a bit hard. (They'll continue to cook when they're in the oven.)

🌿 Stuff the shells with even portions of the spinach-ricotta filling. Pour half the sauce on the bottom of a baking dish large enough to hold the shells side by side, then place the stuffed shells over the sauce. Pour the remaining sauce evenly on top. Sprinkle with the Parmesan cheese and cover loosely with foil.

🍃 Bake until the cannelloni are cooked through, about 15 minutes. Remove the foil and bake until bubbly, about 5 minutes more.

[PER SERVING FOR SPINACH AND RICOTTA IN CALAMARI: CAL. 523 / FAT 19.3 G* / PROTEIN 50 G / CARB. 27.1 G / CHOL. 436.3 MG / SODIUM 558.9 MG**] *MADE WITH PART-SKIM RICOTTA. FOR LESS TOTAL FAT AND CHOLESTEROL, SWITCH TO NONFAT. **VALUE GIVEN IS BEFORE SALTING. % RDA: 114 VIT. A; 134 VIT. C; 36.3 IRON; 64.9 CALCIUM.

[PER SERVING FOR SPINACH AND RICOTTA IN CANNELLONI: CAL. 682 / FAT 20.2 G* / PROTEIN 35 G / CARB. 80.4 G / CHOL. 45 MG / SODIUM 1,179 MG**] *MADE WITH PART-SKIM RICOTTA. FOR LESS TOTAL FAT AND CHOLESTEROL, SWITCH TO NONFAT. **VALUE GIVEN IS BEFORE SALTING. % RDA: 111.7 VIT. A; 120 VIT. C; 47.1 IRON; 70.7 CALCIUM.

desserts

· · · · · ·

Apple Crepes 🍃 Chunky Apple Maple Sauce 🍃 Apple Yogurt Parfait 🍃 Apple Flan 🍃 Fruit Yogurt Soufflés 🍃 Peach Scone Cakes 🍃 Seasonal Clafouti 🍃 Strawberry Risotto 🍃 Sweet Baked Ricotta with Lemon or Pumpkin 🍃 Chocolate Pudding in Orange Shells (The Emperor's New Dessert) 🍃 Steamed Holiday Pudding 🍃 Banana Ricotta Cream 🍃 Banana Cake 🍃 Chocolate Bundt Cakes 🍃 Sweet Potato Pudding 🍃 Custard-Style Indian Pudding 🍃 Fruit Cups 🍃 Vanilla Cheesecake Ice Cream 🍃 Fresh Fruit Compote

You can toy all you'd like with other courses—serving side dishes for supper, making soup the entrée—but when it comes to dessert, you mustn't mess with convention. Dessert has to be good, and it has to be sweet. After all, dessert is a treat *by definition*, so to serve something simply because it's wholesome regardless of how it tastes is not only unfair, it's incorrect.

Conversely, nothing says you can't serve a wholesome dish as the final course, as long as it's delicious. Each of these is nourishing enough to count as part of the meal, and good enough to be, unmistakably, dessert.

HOW TO PICK FRESH FRUIT

To choose the best fruit, smell it. If the peaches, plums, or pineapple smell like peaches, plums, or pineapple, chances are they're good. If you can't smell anything, they're going to be bland. If they smell cloying, tinny, or just plain bad, they're probably too far gone. Check for soft spots, bruises, and mold. If a fruit has a luster not commonly found in nature, ask whether it's been waxed. If so, peel the fruit before you eat it.

When you're choosing fruit for cooking, you don't have to be as finicky as you are when planning to serve it raw. Bruised fruit is fine, as long as the bruise is only a bruise and not a symptom of decay. Just cut away the soft spot before you add it to the dish.

APPLES

In the many places where they're grown, apples are *not* apples. They're pippins or Jonathans or russets or Romes, Cortlands, Delicious (Golden or Red), Granny Smiths, Newtowns, Macouns. They're for eating or baking or reducing to sauce. In fact, the flavor and texture of apples can differ to such a degree that to try to describe how a McIntosh tastes, for example, in relation to a Stayman is like comparing, well, apples and apples.

The best apples are firm and have a natural sheen. Check for soft spots, bruises, and sallow skin. Hard, tart apples such as Granny Smith, Stayman, Macouns, Cortlands, and Romes, are as good for baking and cooking as they are for eating. Also good for eating are the softer, sweeter types, such as Golden and Red Delicious and McIntosh.

Peak season for most apples is autumn and winter.

To store apples, put them in a plastic bag and keep refrigerated, preferably in the crisper. Gases given off by decaying apples can cause the others to go bad, so discard the rotten ones.

Try them in maple-sweetened filling for crepes (see Chunky Maple Apple Sauce, page 216) or Apple Flan (see page 217).

APRICOTS

Fresh apricots are in season so briefly, I know lots of people who've never had a fresh one. That is either a shame or not, depending on the quality of the crop. Apricots are temperamental, a bit underripe and they're bitter; 1 second overripe, and they're mushy and bland. But when they're perfect, they're *perfect*, much like peaches, only firmer and not as sweet.

The best apricots are rich yellow-orange and soft, with a light, sweet scent.

Peak season for apricots is late spring/early summer.

To store unripened apricots, place them in a paper bag and leave them at room temperature away from direct sunlight for a day or two.

Ripened apricots placed in a plastic bag and refrigerated will keep for only about 2 days.

Try them instead of peaches in scone cakes (see page 219).

BANANAS

They're the most popular fruit in the world, and I think I know why. Bananas are easy to transport and able to withstand long spells in storage, so people in far-flung places can get good bananas whatever the season. Frozen and pureed, they're just like ice cream.

The best bananas are firm and chubby and blazing yellow. Some dark streaking is fine, but big black blotches mean they'll be better mashed for banana bread than for eating straight from the skin.

Peak season is all year.

To store unripened bananas, put them in a paper bag at room temperature, away from direct sunlight. To speed up the ripening process, put a ripened banana in the bag with the green ones. Store ripened bananas in the refrigerator for up to 5 days.

Try them frozen and pureed with yogurt, ricotta cheese, honey, and vanilla (see Banana Ricotta Cream, page 224).

BLUEBERRIES

Their season has been enhanced and extended thanks to widespread blueberry cultivation. That's the good news. The bad news is that cultivated berries aren't always as flavorful as those that grow in the wild. But they're still good for baking, bursting in the batter to make those sweet moist spots in muffins.

The best blueberries are deep blue, almost purple, plump, and dusted with fine white powder (a natural occurrence). Check carefully for fuzzy mold and withered fruit.

Peak season for blueberries is midsummer.

To store blueberries, refrigerate them, unwashed and covered with plastic. They'll keep for roughly 4 days.

Try them in Fruit Cups (see page 228) or Seasonal Clafouti (see page 219).

CANTALOUPE

This melon is a rich source of cancer-fighting beta-carotene. This is a convenient fact for those of us who've been looking for a way to justify going through a ton of it each year.

The best cantaloupe is well formed (round or slightly oval) with even netting and a faintly sweet aroma. It should give slightly when pressed. Avoid bald or soft spots.

Peak season for cantaloupe is summer.

To store uncut cantaloupe, refrigerate it for up to 4 days. To store cut cantaloupe, remove the rind, cut the fruit into cubes, and refrigerate in a covered container for up to 3 days.

Try it split and seeded and filled with yogurt and fresh berries (see Fruit Cups, page 228).

CHERRIES

In season just long enough to tease your appetite, cherries are never here long enough to satisfy it.

The best cherries are deep red, plump, firm, and naturally glossy. Check for white fuzzy mold, bruising, and stickiness, which indicate they're rotting.

Peak season for cherries is mid-June to early July.

To store cherries, refrigerate them, unwashed, in a perforated plastic bag for up to 4 days.

Try them baked in vanilla-flavored batter for a custardy cake (see Seasonal Clafouti, page 219) or in Fruit Cups (see page 228).

KIWI

Having gone in and out of fashion, kiwi is finally just another fruit. Actually, it's more than that: one large kiwi has more vitamin C than an orange twice its size.

The best kiwis are plump and smooth and give slightly when you squeeze them. If they're hard, they'll be bland and indigestible.

Peak season is all year.

To store unripened kiwis, put them in a paper bag and keep them at room temperature, away from direct sunlight, until they've softened. Refrigerated, ripened kiwis will keep for up to 10 days.

Try them hollowed out and filled with mixed chopped fruit (see Fruit Cups, page 228).

LEMONS

Count on lemons to spark life into foods that might otherwise be dull. I've found that they cut sweetness, too, so I scatter finely grated rind over beets, sprinkle it on rice pudding, and stir it into the batter whenever I make cheesecake.

The best lemons are sunny yellow and firm, with a smooth, thin skin.

Peak season is all year.

To store lemons for more than 5 days, put them in a plastic bag and refrigerate them. If you plan to use them within a few days of purchase, you can keep them at room temperature, provided they're kept away from direct sunlight or heat.

Try them in a dish that tempers the sting and makes the most of lemon's fresh flavor (see Lemony Risotto, page 130) or in a refreshing cheesecake-style pudding (see Sweet Baked Ricotta with Lemon or Pumpkin, page 221).

MANGOES

The mango has made an optimist of me. After all, how bad can this world be when something this good occurs naturally?

The best mangoes give slightly when you press, and smell sweet. Don't buy one that's too hard, since they tend to ripen unevenly at home, or one that's mushy with withered skin.

Peak season for mangoes is spring and summer.

To store whole mangoes, refrigerate them for up to 2 weeks. If you've taken a slice out of a mango, keep the rest by wrapping it in plastic and returning it to the refrigerator, where it will keep for about 4 days more.

Try them with nuts and sweet spices in refreshing Rice Salad with Mango and Chickpeas (with or without Chicken) (see page 77).

NECTARINES

(see Peaches)

ORANGES

They're not native to Florida, and some of the best aren't even orange. The fruit landed in the Sunshine State with Columbus, who brought them from the Old World, and juice oranges grown in the tropics are actually green (until the distributors dye them). While not the *best* source of vitamin C (kiwis and strawberries have more), oranges have plenty nonetheless.

The best juice oranges are small and heavy with thin, tight-fitting skin. Good navel oranges have smooth skin and a light, sweet aroma. Check for blackening around the navel and moist indentations in the skin, both signs of decay.

Peak season is all year.

To store oranges, refrigerate them or keep them at a cool room temperature. Either way, they'll stay good for up to 2 weeks.

Try them filled with chocolate pudding (see Chocolate Pudding in Orange Shells (The Emperor's New Dessert), page 222).

PEACHES

A candy among fruits, peaches are sweet and delicious, but not all that nutritious compared with many other fruits. Nectarines are smoother, sweeter, and less fragile.

The best peaches are pale yellow, orange, and red, and smell so good you can taste them. Ripe peaches are fragile, so check for bruises. Nectarines should have vivid coloring and should give slightly when pressed. When you sniff, you should be tempted.

Peak season for peaches and nectarines is summer.

To store unripened peaches or nectarines, place them in a paper bag, away from direct sunlight, until they soften. Refrigerate ripened peaches and nectarines for up to 3 days.

Try them with vanilla yogurt for a wholesome shortcake (see Peach Scone Cakes, page 219) or in a sweet-and-sour condiment for grilled foods (see Nectarine Relish, page 107).

PEARS

They can be exasperating, ripening unevenly on the tree and unpredictably at home. That's why a good pear is a prize: soft, but not mealy, and sweet, but not too much so.

The best pears are perfectly smooth and soft enough to give when you press them. Just make sure someone else didn't give them the press test before you got there! A solution is to order pears by mail from orchards that guarantee perfect fruit (see pages 235–36).

Peak season for pears is autumn and winter.

To store unripened pears, place them in a paper bag away from direct sunlight. To speed the ripening, put a ripe banana in the bag with them. Keep ripened pears in the refrigerator. Never seal pears in plastic bags, or they'll go mealy in the middle.

Try them in place of apples in Chunky Maple Apple Sauce (see page 216).

PINEAPPLES

Mercifully, pineapples appear in markets in midwinter, when we're ready for something besides apples and pears.

The best pineapples have gone a bit golden under the eyes and have a light scent of pineapple. They shouldn't look shriveled, and they shouldn't be leaking. Even following the guidelines, you can go wrong, which is why degrees in wizardry should be awarded to anyone who can pick perfect pineapples with regularity.

Peak season for pineapple is winter.

To store an uncut pineapple, put it in a plastic bag and refrigerate it for up to 4 days. You can keep cut pineapple refrigerated in a covered container for up to 4 to 5 days.

Try it filled with seasonal fruits and slivered toasted almonds (see Fruits Cups, page 228).

PLUMS

There are at least 140 varieties, some sweet, some so tart they sting.

The best plums have brilliant even color; thin, smooth skin; and they should yield when you squeeze them.

Peak season for plums is mid- to late summer.

To store unripened plums, put them in a paper bag and keep them at room temperature until they soften.

Refrigerated, ripe plums will keep for up to 4 days.

Try them with black beans as an accompaniment to grilled foods (see Spicy Black Beans with Fresh Plums, page 157).

RASPBERRIES

Since raspberries don't keep, the best strategy is to eat them—*all* of them!—right away.

The best raspberries are opaque red-pink and plump. Check for mold and soggy bottoms.

Peak season for raspberries is summer.

To store raspberries, you must be willing to risk losing them. The best you can do is place them, unwashed, in a single layer on a plate, cover them with a paper towel, then wrap the whole works in plastic. They may last a day or two.

Try them in Fruit Cups (see page 228) or sprinkled on Peach Scone Cakes (see page 219).

STRAWBERRIES

In free association, strawberries lead naturally to shortcake, to summer, to sunshine, to bliss.

The best strawberries are rich red from stem to tip, very juicy and smell like an open jar of strawberry preserves.

Peak season for strawberries is midspring to early summer.

To store strawberries, put them, unwashed, in the refrigerator, where they'll keep for roughly 3 days.

Try them in a thick and creamy rice pudding (see Strawberry Risotto, page 220).

Apple Crepes

Serves 4 to 6

The expression "easy as pie" is a rebuke as far as I'm concerned. Why don't they say "easy as nuclear physics"? It's all the same to me. My crusts turn out tough around the edges and soggy in the center; the filling starts to boil over before the top has browned. I cannot make a decent pie, and I don't appreciate that little adage with its smug assumption that anyone can do it. Besides, it cheats pie makers of the recognition they deserve. They are to be admired, treated with extra kindness and consideration, and encouraged in their work. They are to be invited to dinner and asked to bring dessert.

When I crave apple pie and can't persuade anyone to bake one for me, I make these, which call for the kind of filling I'd put in pie and simple basic crepes, which I can manage more easily than crust.

40 minutes to prepare

2 hours to rest

 You can make the crepe batter and the filling up to 3 days in advance and keep them tightly covered in the refrigerator.

1 tablespoon sugar, preferably raw sugar

1 cup apple juice

1 cup whole wheat or white pastry flour

1 recipe Chunky Maple Apple Sauce, cooled to room temperature (recipe follows)

*i*n a bowl, stir the sugar into the apple juice until dissolved. Whisk in the flour, and set aside, covered, for 2 hours.

❧ Over medium heat, heat an 8-inch nonstick pan. Test it by dropping a teaspoon of batter onto the surface. If it hardens, it's ready to make the crepes.

🍃 Turn the heat down to medium-low. Whisk the batter well and pour ¼ cup of it onto the pan, tilting the pan to distribute it evenly over the entire surface. When the bottom of the crepe has set, loosen it carefully with a wooden spatula, and, with the help of your fingers, flip it over and brown the other side. Transfer the crepes to a plate while you repeat with the rest of the batter.

❧ In the center of each crepe place about ¼ cup of the apple sauce. Fold up the bottom and sides to enclose the filling.

Chunky Maple Apple Sauce

Makes about 4 cups

4 Granny Smith apples, cored, peeled, and chopped

1 teaspoon fresh lemon juice

2 tablespoons pure maple syrup

Pinch mace

Pinch ground cinnamon

½ teaspoon vanilla extract

2 tablespoons apple juice

¼ cup raisins, cooled to room temperature

*i*n a heavy nonreactive saucepan toss the chopped apples with the lemon juice. Add the maple syrup, mace, cinnamon, vanilla, and apple juice and stir.

Over medium-low heat, bring the mixture to a gentle simmer. Cover and cook, stirring often, until the apples soften and break down into a chunky sauce, about 30 minutes.

Remove from the heat and stir in the raisins.

[PER SERVING FOR APPLE CREPES WITH CHUNKY MAPLE APPLE SAUCE: CAL. 292.3 / FAT 0.8 G / PROTEIN 4.8 G / CARB. 66.2 G / CHOL. 0 / SODIUM 5.9 MG]

[PER SERVING FOR CHUNKY MAPLE APPLE SAUCE: CAL. 152.1 / FAT 0.4 G / PROTEIN 0.8 G / CARB. 29.5 G / CHOL. 0 / SODIUM 3.3 MG]

Variation

Soft-Crust Apple Cobbler

Make the batter and the apple sauce. Heat the oven to 450°F. and distribute equal portions of the apple sauce among 4 ovenproof bowls. Pour equal portions of batter on top and bake at until it has browned and set, about 40 minutes.

Apple Yogurt Parfait

Serves 6

1 recipe Chunky Maple Apple Sauce (see page 216), cooled to room temperature
⅓ cup toasted slivered almonds (see page 77)
2 cups low-fat or nonfat vanilla yogurt

Combine the cooled apple sauce and almonds in a small bowl. Mix well, and fold into the yogurt in a large bowl. Spoon into wineglasses and chill for at least an hour.

Apple Flan

Serves 4

There is no fixed definition of flan. It can be a plain egg custard, a sweet pastry containing egg custard, or a custard that contains fresh fruit. Here's a lovely example of the latter, made with cinnamon spiced apples.

10 minutes to prepare
40 minutes to cook

This flan is best hot from the oven, but can also be served cold for breakfast. To store, let it cool, wrap in plastic, and refrigerate for up to 3 days.

3 Granny Smith apples, peeled, cored and thinly sliced
1 tablespoon fresh lemon juice
⅔ cup skim milk
¼ cup nonfat milk powder
2 tablespoons all-purpose flour
1 teaspoon cinnamon

½ teaspoon allspice

1 teaspoon vanilla

1 large egg, lightly beaten

3 tablespoons brown sugar

 eat the oven to 375°F. Lightly grease an 8-inch skillet or coat with nonstick spray. Lay the apple slices evenly over the bottom of the skillet. Sprinkle with the lemon juice.

🍃 Stir together the skim milk, milk powder, and flour in a large bowl and whisk briskly until smooth. Add the cinnamon, allspice, vanilla, egg, and sugar, and mix well. Pouring the batter through a sieve, cover the apple slices and bake until set, about 40 minutes. Serve with ice cream or frozen yogurt, if you'd like.

[PER SERVING: CAL. 259 / FAT 1.6 G / PROTEIN 6.6 G / CARB. 54 G / CHOL. 70 MG / SODIUM 89 MG] % RDA: 18.5 CALCIUM.

Fruit Yogurt Soufflés

Serves 4

The only trick is the timing. If you're serving this to guests, excuse yourself halfway through the main course, whip it up, and put it in to bake. If you have the ingredients and gear set out and ready to go, you won't miss much of what's said at the table. Serve it as swiftly as possible; it looks spectacular while it's standing, but inevitably, it will collapse.

10 minutes to prepare

30 minutes to bake

 This soufflé must be made right before serving or it will fall.

6 large egg whites

Pinch cream of tartar

4 cups low-fat or nonfat lemon yogurt (blended, not fruit-on-the-bottom)

½ cup pure-fruit strawberry syrup (see pages 235–36)

 et the oven at 475°F.

🍃 Beat the egg whites until soft peaks form. Sprinkle with cream of tartar and resume beating until the whites are stiff. Gently fold in the yogurt.

🍃 Spoon the mixture into four 2-cup capacity soufflé dishes or ovenproof soup bowls. Bake until nicely browned, about 30 minutes.

🍃 Toward the end of the baking time, heat the syrup in a small saucepan over medium-low heat. As you serve each soufflé, puncture the top with a knife and swiftly pour in 2 tablespoons of syrup.

[PER SERVING: CAL. 226.8 / FAT 1.9 G* / PROTEIN 11 G / CARB. 41.4 G / CHOL. 7.2 MG / SODIUM 150.9 MG] *MADE WITH LOW-FAT YOGURT. % RDA: 28.8 CALCIUM.

Peach Scone Cakes

Makes 6 to 8 scone cakes

A sweet, light, delicious departure from standard rich shortcake.

20 minutes to prepare

15 to 20 minutes to bake

You can make the scones up to a week ahead, keeping them well wrapped in the freezer. Give them 3 hours to defrost at room temperature, then reheat them, wrapped in foil, in a 300° F. oven for 10 minutes before serving topped with fruit.

3 cups all-purpose flour

1 tablespoon baking powder

Pinch salt

1 teaspoon sugar

1 cup warm low-fat or nonfat milk, plus about ¼ cup for brushing the scones

2 cups low-fat vanilla yogurt

6 fresh peaches or nectarines, peeled, pitted, and chopped

*h*eat the oven to 425° F.

❧ Into a large mixing bowl, sift together the flour, baking powder, salt, and sugar. Stir in 1 cup of the milk and mix well until a soft dough forms.

❧ Lightly flour a work surface and turn out the dough. Shape into a 10 × 12-inch rectangle about 2 inches thick, then, using a sharp knife, cut into 6 to 8 smaller squares.

❧ Place the squares on a lightly greased baking sheet about 1 inch apart and brush the tops with the remaining milk.

❧ Put the scones in the oven and lower the heat to 400° F. Bake until golden, about 15 to 20 minutes.

❧ Let the scones cool on a wire rack.

❧ Serve the scones topped with the vanilla yogurt and chopped peaches or nectarines.

[PER SERVING: CAL. 355.4 / FAT 1.4 G* / PROTEIN 12.1 G / CARB. 73.5 G / CHOL. 4.3 MG / SODIUM 463.6 MG] *MADE WITH LOW-FAT YOGURT. FOR LESS FAT AND FEWER CALORIES, USE NONFAT. % RDA: 32.8 CALCIUM.

Seasonal Clafouti

Serves 4 to 6

The fact that it's simple doesn't explain my enthusiasm for this half-cake/half-custard dessert. I would love it even if it was twice as difficult.

5 to 10 minutes to prepare, depending on fruit

30 to 35 minutes to bake

You can make the clafouti up to 2 days ahead, keeping it refrigerated, well wrapped. If you make it in advance, serve it cold. Clafouti doesn't reheat well.

½ cup low-fat or nonfat milk

½ cup nonfat or part-skim ricotta cheese

2 large eggs

½ cup sugar

½ cup all-purpose flour

1 teaspoon vanilla extract

2 cups fruit (see page 220)

Don't wash fruit before you refrigerate it, or it will go moldy. Wait until you're about to eat it before rinsing.

et the oven at 425°F.

In a food processor or blender combine the milk, ricotta, eggs, sugar, flour, and vanilla, and process until smooth.

Spread the fruit evenly over the bottom of an 8-inch ovenproof skillet or deep-dish pie plate. Pour the batter evenly over the top.

Bake until puffed and golden brown, about 30 to 35 minutes.

Serve warm, or room temperature, or chilled, cut in wedges.

Fruits for Clafouti

Pitted fresh cherries or dried cherries plumped
  in hot water to cover for 1 hour
Blueberries
Peaches, peeled and diced
Apples, peeled and diced, sprinkled with 2
  teaspoons lemon juice and 2 tablespoons
  brown sugar
Pears, peeled and diced, sprinkled with 2
  teaspoons lemon juice, 1 tablespoon maple
  syrup
Stewed pitted prunes, coarsely chopped

[PER SERVING: CAL. 222.1 / FAT 2.9 G / PROTEIN 8.5 G / CARB. 39.6 G / CHOL. 138.5 MG / SODIUM 87.6 MG]

Strawberry Risotto

Serves 3 to 4

I love rice pudding and cannot, even for the sake of a preface to a recipe, declare any single version my absolute favorite. This one is a favorite, though, especially in late spring when I'm stricken by a boundless greed for fresh strawberries. Here the fruit isn't a mere garnish; it permeates the pudding, making the most of risotto's unique ability to absorb and amplify the flavor of anything that's cooked with it.

1 hour to make
3 hours to chill

 *You can make the yogurt cheese up to 3 days in advance, keeping it refrigerated in a tightly covered container until ready to use. You can make the risotto up to 3 days ahead, also keeping it tightly wrapped and refrigerated.*

½ cup low-fat or nonfat strawberry yogurt
  (blended, not fruit-on-the-bottom)
2½ cups low-fat or nonfat milk
Zest of 1 lemon
2 tablespoons sugar
½ cup arborio rice
1 cup sliced fresh strawberries

at least 6 hours before preparing the rest of the dish (up to 2 days in advance), make the strawberry yogurt cheese; spoon the yogurt into a sieve lined with a paper coffee filter or cheesecloth. Set it over a jar or widemouthed glass, put it in the refrigerator, and let the yogurt drain until it's the consistency of cream cheese, at least 6 hours.

🍂 Warm the milk in a small saucepan over low heat and steep the lemon zest in it for 10 minutes, keeping the milk just below a simmer the whole time.

🍐 Dissolve the sugar in the milk, then strain to remove the lemon zest.

🍂 Put the rice in a heavy saucepan and pour in enough of the hot milk to just cover the kernels. Stir over low heat until the milk is absorbed. Keep adding hot milk and stirring until you've used up all of the milk and the rice kernels are plump and chewy, about 40 minutes.

🍐 Take the risotto off the heat and let it cool a bit, stirring often to help it along, for 5 minutes. Stir in the yogurt cheese and let the mixture cool completely. Stir in the fresh strawberries.

🍂 Refrigerate the risotto for at least 3 hours, covered, until chilled through. Stir well before serving.

[PER SERVING: CAL. 132.4 / FAT 0.6 G* / PROTEIN 5.8 G / CARB. 25.4 G / CHOL. 2.9 MG / SODIUM 69.6 MG] *MADE WITH NONFAT MILK AND LOW-FAT YOGURT.

Lemon zest is the fine, yellow top layer of the lemon peel, and as the name implies, it brings flavors to life. Make sure only to include the zest, because the white peel is very bitter.

To zest a lemon or orange, use the fine-grate side of a sharp grater. You can avoid cutting into the peel by rubbing the fruit over the grater not too rigorously and rotating it as you shave away.

Sweet Baked Ricotta with Lemon or Pumpkin

Serves 4 to 6

I've always preferred ricotta cheesecake to the richer, sweeter kind made with cream cheese. Ricotta's light, clean taste complements and conveys other fresh flavors, including lemon and pumpkin.

5 minutes to prepare

45 to 50 minutes to bake

 This is a do-ahead dessert, requiring at least 3 hours to chill. It will keep well, tightly covered, for 3 days.

2 cups nonfat or part-skim ricotta cheese
   (see Note)
2 large eggs
½ cup sugar
½ cup all-purpose flour
2 teaspoons grated lemon zest or
   ½ cup canned pumpkin
2 tablespoons molasses
Pinch ground cloves
Pinch ground cinnamon
Pinch ground nutmeg or mace
Pinch ground ginger

eat the oven to 425° F.

🍂 For either version, combine all of the ingredients in a food processor or blender. Pour the batter into an 8-inch springform pan.

🍐 Bake for 45 to 50 minutes, until a knife inserted in the center comes out clean.

Let cool on a wire rack, then chill, covered, for at least 3 hours. Serve cold.

Note: If the ricotta is watery, drain it by pouring it into a sieve lined with cheesecloth or a coffee filter. Let it drip into a bowl, refrigerated, for several hours.

[PER SERVING FOR SWEET BAKED RICOTTA WITH LEMON: CAL. 238.2 / FAT 8 G* / PROTEIN 13.2 G / CARB. 27.2 G / CHOL. 116.7 MG / SODIUM 126.6 MG*] *MADE WITH PART-SKIM RICOTTA. FOR LESS TOTAL FAT AND CHOLESTEROL, SWITCH TO NONFAT. % RDA: 23.7 CALCIUM.

[PER SERVING FOR SWEET BAKED RICOTTA WITH PUMPKIN: CAL. 268.4 / FAT 8 G* / PROTEIN 13.4 G / CARB. 34.5 G / CHOL. 116.7 MG / SODIUM 136.9 MG*] *MADE WITH PART-SKIM RICOTTA. FOR LESS TOTAL FAT AND CHOLESTEROL, SWITCH TO NONFAT. % RDA: 56.8 VIT. A; 24.8 CALCIUM.

Chocolate Pudding in Orange Shells (The Emperor's New Dessert)

Serves 8

I offer this dessert on a hunch that most people who grew up in the United States would rather eat goopy old chocolate pudding than *mousse au chocolat* any day.

If that's you, here's a way you can indulge at no cost to your dignity. Orange, an ingredient in some of the grandest chocolate desserts, belies the fact that this is one of the humblest.

30 minutes to prepare

3 hours to chill

 You can make the pudding up to 3 days in advance and refrigerate, tightly covered. Fill the oranges shortly before serving.

½ cup powdered hot-chocolate mix
2 tablespoons arrowroot or cornstarch
2 cups low-fat or nonfat milk
4 large navel oranges

*i*n a large saucepan whisk together the hot-chocolate mix, arrowroot or cornstarch, and milk. Heat gently over medium-low heat, whisking often so no lumps form. Continue cooking until the mixture thickens, about 10 minutes.

Turn off the heat and let it cool to room temperature. Once it's cooled throughout, beat it with an electric beater or a whisk until smooth.

Cut the oranges in half and carefully scoop out the fruit, keeping the shells intact. Place the orange pulp in a large mixing bowl. Remove the seeds, if there are any, and strip away large strings of membrane. Carve off the bottom of each shell so it sits squarely on a plate.

Stir the pudding into the orange pulp, and distribute evenly among the shells. Chill for 3 hours, covered, before serving.

Note: Since I tend to stress fresh foods, you might wonder why this recipe calls for hot-chocolate *mix*. A mix makes it easy to get the proportion of cocoa to sugar just right. And there are several wholesome brands on the market, containing only nonfat dried milk, pure cocoa powder, real vanilla, and natural sweeteners.

[PER SERVING: CAL. 85 / FAT 0.2 G / PROTEIN 3.5 G / CARB. 17 G / CHOL. 1.3 MG / SODIUM 102 MG] VALUES WILL VARY DEPENDING ON THE BRAND OF HOT CHOCOLATE MIX YOU USE.

Steamed Holiday Pudding

Serves 6 to 8

This pudding is so rich with delicious dried fruit, no one will miss the suet or shortening that ordinarily bind desserts of this kind. Beautiful to behold, it makes a great gift.

30 minutes to prepare

2 hours 15 minutes to steam and cool

 This pudding keeps well at room temperature, tightly wrapped, for up to 5 days, and freezes indefinitely. To defrost and reheat, wrap tightly in foil and place in a 325° F. oven for 30 to 40 minutes.

½ cup fresh orange juice or prune juice

2 cups mixed chopped dried fruit (such as figs, pitted prunes, apricots, pitted cherries)

1 cup whole wheat pastry flour or all-purpose flour

1 teaspoon baking powder

½ teaspoon baking soda

Pinch ground cinnamon

Pinch ground nutmeg

Pinch ground ginger

½ cup buttermilk, nonfat if desired

1 large egg white, beaten to soft peaks

*i*n a heavy saucepan, combine the fruit juice and dried fruit. Bring to a boil over medium-high heat. Turn down the heat to medium-low, cover, and simmer the fruit until soft, about 20 minutes. Using a slotted spoon, transfer the fruit to a bowl and set aside. Discard the juice or save for another use.

Combine the flour, baking powder, baking soda, cinnamon, nutmeg, and ginger in a large bowl using a long-tined fork or whisk to blend well. Add the fruit and stir well. Stir in the buttermilk to blend. Gently but thoroughly fold in the egg white.

Line a 3-cup pudding mold with aluminum foil. Spoon the batter into the mold and fasten the lid. If your mold doesn't have a lid, cover with foil and tightly tie it in place with kitchen twine. Place the mold inside a saucepan big and deep enough to hold it. Add boiling water halfway up the pudding mold, place the saucepan over medium heat, cover, and simmer for 2 hours, checking often and replenishing the water as necessary.

Let the pudding cool for 15 miutes before removing the cover. Invert by standing the pudding on a table, and placing a plate upside down on top of the mold. Holding the plate and the mold together, flip the mold over, and lay the plate flat on the table with the mold standing on top. Lift up the mold, and carefully peel the foil off the pudding. Serve hot, room temperature or cold, with vanilla ice cream, whipped cream, frozen vanilla yogurt, or hard sauce.

[PER SERVING (USING LOW-FAT BUTTERMILK): CAL. 329 / FAT .5 G / PROTEIN 6.2 G / CARB. 73 G / CHOL. 0 / SODIUM 179 MG] % RDA: 24 VIT. A; 19 IRON.

Banana Ricotta Cream

Serves 4 to 6

More proof that dessert doesn't have to be difficult to be delicious.

3 hours to freeze the bananas

10 minutes to prepare

 You can freeze the bananas, wrapped in plastic, up to 3 months in advance, letting them soften for 15 minutes at room temperature before proceeding with the recipe. Make the dessert just before serving.

2 cups nonfat or part-skim ricotta cheese

2 tablespoons sugar

2 teaspoons vanilla extract

2 teaspoons grated lemon zest

4 bananas, peeled and frozen not quite solid

*i*n a food processor, puree the ricotta cheese until smooth.

🍃 Add the sugar, vanilla, and lemon zest, and process to blend.

🍃 Cut each banana into 4 pieces of equal size, and add to the ricotta mixture. Process until smooth.

🍃 Serve immediately in individual parfait glasses or bowls.

[PER SERVING: CAL. 298.5 / FAT 9.4 G* / PROTEIN 16 G / CARB. 35.8 G / CHOL. 38 MG / SODIUM 156 MG] *MADE WITH PART-SKIM RICOTTA. FOR LESS TOTAL FAT AND CHOLESTEROL, SWITCH TO NONFAT.

Banana Cake

Serves 6

Serve this cake for dessert then heat the leftovers for breakfast the next day. Note: Once the outside has browned, the center may seem unusually moist. This is right; the apple butter gives it that consistency.

15 minutes to prepare

1 hour 15 minutes to bake

 This cake keeps well, tightly wrapped, for up to four days at room temperature. You can freeze it indefinitely.

⅔ cup pitted prunes

3 tablespoons water

¼ cup brown sugar

¼ cup malt powder (see Note)

1 teaspoon vanilla extract

2 ripe bananas, mashed

2 tablespoons apple butter (see Note)

½ cup nonfat yogurt or buttermilk

2 cups whole wheat pastry flour

1 teaspoon baking powder

½ teaspoon baking soda

½ teaspoon cinnamon

¼ teaspoon salt

1 large egg white

*h*eat the oven to 350° F. In a food processor or blender, combine the prunes and water to make a puree.

🍃 Transfer to a large mixing bowl, and beat in the sugar, malt, vanilla, bananas, apple butter, and yogurt until smooth.

In a separate bowl, combine the pastry flour, baking powder, baking soda, cinnamon, and salt. Stir well with a fine whisk or a long-tined fork to blend thoroughly. Stir into the banana mixture until just combined. In a small bowl, beat the egg white until stiff but not dry, and fold gently but thoroughly into the batter.

Pour the mixture into a nonstick 6-cup or lightly greased bundt pan, and bake until golden brown, and a knife inserted at the top tests clean, about an hour. Let the cake cool in the pan on the rack for 1 hour. Turn the cake out onto the rack and let cool completely.

Note: My favorite apple butter is Apple Essence from Walnut Acres. Malt powder is available at health-food stores and through the King Arthur Baker's Catalog. See page 235 for mail-order information.

[PER SERVING: CAL. 302 / FAT .8 G / PROTEIN 7.1 G / CARB. 47 G / CHOL. 0 / SODIUM 121 MG]

If they were to give a Nobel Prize for peace of mind, my candidate would be whoever discovered that pureed prunes can substitute for butter or oil in many baked goods. The puree acts like shortening, adding moisture and depth, while replacing empty fat calories with fast burning complex carbohydrates and fiber, iron, and vitamin A. The California Prune Board recommends substituting pureed prunes for fat measure to measure in all cake and cookie recipes (e.g., 1 tablespoon pureed prunes to 1 tablespoon butter), but the results aren't always as good as the original. Experiment with your favorite recipes to see whether "pruning" the fat works for you.

BASIC PRUNE PUREE
Makes 1 cup
(developed by the California Prune Board, Pleasanton, CA)

In a food processor or blender, combine 1⅓ cups pitted prunes (8 ounces) and 6 tablespoons water. Puree in pulses.

Chocolate Bundt Cakes

Serves 6

You'd never guess that this modest-looking cookbook contains the key to world domination, but here it is: a fat-free chocolate cake. Prune puree takes the place of shortening without affecting the flavor, and the result is a cake so good that you may end up like me, besieged by special orders. If you are inclined to connive, you could turn the situation to your advantage, asking favors of any kind in return. You would not be refused. Only two words of caution: Don't overbake. Fat-free cakes baked too long can turn out tough.

20 minutes to prepare

45 minutes to bake and cool

 You can puree the prunes up to 2 weeks in advance, keeping the puree refrigerated in a covered container. The cake keeps well at room temperature for up to 4 days, and freezes indefinitely. To defrost and reheat, wrap in foil and place in a 325° F. oven for 20 minutes.

8 ounces (about 1 ⅓ cups) pitted prunes

6 tablespoons plus ⅓ cup prune juice, divided

1 cup sifted cocoa powder

1 cup whole wheat pastry flour

½ cup granulated brown sugar

1 teaspoon baking soda

½ teaspoon baking powder

¼ teaspoon salt

⅔ cup nonfat buttermilk

2 large egg whites

1 teaspoon vanilla extract

eat oven to 350° F. Put the prunes and 6 tablespoons prune juice in the work bowl of a blender or food processor. Process in short pulses to make a thick puree.

Into a large mixing bowl, sift together the cocoa, flour, sugar, baking soda, baking powder, and salt. In a separate bowl, beat together the buttermilk, prune puree, egg whites, vanilla, and the remaining ⅓ cup prune juice. Stir the wet ingredients into the dry, and stir well to blend thoroughly.

Pour into six nonstick bundt muffin tins (or large muffin tins) and bake until firm but springy to the touch, about 25 minutes. Let cool on a cake rack 20 minutes before removing from pan. Let cool on the rack completely before serving. Serve the cakes with ice cream, frozen yogurt, whipped cream, or fruit preserves if desired.

[PER SERVING: CAL. 300 / FAT 2.7 G / PROTEIN 9 G / CARB. 59.9 G / CHOL. 0 / SODIUM 229 MG] % RDA: 26 IRON.

Sweet Potato Pudding

Serves 4

No one will know that this dessert is really an extra vegetable course, but check out the vitamin values below, and keep the secret to yourself.

15 minutes to prepare

1 hour to bake

 You can make this up to 3 days in advance, keeping it refrigerated tightly covered with plastic. Serve cold or at room temperature, or cover with foil and reheat at 325°F. for 15 minutes.

¼ cup dry nonfat milk powder

1 cup skim milk

1 large egg

1 large egg white

1 pound sweet potatoes, baked and mashed (see box, page 97), about 1½ cups sweet potato puree

⅓ cup brown sugar

1 tablespoon molasses

1 teaspoon ground ginger

1 teaspoon ground cinnamon

Vanilla ice cream or frozen yogurt

eat the oven to 370°F. Lightly grease or coat with nonstick spray a 3- to 4-cup baking dish (a small dish is perfect for this).

☙ In a large mixing bowl, whisk together the nonfat milk powder and skim milk. In a separate bowl lightly beat together the egg and egg white and add them to the milk. Beat in the sweet potatoes, brown sugar, molasses, ginger, and cinnamon, until smooth.

☙ Pour into the baking dish. Bake until firm and springy when you press it with your finger, about 1 hour. Serve hot, cold, or room temperature topped with vanilla ice cream or frozen yogurt.

[PER SERVING: CAL. 193 / FAT 1.5 G / PROTEIN 8.2 G / CARB. 36.6 G / CHOL. 71 MG / SODIUM 116 MG] % RDA: 20 CALCIUM.

Custard-Style Indian Pudding

Serves 4 to 6

I've heard people refer to Indian pudding as "ordeal by dessert," and although I've always loved the spicy gingerbread taste, I agree that the conventional cornmeal and molasses combination goes down like an anvil. But made in a water bath as follows, it becomes a luscious custard as flavorful as the classic version, but mercifully light.

40 minutes to prepare

1 hour 40 minutes to bake

 You can prepare this pudding up to 3 days in advance, keeping refrigerated tightly covered with plastic. Serve at room temperature, or cover with foil and reheat at 325°F. for 20 minutes before serving.

3½ cups nonfat milk, divided

½ cup cornmeal, preferably stone ground

½ cup molasses

1 teaspoon ground cinnamon

1 teaspoon ground ginger

½ teaspoon ground mace or nutmeg

1 tablespoon arrowroot
2 large eggs, lightly beaten
Vanilla yogurt (optional)

*h*eat the oven to 350°F.
🍃 Pour 2¾ cups of the milk into a heavy saucepan and scald (bring almost to the boiling point) over medium-high heat. Meanwhile, in a small mixing bowl, whisk the cornmeal into ½ cup of the milk. When the milk in the saucepan has scalded, whisk in the cornmeal mixture, pouring in a steady stream. Continue whisking over medium-low heat until the mixture is thick and smooth, about 20 minutes. Whisk in the molasses, cinnamon, ginger, and mace or nutmeg. Remove from the heat.

🍃 In a large mixing bowl, stir together the arrowroot and the last ¼ cup of the milk, then beat in the eggs.

🍃 Stirring constantly, add ½ cup of the hot cornmeal mixture. Add another ½ cup and stir thoroughly. Add the rest, and stir until smooth.

🍃 Pour the mixture into a lightly greased 1½-quart baking dish. Place this dish inside a deep roasting pan, and add enough water to come halfway up the sides of the baking dish. Bake until set and lightly brown on top, about 1 hour 40 minutes.

🍃 Serve warm, room temperature, or chilled, topped with vanilla yogurt if you'd like.

[PER SERVING: CAL. 285 / FAT .9 G / PROTEIN 11.1 G / CARB. 58 G / CHOL. 3.5 MG / SODIUM 192 MG] % RDA: 31 CALCIUM.

Fruit Cups

Any fruit that can be hollowed out can be used to hold assorted chopped fruits. This is one of my favorite dessert devices because it always looks as if it took a lot more effort than the scooping, chopping, stirring, and stuffing actually involved.

Fruit
Cantaloupe
Orange
Grapefruit
Pineapple
Yogurt cheese (see box, page 133), made with plain or fruit flavored yogurt
Berries or chopped or sliced bananas or chopped dried fruit, such as figs, prunes, apples, apricots, cherries

*C*ut the fruit in half crosswise, hollow out the pulp, and set it aside. To make rounded fruits, such as cantaloupes, grapefruits, or oranges, sit upright on a serving plate, slice off the curved part of the rind, being careful not to cut into the fruit.

🍃 Mix the yogurt cheese with your choice of berries, bananas, or dried fruit, and fill the hollowed-out shell with this mixture, plus the reserved pulp. Chill covered loosely with plastic wrap, or serve it right away.

Vanilla Cheesecake Ice Cream

Yields 2¹/₂ pints

Appliances are my weakness.

I haven't bought shoes in two years, a new dress in one, a lipstick in six months. Clothing and cosmetics catalogs go straight into the recycle bin, and designer sportswear sales don't lure me to the mall.

But I will stand in line for a waffle iron, drive all over the map for a particular immersion blender, and replace my toaster oven regularly with a model promising faster broiling and better browning. I have three food processors, a giant mixmaster, two electric beaters, and three espresso machines. Yet for the longest time, I drew the line at ice cream makers. I have now crossed it.

My incentive was curiosity. I wondered whether it was possible to make fat-free frozen desserts that tasted rich and creamy. Now my curiosity is satisfied, and so are my frequent cravings for this wonderful treat.

5 minutes to prepare
Freezing time depends on your ice cream maker

 You can make this ice cream anytime, and keep it frozen indefinitely.

1½ cups part-skim ricotta cheese
1 cup nonfat vanilla yogurt
¼ cup plus 2 tablespoons maple syrup
2 teaspoons vanilla extract

*i*n a food processor or blender, combine all of the ingredients. Transfer the mixture to your ice cream maker and freeze according to manufacturer's directions.

[PER SERVING: CAL. 179 / FAT TR. / PROTEIN 15 G / CARB. 29 G / CHOL. 1.5 MG / SODIUM 151 MG] % RDA: 59 CALCIUM.

Variation

Strawberry Cheesecake Ice Cream

Substitute strawberry yogurt (blended, not fruit-on-bottom) for the vanilla yogurt, and 2 teaspoons natural strawberry flavoring for vanilla extract. Natural strawberry flavoring is available in the spice and seasoning section at food specialty stores, and by mail from the King Arthur Baker's Catalog (see page 235).

Fresh Fruit Compote

Serves 4

This chilled dessert makes good use of not-so-great fruit. A catchall stewed salad, it may be the best way to savor the last bit of flavor in fruit that's no longer perfect.

30 minutes to prepare

3 hours to chill

 This is a do-ahead dish. Covered and refrigerated, it will keep for up to 3 days.

1 lemon

1 cup water

½ cup light honey

6 cups mixed sliced fresh fruit of any kind, such as apples, peeled and cored; pears, peeled and cored; peaches, peeled and pitted; oranges; grapes; strawberries

⅓ cup apricot or raspberry preserve

Plain low-fat or nonfat yogurt (optional)

Cut the lemon in half and squeeze the lemon juice into a large non-reactive saucepan. Peel away two 2-inch-long strips of the rind and put it into the saucepan, too. Add the water and the honey and stir over low heat until thickened, about 15 minutes. Add the fruit and stir over medium-low heat, uncovered, until the fruit is very soft, about 15 minutes more.

Using a slotted spoon, transfer the fruit to a mixing bowl. Stir in the fruit preserve, mixing thoroughly. Chill, covered, for at least 3 hours before serving, topped with yogurt if you'd like.

[PER SERVING*: CAL. 194.1 / FAT 0 / PROTEIN 0.9 G / CARB. 41 G / CHOL. 0 / SODIUM 2.2 MG] *DEPENDS ON THE FRUIT YOU USE. THESE VALUES REPRESENT A MIXTURE OF THOSE FRUITS LISTED IN RECIPE. % RDA: 77.6 VIT. C.

How to Choose and Use Basic Kitchenware

I move so often, "basic" means just that for me. To control the cost and trouble involved in hauling things from place to place, I've had to whittle away what I want to what I truly need. Here are my recommendations.

You can't have enough bowls for mixing, tossing, beating, and whisking, and for organizing your time and space by holding ingredients until you're ready to use them. I prefer clear Pyrex bowls because you can see what's in them, and because they're heat resistant, microwavable, and inexpensive.

You'll need a heavy **4-quart casserole** with a cover for stewing and for sautéing large quantities of onions, peppers, and such. If you get a **rack** that fits inside it, you'll be able to use it to poach chicken breasts and fish (see page 172 and 190).

"There Are No Stupid Questions" Department

Q. *What is a nonreactive pan?*
A. That term appears—undefined—in so many recipes that you may have the feeling you're the only one who doesn't know what it means. But I wasn't really so sure until I decided to consult several authoritative sources for the purpose of offering an accurate explanation in this book. Here's what I found.

For practical purposes, a nonreactive pan is one that won't discolor acidic foods such as eggs, fruits, vegetables, and anything prepared in a wine or citrus marinade. Enamel cookware and *anodized* aluminum are nonreactive.

COOKWARE: A TRUE FABLE

Exotic ingredients were hard to come by in Milan. But one day I scoured the city to scrape together the ingredients for a Tunisian fish stew. My guests were coming at eight, and at five-thirty, everything was bubbling along beautifully. I turned off the heat (or so I thought) and went to lie down for a few minutes. When I woke up nearly an hour later, I found that I hadn't turned off the heat, and my stew had cooked down to a mere condiment. But it hadn't burned, thanks to my cookware—a casserole made of heavy-duty aluminum alloys. I was able to restore it to stew by adding a couple of pounds of peeled chopped tomatoes.

A **long, wide chopping board** extends your work space and makes it easy to clean. Wood looks pretty, but I've found heavy plastic is more practical. Odors rinse right out of plastic, but cling to wood, making the strawberries that were sliced for dessert taste something like the onions served with dinner. Whichever surface you choose, make sure to clean the board thoroughly after each use, even scrubbing down the cracks so bacteria won't lodge in them.

Get a **stainless-steel colander** for draining pasta, rinsing fruits and vegetables, and straining large quantities of broth. Mine has a hinge on one side and a long handle on the other, so it can rest over the sink for total convenience. You'll need a **sieve**, too, which is smaller than a colander, and with finer mesh. You'll use it to sift dry ingredients, to strain broth, and to drain yogurt for a low-fat spreadable cheese (see page 133).

For lasagna and other big baked dishes, you'll need **ovenproof baking pans** in at least two sizes (8 × 8 inches square and 11 × 7 inches rectangular). I prefer Pyrex, which is sturdy and inexpensive. I don't like nonstick pans for this purpose because it's too easy to scrape them when you serve.

A **compact or full-size food processor** chops, blends, and purees swiftly and efficiently. Get several work bowls so you can process and set aside a number of ingredients at once. The compact is easier to clean and so possibly more practical when you don't need much capacity. But if you're feeding a family, entertaining often, baking bread, or generally making food in big batches, go for the larger model, if you're buying just one.

Kitchen shears are easier to handle and more efficient than knives for mincing herbs and cutting poultry.

And you'll need a **ladle with a 1-cup capacity** for adding broth to risotto and for serving soup or stew.

Because it takes lots of water to boil pasta, you'll need an **8-quart stockpot** for that purpose. It doesn't have to be expensive (mine is Revere Ware), but it should heat up fast.

For roasting chicken, turkey breast, and fish, you'll need a **large rectangular roasting pan**. Look for one with a removable rack; when you roast the chicken on the rack, the fat drips off and drains away. (I use a disposable aluminum roasting pan on the rare occasions when I make a full-size turkey, because I don't have space in my sink to wash a pan of that size).

Inquisitive Cooks Want to Know . . .

Q. Why do cookware prices vary so much?

A. The high price of costly cookware usually indicates that it's made out of expensive metals. The metals are likely to have been chosen for their ability to conduct and control heat.

Q. Is costly cookware always best?

A. No. Pick and choose expensive pieces, depending on what you'll be making in them. For example, I prefer a nonstick surface for crepes and omelettes, so I have an expensive 6-inch heavy-duty nonstick anodized aluminum pan for that purpose. I also paid a lot for a heavy enamel saucepan because I make risotto often, and it gives me as much heat as I want and a slick surface that keeps rice from sticking. I bought an expensive 11-inch skillet and 6-quart casserole because I want optimum control over the heat when I sauté and stew. I also have several inexpensive Revere Ware saucepans, covered pots, and skillets, which are fine for everyday use.

Simply, having a complete set may look nice, but it's not necessarily practical or economical. Buy a complete set only if you're sure that: (a) you'll use everything in it, or enough of it to justify the total cost, or (b) there's some real advantage to having everything made of this particular material.

Often you don't need an expensive piece—for instance, a modestly priced Revere Ware stockpot is fine for boiling pasta, and costs much less than a stockpot made by Caphalon or Cuisinart.

You'll be glad to have **three heavy saucepans** (1 quart, 2 quart, and 3 quart). *I'm* glad that one of mine is enameled because it's easy to clean and slick enough to require less

NICE, BUT NOT NECESSARY

I use my compact microwave oven for blanching and steaming fresh vegetables and for baking potatoes. It's faster and neater and more precise.

I also have an immersion blender, a long-handled, single-blade gadget that purees ingredients right in the bowl or saucepan, saving me the trouble of transferring them to the food processor. It's also perfect for mayonnaise because I can run it steadily with one hand and pour in the oil with the other. An electric beater makes it possible to prepare souffles and all other dishes that depend on well-whipped egg whites.

cooking fat than most made of metal. You'll be as glad to own a **9-inch sauté pan** and an **11-inch skillet**.

Get a good **timer** because precision counts when you're cooking foods such as pasta, fish, and rice.

A **slotted spoon** comes in handy for fishing foods out of cooking, poaching, or soaking liquid. The most versatile are round and wide, essentially a cross between a ladle and a spatula with holes.

After you've taken them out of the oven, dishes should cool on a **wire rack**. The rack should stand about an inch high so air can circulate around it.

Lay in a number of **wooden spoons** and **spatulas** for handling pasta, tossing salads, and cooking on nonstick pans (metal utensils scrape off the treated surface). You'll need a **metal spatula** for tasks such as removing cookies from a baking sheet.

A **cheese grater** isn't just for cheese. You'll use it to grate ginger (grating releases more flavor than chopping or mincing), garlic, and the zest of lemons and oranges.

You'll use a **potato or vegetable peeler** for carrots, apples, artichoke stems, and many other fruits and vegetables.

Nothing beats a **wire whisk** for eggs, sauces, and some soups.

Have at least four **good knives**: one large serrated knife to slice bread; one sharp heavy knife to cut meat and crush garlic cloves; one sharp medium-blade knife for slicing and chopping vegetables; and one paring knife for fruit. Good knives are expensive, but you won't save any money by getting cheap ones, because they'll go dull on you before long, and you'll have to replace them.

Ordering by mail is often convenient, but rarely a bargain. Before you hit the 800 numbers or send off your checks, go comparison shopping. A specialty store or health-food market near you may carry many of the goods featured in the catalogs and charge less for them. And remember, if you're unhappy with the products you receive, write or call the company with your complaints. It's risky buying goods sight unseen, but if the flavor or quality doesn't match the description in the catalog, let them know and demand a refund.

With that caveat out of the way, here are some companies whose products and services I recommend.

Walnut Acres has been my favorite mail-order food retailer for many years. Thanks to their reliable delivery service and high standards, I've been able to enjoy the best organic cereals, dried beans, dried herbs, dried fruits, and other ingredients in each of the many places I've lived, from Los Angeles to Cape Cod to Milan. The goods aren't cheap, but prices compare favorably with other mail-order firms that aren't as dependable.

Walnut Acres Organic Farms
Walnut Acres Road
Penns Creek, PA 17862
(800) 433-3998

I order from **King Arthurs Baker's Catalog** for two reasons. First, King Arthur makes better flour and distributes better products than anyone else. I'm convinced King Arthur's basic white and whole wheat flours have a magical property that compensate for lousy technique, because my breads—otherwise lumpen and doughy—never fail when I use them. The catalog also offers baking utensils, and while I don't recommend ordering cooking equipment by mail generally, this company is so dependable, I've come to feel that trusting them is the same as picking it out myself.

Second, the King Arthur company supports its products with informative recipe inserts written with earnest and painstaking consideration for amateurs. Each insert is a seminar on its subject, whether how to use the sourdough starter, make semolina bread, or prepare the world's best popovers.

The Baker's Catalog
P.O. Box 876
Norwich, VT 05055
(800) 827-6836

Some of the best rices on the market come from **Lundberg Family Farms,** which has been procuring and cultivating unusual strains of rice for several generations. Much of their crop is grown without synthetic chemicals. Their mahogany colored Wehani brand is so sweet and chewy, it's virtually rice pudding. Also try their Black Japonica brand, Jubilee Blend, and Sweet Brown (a sticky rice perfect for sushi).

Lundberg Family Farm
P.O. Box 369
Richvale, CA 95974
(916) 882-4551

My favorite herb-infused vinegars for cooking and salad dressing come from **Wild Thyme Farm** in Medusa, New York, and **American Spoon Foods** makes outstanding jams and fruit purees (marketed as Spoon Fruits and Fruit Butters).

Wild Thyme Farm
Medusa, NY 12120
(518) 239-4756

American Spoon Foods
P.O. Box 566
Petoskey, MI 49770-0566
(800) 222-5886

You can avoid hunting down Asian seasonings by ordering them from **The Spice Merchant,** which sells virtually everything you need for Far Eastern and Middle Eastern dishes at prices that compare well with specialty shops.

The Spice Merchant
P.O. Box 524
Jackson Hole, WY 83001
(800) 551-5999

Throughout the book, I indicate a preference for organically grown potatoes, which tend to taste much better than plain old mass-produced potatoes, but which can be hard to find. That's why I buy potatoes by mail from Jim and Megan Gerritsen at **WoodPrairie Farm,** who raise and ship potatoes of many kinds, all organically grown, and gently cleaned without chemicals. It may seem crazy to spend up to three times more for a vegetable that you can buy by the sackful at your supermarket. But most ordinary chain grocery stores don't carry potatoes anywhere near as sweet and creamy as the Gerritsen's Yukon Golds, Reddales, or fingerling varieties.

WoodPrairie Farm
RFD 1 Box 164
Bridgewater, ME 04735
(800) 829-9765

If you live West of the Mississippi, where the cost of postage from Maine may be prohibitive, try:

Ronniger's Seed Potatoes
Star Route Road 73
Movie Springs, ID 83845

For more information, consult *Green Groceries* by Jeanne Heifetz (HarperPerennial), a comprehensive catalog of good food-by-mail companies. And if you want to know what's new in the mail-order marketplace, subscribe to the newsletter *Mail Order Gourmet*, P. O. Box 1085, New York, NY 10011, (800) 989-5996.

Bibliography
A Personal Recommended Reading List
for the Almost Vegetarian

It used to be that whenever someone asked me to name my favorite cookbook, my answer would depend on my mood or the time of year. A French volume in the winter; something southwestern in summer; a book of thick, chewy pastas when I was feeling lost and insecure; a collection of crisp vegetable curries when my confidence returned.

But then something happened, and I discovered I have a favorite above all others, a favorite for life, a cookbook I love so much I still consult it even though I know all of the recipes and most of the text by heart.

Here's what occurred.

I came down with influenza. This was no mere flu. This was an illness of four syllables. It was so bad I had to spend an entire day in the emergency room. It was so bad, I couldn't imagine ever eating again; I couldn't imagine *wanting* to eat ever again.

The fever cooled gradually, but my appetite didn't return. I was moving to Europe in a week and needed strength for the trip. Fifteen pounds underweight and barely able to walk around the block, I had to eat. But I couldn't.

I flipped through every cookbook in my collection looking for *something* that made me hungry. I found it in my jam-stained, syrup-splattered, batter-blotched copy of Marion Cunningham's *Breakfast Book* (Knopf): a baked apple. A baked apple and a cup of cocoa. And then a bowl of Indian pudding. Even writing this now, on a full stomach, restored to my fighting weight a year and a half later, it makes me hungry.

The recipes in that book will always make me hungry because they appeal not to particular cravings but to two fundamental, enduring desires: the desire for comfort and for nourishment. I will be fickle about the runners-up, loving first some new Chinese cookbook, then the most recent recipe collection from Tunisia, Italy, or Provence. I'll be thrilled by what's new, exotic, and bold for a time, but I'll cherish *The Breakfast Book* for *all* time.

The nutritional information in this book comes largely from *The Wellness Encyclopedia of Food and Nutrition*, published and written by the University of California Wellness Letter Editors and Sheldon Margen. I own three copies of the five-hundred-page-volume. I keep one in my kitchen, one in my study, and one in more or less permanent circulation among friends. The title is dull, but the book is a lively, thorough guide to foods of all kinds.

Techniques of Healthy Cooking, published by the Culinary Institute of America, may be the best book there is on the title subject. Although it's meant for professional chefs, anyone with a working knowledge of pots and pans will find it easy to follow. It's full of neat tricks for reducing fat and boosting flavor, as well as basic recipes that inspire imaginative adaptations.

I found Emelie Tolley and Chris Mead's beautiful, compact *The Herbal Pantry* (Clarkson Potter/Publishers) an excellent introduction to cooking with herbs, and if there were never another word written on the subject of Mediterranean seafood, it wouldn't be missed by anyone who has a copy of Alan Davidson's exhaustive book by that name (Penguin). An odd combination of encyclopedia, commentary, and recipe collection, it's one of my favorite books on any subject.

In effect I had only half of a microwave oven until I bought Barbara Kafka's inspirational, instructive *Microwave Gourmet* and *Microwave Healthstyle* cookbooks (Morrow). While I use my microwave mostly for defrosting, Kafka tested its potential and found it nearly limitless, sharing in these books eclectic, appetizing recipes, which are unfailingly accurate. I'm grateful for the work she's done so that the rest of us can have splendid, healthy meals at the push of a button.

The most comprehensive and practical single cookbook/reference book I can recommend is Anne Willan's *La Varenne Pratique* (Crown)—the one I consult for precise infor-

mation on any subject pertaining to food preparation.

I was a novice baker when I bought *The King Arthur Flour 200th Anniversary Cookbook* (The Countryman Press), but having baked from it almost daily since then, I feel like a pro. Compiled by Brinna Sands, who married into the family that founded King Arthur two centuries back and continues to manage it today (see page 235), the book shares the cumulative wisdom of generations of avid bakers so that you can make terrific yeast breads, waffles, pancakes, muffins, sourdoughs, pretzels, pastas . . . virtually anything calling for batter or dough.

Finally, subscribing to *Cook's Illustrated* magazine is better than enrolling in a master class. If it's slimmer than other food magazines, it's not because it's slighter, but because its serious, scrupulous editors don't accept advertisements. Named for the wonderful step-by-step drawings that accompany the recipes, *Cook's Illustrated* is instructive, informative, and the one food magazine I wouldn't want to do without.

INDEX

Almost Vegetarian(s), 3
  Holiday Dinner, 186–87
  nutrition for, 7–8
Apple(s), 210
  Crepes, 216
  Flan, 217–18
  Sauce, Chunky Maple, 216–17
  Yogurt Parfait, 217
Apricot(s), 210–11
  and Carrot Terrine, 87
arborio rice, 38. See also Risotto
aromatic rices (Jasmine, basmati,
    Texmati), 38
Artichoke(s) 14; cooking, 173
  or Poached Chicken Breasts with
    Artichoke Stuffing, 172–74
  Soup, 47–48
Asian Snow Pea and Mussel Salad,
    75–76
Asparagus, 15
  and Leeks, Pasta with, 116
  Torta, Herbed, 80–81
avocado, 15

B-vitamin, dishes rich in, 7
Baba Ganoush, 71
baking and cooking terms, 5–6
balsamic vinegar, 40
Banana(s), 211
  Cake, 224–25
  Ricotta Cream, 224
Barbecued or Broiled Turkey Burgers
    with All the Fixin's, 184
Barley, Mushroom, 102–3
basil, fresh, 31; cooking with, 54
Bean Curd
  or Chicken, Tea Steamed, with
    Vegetables, 170–71
  and Mushrooms (and Scallops) in
    Thai Peanut-Coconut Curry
    Sauce, 162–63

Beans (legumes), 35–36; soaking, 35,
    37; cooking, 36. See also Black
    Beans; soybeans; White Beans
    or Seafood, Chili with, 204–5
Béchamel Sauce, Light(er), with
    Parmesan, 125–26
Beet(s), 16; cooking, 154
  Risotto, 132
  Tabbouleh, 72–73
Bell Pepper. See Pepper
Black Beans, Spicy, with Fresh Plums,
    157
blanch, defined, 5
blanching or steaming vegetables in
    microwave, 144
blueberries, 211
bouquet garni, how to make, 44–45
braise, defined, 5
Broccoli, 16; Pesto, 160
broil, defined, 5
Broiled. See Barbecued; Grilled
broth, 44; homemade, 44
  chicken, very basic, 46; how to
    defat, 46
  mushroom, light, for risotto and
    soups, 47
  vegetable, basic, 44–45
brown rice, 37, 38
brussels sprouts, 17
button mushrooms, 22–23

Cabbage, 17
  with Apples and Cheese, 84
  Cakes, 83
  and Cumin, Whole Wheat Penne
    with, 117
  Filled with Spinach, Basmati
    Rice, and Fresh Salmon or
    Spicy Lentil Puree, 199–200
  Red, and Onion Relish, 106

Sweet, Shredded, Chicken Legs
    Filled with, 180
Caesar-Style Salad, Oil-Free,
    Creamy, 67
Cake(s)
  Banana, 224–25
  Chocolate Bundt, 226
  Peach Scone, 219
Calamari
  about cleaning, 207
  or Cannelloni, Spinach and Ri-
    cotta in, 206–7
calcium, in meatless diet, 8
calcium-rich dishes, 8
calories and weight control, 8
Cannelloni or Calamari, Spinach and
    Ricotta in, 206–7
canola oil, 41
cantaloupe, 212
carbohydrate, high-, menus, 10
carbohydrates, simple and complex, 9
Carrot(s), 18
  and Apricot Terrine, 87–88
  -Ginger Risotto, 129–30
  Pie, Savory, 163–64
  and Spinach Lasagna with Lemon
    Sauce, 123–24
Cauliflower, 18
  Soup, Peerless Pureed, 57–58
celery, 18–19
Cheddar Buttermilk Spoon Bread,
    103–4
Cheese and Potato Pierogin, 150–51
Cheesecake Ice Cream, Vanilla, 229;
    Strawberry, 229
cherries, 212
Chicken, 168–82. See also Turkey
  buying, handling, etc., 168–69
  and Lentil Stew, 179
  Roasted with Garlic, 181–82

Chicken Breasts
  Gnocchi with Sun-Dried Tomatoes and, 126
  and Mushrooms, 174–75
  Poached, or Artichokes with Artichoke Stuffing, 172–74
  (or Pressed Tofu) with Sweet Mustard Glaze, 176
  Rice Salad with Mango and Chickpeas, 77
  Tandoori Spice Marinade for, 177
  Tapenade, Braised, 169–70
  Tea Steamed, or Bean Curd with Vegetables, 170–71
  Vegetable-Tofu Stir-Fry with, 147–49
chicken broth, very basic, 46; how to defat, 46
Chicken Legs
  Filled with Sweet Shredded Cabbage, 180
  Stewed with Fennel, Tomatoes, and Saffron, 178
Chickpea(s)
  Curry, 156
  and Mango, Rice Salad (with or without Chicken), 77
  or Shrimp, Fresh Tomatoes and Feta Cheese with, 203–4
Chili with Seafood or Beans, 204–5
chives, fresh, 31
Chocolate
  Bundt Cake, 226
  Pudding in Orange Shells (The Emperor's New Dessert), 222
chop, defined, 6
Chowder, Corn, Chilled, 59–60
Cilantro (coriander), fresh, 31
  Pesto, 161
Clafouti, Seasonal, 219–20
clove, about using, 85
Compote, Fresh Fruit, 230

cooking and baking terms, 5–6
cooking well, tips for, 4–5
cookware and utensils
  choosing and using, 231–34
  luxury items, 233
  non-stick pans, 232
coriander (cilantro), fresh, 31
Corn, 19
  Chowder, Chilled, 59–60
  Potato, and Egg Salad with Chives, 69–70
Corncakes, Sweet, with Mixed Pestos or Crab Filling, 158–59
Cornmeal, Cheddar Buttermilk Spoon Bread, 103–4
Court Bouillon, 192
Couscous, 198
  with Vegetables (and Fish), 197–98
Crab Filling, Sweet Corncakes with, 158–59
Cream-Style Low-Fat Basic Dressing, 66
cremini mushrooms, 23
Crepes, Apple, 216
cruciferous vegetables, 9
Cucumber, 19–20; seeding, 60
  Soup, Chilled, 60
cumin, dried, ground, 32
Curry
  Chickpea, 156
  Sauce, Thai Peanut-Coconut, Mushrooms and Bean Curd and Scallops in, 162–63

Dessert, 216–30
  Apple Crepes, 216
  Apple Flan, 217–18
  Apple Sauce, Chunky Maple, 216–17
  Apple Yogurt Parfait, 217
  Banana Cake, 224–25
  Banana Ricotta Cream, 224
  Chocolate Bundt Cakes, 226
  Chocolate Pudding in Orange Shells (The Emperor's New Dessert), 222
  Fresh Fruit Compote, 230
  Fruit Cups, 228

Fruit Yogurt Soufflés, 218
  Holiday Pudding, Steamed, 223
  Indian Pudding, Custard-Style, 227–28
  Peach Scone Cakes, 219
  Prune Puree, Basic, 225
  Ricotta, Sweet Baked, with Lemon or Pumpkin, 221–22
  Seasonal Clafouti, 219–20
  Strawberry Risotto, 220–21
  Sweet Potato Pudding, 227
  Vanilla Cheesecake Ice Cream, 229
dice, defined, 6
dill, fresh and dried, 32
Dip, Hummus, 72
Dough for Savory Pie, 165
Dressing. See Salad Dressing

Egg, Potato, and Corn Salad with Chives, 69–70
Eggplant, 20; salting, 82
  Pancakes, 82–83
  and Peppers, Mediterranean, 81–82
  and Radicchio Sandwich, Baked, 147
  Salad, Baba Ganoush, 71
eggs, using raw, 159
Endive and Leek Fondue, 105

Fajita Salad, Grilled (with Turkey), 182–83
Fat-Free Buttermilk Salad Dressing, 65
  in a meatless diet, 7
  and weight control, 8
Fennel, 20–21; seed, 32
  and Leek Flans, Gingered, 90–91
  Tomatoes, and Saffron, Chicken Stewed with, 178
Fettuccine, Spinach, with Tangy Tofu Sauce and Mushrooms, 118
Fish, 190–203. See also Seafood
  about buying fresh, 190; cooking, 190; serving whole, 191
  Braised, with Winter Greens, 192–93

Court Bouillon for poaching, 192
Couscous with Vegetables and,
    197–98
Milk Poached with Chive Cream,
    193–94
Monkfish with Mushrooms and
    Lentils, 194–95
Poached, 190–91
Salmon, Fresh, or Spicy Lentil
    Puree, Cabbage Filled with
    Spinach, Basmati Rice and,
    199–200
Sandwich, Grilled Niçoise-
    Style, 202–3
Skate, Broiled with Citrus Glaze,
    196–97
Tuna, Fresh, and White Beans,
    201–2
Flan(s)
Apple, 217–18
Leek, Gingered, 90–91
Focacce, 138–39; variations, 139
    for Pizzas, 139
French Toast Sandwich, Savory, 146
fresh fruit directory, 210–15. *See also*
    Fruit; Name of Fruit
fresh vegetable directory, 14–30. *See
    also* Vegetables; Name of Veg-
    etable
Fruit. *See also* Name of Fruit
    choosing, 210; washing, 219
    Compote, Fresh, 230
    Cups, 228
    dried, Steamed Holiday Pudding,
        223
    fresh, directory, 210–15
    Seasonal Clafouti, 219–20
    Yogurt Soufflés, 218

Garlic, 21; grating, 149; peeling, 193
    Pesto, Roast, 139
    Roasted, Wholly Wholesome
        Mashed Potatoes with, 100
Ginger, fresh, 32; grating, 149
    -Carrot Risotto, 129–30
Gingered Leek and Fennel Flans,
    90–91
Gnocchi, 124–25
    with Leeks and Ricotta, 127

with Sun-Dried Tomatoes (and
    Chicken), 126
Grape Leaves, Stuffed, 96–97
Grilled, 143
    Assorted Vegetables, 143–45
    or Broiled Pressed Tofu, 145
    Fajita Salad (with Turkey), 182–83
    Niçoise-Style Sandwich, 202–3

Herbed Asparagus Torta, 80–81
herbs
    bouquet garni, how to make,
        44–45
    fresh, for pasta sauce, 110
    and spices, organic, 89
    storing fresh, 70; washing, 73
high-carbohydrate menus, 10
high-fiber cruciferous vegetables, 9
high-fiber menus, 9
Holiday Dinner, Almost Vegetarian,
    186–87
Holiday Pudding, Steamed, 223
Hummus, 72

Ice Cream, Vanilla Cheesecake, 229;
    Strawberry Cheesecake, 229
Indian Pudding, Custard-Style,
    227–28
iron-rich dishes, 7

kiwi, 212

Lasagna, Carrot and Spinach, with
    Lemon Sauce, 123–24
Leek(s), 21–22; cleaning, 91
    and Asparagus, Pasta with, 116
    and Endive Fondue, 105
    and Fennel Flans, Gingered, 90–91
    and Potato Soup, Aromatic, 50
    and Ricotta, Gnocchi with, 127
legumes (beans), 35–36; cooking, 36;
    soaking, 35, 37
Lemon(s), 212–13 ; zest, 221
    or Pumpkin, Sweet Baked Ricotta
        with, 221
Lemony Risotto, 130–31
Lentil(s)
    and Chicken Stew, 179
    and Mushrooms, Monkfish with,
        194–95

Puree, Spicy, 201; Cabbage Filled
    with Spinach, Basmati Rice, and
    Fresh Salmon or, 199–200
Salad with Sun-Dried Tomatoes
    and Feta Cheese, 74–75
Soup with Parmesan, Chunky,
    56–57
lettuce(s), 22; cleaning, 66
Linguine with Mussels and Shrimp,
    121–22
long-grain rice, 38
Low-Fat Cream-Style Basic Dressing,
    66
low-fat menus, 9

mail-order sources for food, 235–36
mangoes, 213
Marinade, Tandoori Spice, for
    Chicken (or Pressed Tofu), 177
Mayonnaise, 159–60
meatless diets, risks of, 7–8
Meatless Main Dish, 141–65
    about combining for, 141–42;
        compensating for flavor and
        nutrients, 142
    Black Beans, Spicy, with Fresh
        Plums, 157
    Carrot Pie, Savory, 163–64
    Cheese and Potato Pierogin, 150–51
    Chickpea Curry, 156
    Corncakes, Sweet, with Mixed
        Pestos or Crab Filling, 158–59
    Eggplant and Radicchio Sandwich,
        Baked, 147
    French Toast Sandwich, Savory,
        146
    Grilled Assorted Vegetables,
        143–45
    Grilled or Broiled Pressed Tofu, 145
    Mushroom Pie, Savory, 164–65
    Mushrooms and Bean Curd (and
        Scallops) in Thai Peanut-
        Coconut Curry Sauce, 162–63
    Potato Frittata, 149–50
    Potato Tortas, Individual, 151–53
    Vegetable Ragu, 153–54
    Vegetable-Tofu Stir-Fry (with
        Chicken), 147–49
    Winter Slaw, Wonderful Warm,
        154–55

meatless meals, a collection of side dishes, 80

Mediterranean Eggplant and Peppers, 81–82

medium-grain rice, 38

Menus

all vegetarian, 12, 13; almost vegetarian, 13

Almost Vegetarian Holiday Dinner, 186–87

high-carbohydrate, 10

high-fiber, 9

low-fat, 9

one-dish dinners, 12

special occasion, 13

mesclun, American, for salad, 68

metabolism, mystery of, 8

microwave, blanching or steaming vegetables in, 144

milk, scalding, 125

mince, defined, 6

Minestrone with Creamy Pesto, My Favorite, 54–56

Monkfish with Mushrooms and Lentils, 194–95

morel mushrooms, 23

multivitamins, the better, 9

Mushroom(s), 22–24; varieties of, 22–24

Barley, 102–3

and Bean Curd (and Scallops) in Thai Peanut-Coconut Curry Sauce, 162–63

broth, light, for risotto and soups, 47

and Chicken, 174–75

and Lentils, Monkfish with, 194–95

Noodle Pudding, 119–20

Pie, Savory, 164–65

and Tangy Tofu Sauce, Spinach Fettuccine with, 118

Mussel(s)

about cleaning, 122

Risotto with, 135–36

and Shrimp, Linguine with, 121–22

and Snow Pea Salad, Asian, 75–76

Nectarine(s). See also Peaches

Relish, 107

"nonfat buttermilk," 65

Noodle Pudding, Mushroom, 119–20

Not-So-Sloppy Joes, 185

nutrition for almost vegetarians, 7–8

nutritional content per serving, 11

Oil(s)

cooking with, 41; varieties of (canola, safflower, peanut, etc.), 41

-Free Creamy Caesar-Style Salad, 67

and Vinegar Salad Dressing, Classic Reliable, 65

olive oil, 41; for pasta sauce, 110

one-dish dinners, 12

Onion(s), 24

Braised, with Sweet Rice Stuffing, 94–95

and Red Cabbage Relish, 106

Orange(s), 213

Shells, Chocolate Pudding in (The Emperor's New Dessert), 222

Tahini Dressing, 73

oregano, fresh and dried, 32–33

organic herbs and spices, 89

oyster mushrooms, 23

Panzanella Soup, 50–51

Parmesan cheese, for pasta sauce, 110

parsley, fresh, 33

Pasta, 110–27

about, 110–11; favorite brand, 112; perfect, 111; herbs, imported cheese, olive oil for, 110

with Asparagus and Leeks, 116

Cannelloni or Calamari, Spinach and Ricotta in, 206–7

Gnocchi, 124–25

Gnocchi with Leeks and Ricotta, 127

Gnocchi with Sun-Dried Tomatoes (and Chicken), 126

Lasagna, Carrot and Spinach, with Lemon Sauce, 123–24

Linguine with Mussels and Shrimp, 121–22

Mushroom Noodle Pudding, 119–20

Quick Creamy, 120–21; variations, 121

Sauce, Light(er) Béchamel, with Parmesan, 125–26

Sauce, Perfect Tomato, 112–13; Perfect Tomato Too, 113–14

Spinach Fettuccine with Tangy Tofu Sauce and Mushrooms, 118

Whole Wheat Penne with Cabbage and Cumin, 117

Peach(es), 214

Scone Cakes, 219

pears, 214

peas, 25

Penne, Whole Wheat, with Cabbage and Cumin, 117

Pepper(s), 25–26

bell, roasting, 88

Bell, Soup, 58–59

and Eggplant, Mediterranean, 81–82

Filled Peppers, 92

Red Roasted, Terrine, 88–89

Perfect Tomato Sauce(s), 112–14

Pesto(s), 55

Broccoli, 160

Cilantro, 161

Creamy, 55

ice cubes, 160–61

Mixed, Sweet Corncakes with, 158–59

Roast Garlic, 139

pineapples, 214–15

Pissaladière-Inspired Potato Tarts, 97–98

Pizzas, 139

Plums, 215

Fresh, Spicy Black Beans with, 157

poach, defined, 6
porcini mushrooms, 23
portobello mushrooms, 23
Posole-Tomato Soup, 51–52
Potato(es), 26–27; varieties of, 26.
    See also Sweet Potatoes
    baking, 97
    and Cheese Pierogin, 150–51
    Corn, and Egg Salad with Chives,
        69–70
    Frittata, 149–50
    Gratin, 99
    and Leek Soup, Aromatic, 50
    Mashed, Wholly Wholesome,
        99–100; with Roasted Garlic,
        100
    Red, in Saffron Marinade, 101
    Salad, Warm Confetti, 68–69
    Tarts, Pissaladière-Inspired, 97–98
    Tortas, Individual, 151–53
Poultry, 168–87. See also Chicken;
    Turkey
    buying, handling, etc., 168–69
prune juice, for roughage, 10
prune puree, basic, 225
Pudding (dessert)
    Chocolate, in Orange Shells, 222
    Holiday, Steamed, 223
    Indian, Custard-Style, 227–28
    Sweet Potato, 227
Pumpkin. See also Winter Squash
    or Lemon, Sweet Baked Ricotta
        with, 221
    Risotto, 133–34
puree, defined, 6

Radicchio and Eggplant Sandwich,
    Baked, 147
raspberries, 215
recipes, about following, 5
Red Cabbage and Onion Relish, 106
Red Pepper. See Pepper

Red Potatoes. See Potatoes
Relish
    Nectarine, 107
    Red Cabbage and Onion, 106
Rice, 37–39. See also Risotto
    Basmati, Spinach, and Fresh
        Salmon or Spicy Lentil Puree,
        Cabbage Filled with, 199–200
    Grape Leaves, Stuffed, 96–97
    how to steam perfect, 38
    Salad with Mango and Chickpeas
        (with or without Chicken), 77
    Stuffing with Pine Nuts and Dried
        Cherries (for roast turkey),
        186–87
    Stuffing, Sweet, Braised Onions
        with, 94–95
    varieties of, 38. See also
        Name of Rice (arborio, brown,
        wild, etc.)
Ricotta
    Banana Cream, 224
    and Leeks, Gnocchi with, 127
    and Spinach in Calamari or Can-
        nelloni, 206–7
    Sweet Baked, with Lemon or
        Pumpkin, 221–22
Risotto, 128–37; cooking, 111–12
    arborio rice for, 38
    Basic, 128
    Beet, 132
    Carrot-Ginger, 129–30
    Lemony, 130–31
    light mushroom broth for, 47
    with Mussels, 135–36
    Pumpkin, 133–34
    with Shrimp, 136–37
    Strawberry, 220–21
    Summer Garden (with Scallops),
        134–35
roast, defined, 6
rosemary, fresh, 33
roughage. See high-fiber; prune juice
Rutabagas, Simple Baked, 92–93

saffron, dried, 33–34
sage, fresh and dried, 34
Salad(s), 64–77; tips for, 64
    about cleaning lettuce, 66

Asian Snow Pea and Mussel,
    75–76
Baba Ganoush, 71
Beet Tabbouleh, 72–73
Caesar-Style, Oil-Free Creamy, 67
Grilled Fajita (with Turkey),
    182–83
herbs. See Herbs
mesclun, 68; varieties of, 68
Lentil, with Sun-Dried Tomatoes
    and Feta Cheese, 74–75
Potato, Corn, and Egg with
    Chives, 69–70
Potato, Warm Confetti, 68–69
Rice, with Mango and Chickpeas
    (with or without Chicken), 77
two tahini, 70
Salad Dressing, 64–66
    Fat-Free Buttermilk, 65
    Hummus, 72
    Low-Fat Cream-Style, Basic, 66
    oil and vinegar, 64; Classic
        Reliable, 65
    Orange Tahini, 73
    Sesame-Scallion Vinaigrette, 65
    Tahini, Basic, 71
    Walnut-Raspberry Vinaigrette, 65
Salmon, Fresh, or Spicy Lentil Puree,
    Cabbage Filled with Spinach,
    Basmati Rice and, 199–200
salt, using, 104
Sandwich
    French Toast, Savory, 146
    Grilled Niçoise-Style, 202–3
Sauce. See also Pesto
    Béchamel, Light(er), with Parme-
        san, 125–26
    Mayonnaise, 159–60
    Perfect Tomato, 112–13; Perfect
        Tomato Too, 113–14
sauté, defined, 6
Savory Pie, Carrot, 163–64; Mush-
    room, 164–65; Dough for, 165
scalding milk, 125
scallions, 27
Scallops
    and Mushrooms and Bean Curd in
        Thai Peanut-Coconut Curry
        Sauce, 162–63

Summer Garden Risotto with, 134–35
Scone Cakes, Peach, 219
Seafood, 203–7. *See also* Fish
 or Beans, Chili with, 204–5
 Calamari or Cannelloni, Spinach, and Ricotta in, 206–7
 Crab Filling, Sweet Corncakes with, 158–59
 Mussel and Snow Pea Salad, Asian, 75–76
 Mussels, Risotto with, 135–36
 Mussels and Shrimp, Linguine with, 121–22
 Scallops and Mushrooms and Bean Curd in Thai Peanut-Coconut Curry Sauce, 162–63
 Scallops, Summer Garden Risotto with, 134–35
 Shrimp, or Chickpeas, Fresh Tomatoes and Feta Cheese with, 203–4
 Shrimp, Risotto with, 136–37
Seasonal Clafouti, 219–20
seasonings, directory of, 31–34. *See also* Name of Seasoning
Sesame-Scallion Vinaigrette, 65
shallots, 27
shiitake mushrooms, 23–24
short-grain rice, 38
Shrimp
 or Chickpeas, Fresh Tomatoes and Feta Cheese with, 203–4
 cleaning, 122
 and Mussels, Linguine with, 121–22
 Risotto with, 136–37
Side Dishes and Starters, 80–107
 about making a meal of, 80
 Asparagus Torta, Herbed

Cabbage with Apples and Cheese, 84
Cabbage Cakes, 83
Carrot and Apricot Terrine, 87–88
Eggplant Pancakes, 82–83
Eggplant and Peppers, Mediterranean, 81–82
Endive and Leek Fondue, 105
Grape Leaves, Stuffed, 96–97
Leek and Fennel Flans, Gingered, 90–91
Mushroom Barley, 102–3
Nectarine Relish, 107
Onions, Braised, with Sweet Rice Stuffing, 94–95
Pepper Filled Peppers, 92
Potato Gratin, 99
Potato Tarts, Pissaladière-Inspired, 97–98
Potatoes, Mashed, Wholly Wholesome, 99–100; with Roasted Garlic, 100
Potatoes, Red, in Saffron Marinade, 101
Red Cabbage and Onion Relish, 106
Red Pepper, Roasted, Terrine, 88–89
Rutabagas, Simple Baked, 92–93
Spoon Bread, Cheddar Buttermilk, 103–4
Sweet Potato Pancakes, 102
Tomato Timbales in Tender Spinach Casing, Chilled, 89–90
Turnips, Baked Stuffed, 93–94
Winter Squash Gratin, 86–87
Winter Vegetables in Mellow Lemon Marinade, 85
Skate, Broiled with Citrus Glaze, 196–97
Sloppy Joes, Not-So-Sloppy, 185
Snow Pea(s), 76
 and Mussel Salad, Asian, 75–76
Soufflés, Fruit Yogurt, 218
Soup, 43–61
 Artichoke, 47–48
 Bell Pepper, 58–59
 broth, 44; homemade, 44; mushroom, for risotto and soups, 47; vegetable, basic, 44–45

Cauliflower, Peerless Pureed, 57–58
chicken broth, very basic, 46; how to defat, 46
Chilled Corn Chowder, 59–60
Chilled Cucumber, 60
Cold Sweet Potato, 61
Leek and Potato, Aromatic, 50
Lentil, with Parmesan, Chunky, 56–57
Minestrone with Creamy Pesto, My Favorite, 54–56
Panzanella, 50–51
Spinach-Yogurt, Tangy, 48–49
Tomato-Posole, 51–52
Vegetable, Silken, 52–53
Wheat Berry, 53–54
soybeans, 36–37
special occasion menus, 13
spices and herbs, organic, 89
Spinach, 28
 Basmati Rice, and Fresh Salmon or Spicy Lentil Puree, Cabbage Filled with, 199–200
 and Carrot Lasagna with Lemon Sauce, 123–24
 Casing, Tender, Chilled Tomato Timbales in, 89–90
 Fettuccine with Tangy Tofu Sauce and Mushrooms, 118
 and Ricotta in Calamari or Cannelloni, 206–7
 -Yogurt Soup, Tangy, 48–49
Spoon Bread, Cheddar Buttermilk, 103–4
squash. *See* Winter Squash; zucchini
Starters. *See* Side Dishes and Starters
steam, defined, 6
steaming or blanching vegetables in microwave, 144
steep, defined, 6
stew, defined, 6
Stir-Fry, 6
 Vegetable-Tofu (with Chicken), 147–49
strawberries, 215
Strawberry Cheesecake Ice Cream, 229
Strawberry Risotto, 220–21
sugar, eating, 9–10

sugar snap peas, cooking, 76
Summer Garden Risotto (with Scallops), 134–35
summer squash. *See* zucchini
Sun-Dried Tomatoes, 74
    Gnocchi with (and Chicken), 126
    Lentil Salad with, and Feta Cheese, 74–75
Sweet Potato(es), 28
    Pancakes, 102
    Pudding, 227
    Soup, Cold, 61

Tahini
    Dressing, Basic, 71
    Orange Dressing, 73
    salads, two, 70
Tandoori Spice Marinade for Chicken (or Pressed Tofu), 177
Tapenade, Braised Chicken Breasts, 169–70
tarragon, fresh and dried, 34
Tea Steamed Chicken or Bean Curd with Vegetables, 170–71
terrines, making, 87
thyme, dried, 34
Tofu, 37; pressing, 145
    Pressed, Grilled or Broiled, 145
    Pressed, with Sweet Mustard Glaze, 176
    Pressed, Tandoori Spice Marinade for, 177
    Sauce and Mushrooms, Tangy, Spinach Fettuccine with, 118
    Tea Steamed Chicken or Bean Curd with Vegetables, 170–71
    -Vegetable Stir-Fry (with Chicken), 147–49
Tomato(es), 29; peeling, 155. *See also* Sun-Dried Tomatoes

Fennel, and Saffron, Chicken Stewed with, 178
Fresh and Feta Cheese with Shrimp or Chickpeas, 203–4
Panzanella Soup, 50–51
-Posole Soup, 51–52
Sauce, Perfect, 112–13; Perfect, Too, 113–14
Summer Garden Risotto (with Scallops), 134–35
Timbales in Tender Spinach Casing, Chilled, 89–90
Tuna
    Fresh, and White Beans, 201–2
    Grilled Niçoise-Style Sandwich, 202–3
Turkey, 168–69, 182–87
    Burgers, Barbecued or Broiled, with All the Fixin's, 184
    Grilled Fajita Salad with, 182–83
    Not-So-Sloppy Joes, 185
    Roast, 187; Rice Stuffing with Pine Nuts and Dried Cherries, 186–87
Turnips, 29
    Baked Stuffed, 93–94

utensils. *See* cookware and utensils

Vanilla Cheesecake Ice Cream, 229
Vegetable(s). *See also* Name of Vegetable
    blanching or steaming in microwave, 144
    broth, basic, 44–45
    choosing, 14; steaming, 148
    fresh, directory of, 14–30
    Couscous with (and Fish), 197–98
    Grilled Assorted, 143–45
    Minestrone with Creamy Pesto, My Favorite, 54–56
    Ragu, 153–54
    Soup, Silken, 52–53
    Tea Steamed Chicken or Bean Curd with, 170–71
    -Tofu Stir-Fry (with Chicken), 147–49

Winter, in Mellow Lemon Marinade, 85
Winter Slaw, Wonderful Warm, 154–55
Vegetable Main Dishes, 141–65. *See also* Meatless Main Dishes; Name of Vegetable
Vegetable Side Dishes and Starters, 80–107; *See also* Side Dishes and Starters; Name of Vegetable
Vegetarian(s)
    all, menus, 12, 13; almost, 13
    Chili, 205
    meals, collection of side dishes, 80
    part-time, 3
Vinaigrette. *See also* Salad Dressing
    Sesame-Scallion, 65
    Walnut-Raspberry, 65
vinegar, balsamic, about, 40
vinegars and wines, cooking, 39–40
vitamin B, dishes rich in, 7

Walnut-Raspberry Vinaigrette, 65
weight control, 8
Wheat Berry Soup, 53–54
White Beans and Fresh Tuna, 201–2
Whole Wheat Penne with Cabbage and Cumin, 117
wild rice, 39
wines and vinegars, cooking with, 39–40
Winter Greens, Braised Fish with, 192–93
Winter Slaw, Wonderful Warm, 154–55
Winter Squash, 30
    Gratin, 86–87
    or pumpkin, whole, cooking, 86
Winter Vegetables in Mellow Lemon Marinade, 85

Yogurt, 119
    Apple Parfait, 217
    cheese, making, 133
    Fruit Soufflés, 218
    -Spinach Soup, Tangy, 48–49

zucchini, 30

CONVERSION CHART
Equivalent Imperial and Metric Measurements

American cooks use standard containers, the 8-ounce cup and a tablespoon that takes exactly 16 level fillings to fill that cup level. Measuring by cup makes it very difficult to give weight equivalents, as a cup of densely packed butter will weigh considerably more than a cup of flour. The easiest way therefore to deal with cup measurements in recipes is to take the amount by volume rather than by weight. Thus the equation reads: 1 cup = 240 ml = 8 fl. oz.; ½ cup = 120 ml = 4 fl. oz. It is possible to buy a set of American cup measures in major stores around the world.

In the States, butter is often measured in sticks. One stick is the equivalent of 8 tablespoons. One tablespoon of butter is therefore the equivalent to ½ ounce/15 grams.

Liquid Measures

Fluid ounces	U.S.	Imperial	Milliliters
	1 teaspoon	1 teaspoon	5
¼	2 teaspoons	1 dessertspoon	7
½	1 tablespoon	1 tablespoon	15
1	2 tablespoons	2 tablespoons	28
2	¼ cup	4 tablespoons	56
4	½ cup or ¼ pint		110
5		¼ pint or 1 gill	140
6	¾ cup		170
8	1 cup or ½ pint		225
9			250, ¼ liter
10	1¼ cups	½ pint	280
12	1½ cups	¾ pint	340
15	¾ pint		420
16	2 cups or 1 pint		450
18	2¼ cups		500, ½ liter
20	2½ cups	1 pint	560
24	3 cups or 1½ pints		675
25		1¼ pints	700
27	3½ cups		750, ¾ liter
30	3¾ cups	1½ pints	840
32	4 cups or 2 pints or 1 quart		900

Solid Measures

U.S. and Imperial Measures ounces	pounds	Metric Measures grams	kilos
1		28	
2		56	
3½		100	
4	¼	112	
5		140	
6		168	
8	½	225	
9		250	¼
12	¾	340	
16	1	450	
18		500	½
20	1¼	560	
24	1½	675	
27		750	¾
28	1¾	780	
32	2	900	
36	2¼	1000	1
40	2½	1100	
48	3	1350	
54		1500	1½
64	4	1800	
72	4½	2000	2

Equivalents for Ingredients

all-purpose flour—plain flour
arugula—rocket
buttermilk—ordinary milk
confectioners' sugar—icing sugar
cornstarch—cornflour
eggplant—aubergine
granulated sugar—caster sugar
half-and-half—12% fat milk
heavy cream—double cream
light cream—single cream
lima beans—broad beans
scallion—spring onion
squash—courgettes or marrow
unbleached flour—strong, white flour
zest—rind
zucchini—courgettes

Oven Temperature Equivalents

Fahrenheit	Celsius	Gas Mark	Description
225	110	¼	Cool
250	130	½	
275	140	1	Very Slow
300	150	2	
325	170	3	Slow
350	180	4	Moderate
375	190	5	
400	200	6	Moderately Hot
425	220	7	Fairly Hot
450	230	8	Hot
475	240	9	Very Hot
500	250	10	Extremely Hot

Linear and Area Measures

1 inch   2.54 centimeters